Hebrew Myth and Christian Gospel

THOMAS FAWCETT

Hebrew Myth and Christian Gospel

SCM PRESS LTD

334 00606 6

First published 1973
by SCM Press Ltd
56 Bloomsbury Street London

© SCM Press Ltd 1973

Printed in Great Britain by
Western Printing Services Ltd, Bristol

Contents

Acknowledgments

Except when stated otherwise in the notes, the following editions of ancient texts have been cited: *The Apocrypha and Pseudepigrapha of the Old Testament*, ed. R. H. Charles; *The Mishnah*, ed. H. Danby, both published by the Clarendon Press; *New Testament Apocrypha*, ed. E. Hennecke, published by Lutterworth Press; *The Babylonian Talmud*, ed. I. Epstein; *Midrash Rabbah*, ed. H. Freedman and M. Simon, both published by the Soncino Press; *The Midrash on Psalms*, trans. W. G. Braude, published by Yale University Press; *The Loeb Classical Library*, ed. T. E. Page and others, published by W. Heinemann and Harvard University Press. The text of the Revised Version of the Bible has been followed except in those cases where a point has been more clearly brought out in another translation.

The author would like to take this opportunity to express his gratitude for the facilities afforded so willingly by the staffs of St Deiniol's Library, Hawarden, and of the library of Chester College of Education; to colleagues in the Divinity Department of Chester College and in particular to the Rev. A. L. Poulton who kindly read the typescript and made a number of suggestions for its improvement. Once again the largest debt is owed to my wife, Elsie, for the many hours of patience and care spent turning an often illegible script into a readable text.

Introduction

For most Christians living in the eighteenth century, 'gospel truth' meant plain, unvarnished, historical fact. Myth, on the other hand, was regarded as a fanciful story created out of the barbarous and immoral imagination of heathen idolaters. An uncrossable gulf separated the one from the other. The Bible was held to be throughout a historical record of events, knowledge of which had been vouchsafed to the writers by God himself. Because of the status of the Bible, it was believed improper to make any comparisons between biblical and other literatures. The Bible was the direct revelation of God, while other religions were based upon myths which had probably been inspired by devils. Scripture told of history, while the stories of a Mithras or an Osiris were classed with fairy tales. The grandeur of New Testament morality was opposed to the lascivious and sensual accounts of a Krishna and the promiscuity of the fertility rites. The orthodox Christian was thus able to enjoy a kind of splendid isolation from the rest of the world's religions, whose adherents only concerned him as objects for his missionary activity.

This attitude came to an end for a great many during the nineteenth century. There were certain outstanding causes which we can isolate in order to see the effect they had on the idea of the relationship of myth to the gospel.

First, the rationalism which flourished during the eighteenth century left a legacy which we can see at work even to the present day. The mechanistic thinking of science did not allow for the possibility of openness in history and hence rejected the credibility of what was called miracle. We can see this influence at work in the writings of G. L. Bauer (1755–1806) and D. F. Strauss (1808–74). While Bauer cautiously suggested that there were mythical elements in the New Testament, particularly in

the birth narratives of Matthew and Luke, Strauss went much
further and declared mythical all the miraculous elements in the
gospel story. His *Life of Jesus*, translated by George Eliot and
published in English in 1846, was largely concerned with showing that the miracles in the gospels could not have taken place
but were frequently created out of Old Testament material and
so must be classed as mythical.

This kind of criticism was clearly useful to opponents of
Christianity such as the Armenian scholar F. C. Conybeare
(1856–1924), who exemplifies the kind of gospel criticism which
Bauer and Strauss had germinated. Although not questioning
the historical existence of Christ, he argued that many features
of the gospel story were mythical. The word myth is used frequently, but it did not appear in the index of his book, and the
author was content with a passing definition of it as 'a religious
narrative that purports to be historically true, but is not'.[1] His
procedure is exemplified by his treatment of the Lukan passages
concerning Pontius Pilate, whose conduct as recorded in the
gospels is held to be mythical because it is unbelievable. Hence
the story is judged 'good dramatic art' rather than history.[2] He
says that the evangelists whitewashed Pilate in order to place
the blame upon Herod, and claims to have demonstrated the
mythical character of the accounts by their similarity to Old
Testament narratives. The virgin birth and the resurrection of
Christ are of course dubbed as myth, the latter growing out of
the visions noted in I Cor. 15.5–8, which increased as one was
able to 'suggestionize' another.[3]

The second blow to the reserved position claimed for the
Christian gospels was dealt by those who pointed out the
similarities which existed between them and the literature of
the pagan faiths. The work of Sir James G. Frazer (1854–1941)
is most notable in this regard, not because his method or his
conclusions have stood the test of further research by other
anthropologists, but because he worked on a massive scale and
attained a wide popularity. His procedure was simply to gather
examples of myth and cult from every quarter and to place what
he considered to be parallel material together. His importance
for our purpose is not any particular consideration he gave to
the gospels, but the fact that his famous *The Golden Bough*[4]
seemed to many to show that all religion was fundamentally

the same and that its roots were in the sensual barbarism of ignorant savages. Whatever the weakness of his work, Frazer ensured that Christians could no longer ignore those who pointed to similar stories of divine births, last suppers and raisings to heaven in other traditions. To the scandal of particularity was added the problem of similarity.

Finally, there intruded a hypothesis which Frazer did much to inculcate, namely that all religions have progressed in a similar manner everywhere. If this was accepted, it would mean that the Christian could no longer claim that his religion was a direct gift of God and shown to be so by its discontinuity with what had gone before. On the contrary, it would mean that Christianity and even Christ himself would be a product of a law of evolution operating in the sphere of religion. In response to these ideas a number of competing schools of thought came into being with a varying willingness to concede that religion in general and the gospels in particular might be influenced by myth.

The most radical of these was the 'Christ-myth' school, which tended to adopt all three propositions: i.e., they were rationalist, assimilators and believed in a law of religious development. Very largely, their work was inspired by an intention to discredit Christianity by showing that it had no basis in history and that its gospel was entirely mythical. The beginnings of this kind of speculation are found at the end of the eighteenth century in France where both C. F. C. Volney (1757–1820) and C. F. Dupuis (1742–1809) denied any historicity to the gospel story. For them it was just a myth about the sun. There was a tendency at this time to see all myths as nature myths and especially as astral or solar myths. Apart from the attractiveness of a single and simple idea with which to work, this tendency was probably in part due to the growing knowledge about 1800 of the Indo-Germanic languages and peoples, whose myths seemed to be of a nature or astral character. And so Dupuis believed that he had found the simple key to the mysteries of the gospel—Jesus was in reality only the sun. Not unnaturally, he found the sources of this Christian sun-worship in the astral religion of Persia and believed, as the title of his book published in 1794 suggests, that he had found in solar mythology the *Origine de tous les cultes*.

The work of Frazer, who tended to see all mythology as a poetic narrative description of the vegetative cycle of nature, became of direct relevance to the Christ-myth debate when he suggested in the ninth volume of his famous work, *The Golden Bough*, that Jesus might have been forced, as a criminal, to play the part of Haman in the Jewish Feast of Purim when, he conjectured, a rite which ultimately derived from Babylonia was enacted in which a man playing the part of a god was killed.[5] On this hypothesis, the Jesus of Christian piety was no more than another example of the vegetation-deity, annually slain on the sacred tree, which he found in other cults. In the third edition (1913) of *The Golden Bough* he admitted the highly speculative character of this suggestion and, removing it from the main body of the work, placed it in an appendix. Frazer appeared to be deliberately attempting to undermine religion and was attacked by Andrew Lang (1844–1912), among others, on this ground. This was not really fair, however, for Frazer had been brought up in a pious family, attended church during most of his life and explicitly asserted the historicity of Jesus. On the great questions of faith, he would seem to have kept an open mind.[6] His suggestion, however, was to be taken up with enthusiasm by E. Dujardin and others, becoming the seed from which much more elaborate theories were to grow.

Contemporary with Frazer there occurred what C. J. Wright has called a 'small epidemic' of Christ-mythology.[7]

In 1900, J. M. Robertson (1856–1933) published *Christianity and Mythology*, and followed this in 1903 with *Pagan Christs*. In his work we find many of the features which dominated the debate about this time.

(i) Robertson accepted from Frazer the idea that there was a law of evolution for all religions, and held therefore that Christianity must have conformed to this law.

(ii) Further, Robertson claimed, on the basis of apparent similarity, that Christianity had created itself by drawing upon a number of traditions spread across the Near and Far East. The sources of Christianity were to be found not only in Judaism but also in an ancient Akkadian belief in a Deliverer-Messiah, the Mithraic mystery emanating from Persia, the Krishna story of Hinduism, the legend of the Buddha and the many sacrificial cults of the Graeco-Roman world. The fact that the com-

parisons were often being made with material which was much
later than Christ himself did nothing to abate his enthusiasm.

(iii) Robertson also combined the line of thought embodied
in Frazer's prodigious speculation with F. Creuzer's (1771–
1858) theory that myth was invented to explain already existing
rituals.[8] In consequence he argued that the story of the crucifixion in particular was a myth to explain the eucharist, which
retained elements of its origin in an ancient rite of human
sacrifice. The gospel story was not a historical record but
merely a mystery play, another myth similar to those of Osiris
and Tammuz.

(iv) The creation of the Christ-myth, moreover, was held by
Robertson to be merely a development of an already existing
cult. Jesus, he asserted, was no more than a new name for a god
who had been worshipped for generations. Earlier he had been
known as Abraham, Isaac, Moses, Joshua, Samson and David.
These originally Hebrew equivalents of Adonis and Tammuz
had, like Jesus, subsequently been humanized and treated as
though they were real characters in history. This surprising
thesis was arrived at in the following way. First it was assumed
that all deities were at root astral and hence that the gods
commonly worshipped by men were sun-gods. Secondly, the
names were submitted to philological manipulation in order to
show that a number of apparently distinct names were in fact
all one. Thus Robertson argued that David, Dauoid and Dodo
all had an identical philological origin, that Dodo was a name
for the god Tammuz and therefore that David was none other
than that deity.

Robertson's argument that the Christ-myth grew out of an
already existing cult was posited by a number of others. R.
Taylor (1784–1844) had much earlier suggested on the basis of
passages in Philo and Eusebius, that the Therapeutae of Egypt
had possessed the gospel story before the time of Jesus.[9] Robertson's proposal was taken up and developed by W. B. Smith
(1850–1934) in *The Pre-Christian Jesus*, published in 1906. Smith
based his arguments on Acts 18.25 where, it can be argued,
Apollos knows the cultic deity only as proclaimed before the
time of Jesus by the sect of the Baptist.[10] Again the philological
method is made to do service. The troublesome title Nazarene
for Jesus, which many scholars have doubted as a geographical

designation, is traced by Smith to the Babylonian root *NSR* and compared with the Syriac *Nasaryu*, which means 'God is protector'. It is noted that Hippolytus later referred to gnostics known as Naassenes and that Epiphanius mentioned a Jewish sect of Nazarenes. From this evidence the conclusion was drawn that Nazarene was a name used in the pre-Christian cult. A. Drews continued the work of Robertson and Smith, maintaining the hypothesis of a pre-Christian Jesus cult of the sun (for which Joshua, Jason and Jesus were alternative names) and suggesting further that the cult was influenced by the Adonis-type myths of dying and redeeming gods such as Attis, Mithras and Osiris.[11]

About the same time, between 1906 and 1910, an Assyriologist, P. C. A. Jensen, was enthusiastically making use of the new knowledge of Babylonian and Assyrian religion which had been made available from about 1850 onwards by the deciphering of their cuneiform scripts. He was particularly excited by the discovery of the *Epic of Gilgamesh*. As often happens at the time of new archaeological finds, there was a tendency to believe that the answer to all the old problems had been found. So Jensen thought that he could see the source of much Near-Eastern religion in ancient Babylonia and in the Gilgamesh epic in particular—one of his books was called *The Epic of Gilgamesh in the Literature of the World*. This newly-discovered literature also revealed the prevalence of nature and astral myths in ancient Babylonia, and so we find Jensen taking part in the speculations of the new school of nature and astral mythology to which the literature gave rise. His interest for our purpose lies in his thesis that the gospels could be explained against the background of the *Epic of Gilgamesh* and Babylonian astralism. He concluded that Jesus was not a historical person but the astral deity in a myth which, like the *Epic of Gilgamesh*, depicted man's quest for immortality.[12]

In 1924 P. L. Couchoud took up the theme of a pre-Christian myth, which he supposed to describe a drama of redemption involving a suffering Yahweh and a god, Jesus. This Paul had turned into the story of a man which had been filled out by the evangelists from Old Testament prophecy, with further additions provided by the visions of Peter and the collective mystical experience of the early Christians. The elements of the Christ-myth thesis have by this time become monotonously stable and the only improvement over earlier theorizers of this kind which Wright found in Couchoud's work was his recognition of the 'mystic and poetic appreciation of the rôle' which the myth of Jesus had and still has.[13]

The thesis of the Christ-myth school has been repeated in recent times by G. A. Wells in his book *The Jesus of the Early Christians* and by J. M. Allegro in *The Sacred Mushroom and the Cross*. Wells again presented the argument that the gospel represents a syncretistic myth written to explain why men performed a eucharistic ritual and suggests that it fused for this purpose the pagan myths of dying and rising gods with a Jewish belief in a suffering Messiah.[14] Allegro has been much more adventurous and has presented a distinctive thesis of his own. According to this the gospels were written by members of a mushroom cult who indulged in practices repugnant to the Jewish and Roman authorities, particularly the eating of the fungus as a drug and sexual promiscuity. In order to avoid persecution the gospels were written in such a way as to mislead the reader, but were capable of explanation by a group leader. The argument is largely based on philological grounds and frequently upon hypothetical reconstructions of word roots. In this way, veiled references are found to the mushroom throughout as the evangelists enjoy making their puns. The conclusion is probably more radical than any expression of the Christ-myth thesis previously. Not only Jesus but all the disciples are declared to be mythical references to the mushroom, and the message of temperance and love is said to have derived from the mistake made in the early centuries when men failed to recognize the hoax and took the gospels at their face value.[15]

The Christ-myth thesis has not unnaturally called forth a good deal of opposition during its long history. Among its opponents, however, were many who, like Carl Clemen, were not averse to the methods employed in order to arrive at it, but who believed that men like Robertson and Drews had gone beyond the evidence. They wished in fact to rescue the validity and respectability of a scientifico-historical study of Christian origins from the excesses which could bring it into disrepute. These scholars were members of what was known as the history of religions school. They accepted the thesis that there was a law of development in religion and that no example of religious belief and practice could be exempt from explanation in historical terms. They were very ready to see Christianity, with Otto Pfleiderer (1839–1908), as the product of earlier cultures and of the 'same psychological causes' which had produced other religions.[16] At first their concern was largely with the Old Testament, and the influence of the nature-myth school was evident. I. Goldziher (1850–1921), for example, writing on Hebrew mythology in 1876, argued that the stories of the patriarchs were myths about nature deities, not men, and that Jonah was a sun hero.[17] J. F. H. Gunkel (1862–1932) and T. K. Cheyne (1841–1915) argued for the dependence of much Hebrew thinking on Babylonia. This gave rise around 1900 to the Bible–Babel controversy, as scholars reacted to their attempts to gloss over the distinctiveness of the Old Testament faith. For many, however, the issue was sharpest when their theories were applied to the New Testament.

In time many scholars came to accept the influence of non-Hebraic mythological material on the ancient Hebrews, but when Cheyne argued that the birth, descent into Hades, resurrection and ascension of Christ were to be derived ultimately from 'a widely current mythic tradition respecting a solar deity',[18] there was considerably more opposition. Typical of many was Charles Gore (1853–1932), whose liberalism enabled him to accept the presence of myth in the Old Testament, but whose conservatism refused to allow that it was also to be found in the gospel story. The links between the gospel and the myths of ancient Babylonia seemed tenuous and so easily resisted. It seemed possible, however, to make out a much better case for a link with the paganism of the Graeco–Roman world.

The mystery religions of the New Testament period had become much better known through the authoritative work of F. V. M. Cumont (1868–1947). It was clear that there were similarities, especially in their rituals, to aspects of early Christianity. In consequence there began a movement whose participants believed the early church to have been fundamentally affected by the beliefs and practices of the mystery cults.

In 1913, W. Bousset (1865–1920) published his notable contribution to the subject, *Kyrios Christos*. He concentrated particularly upon the similarity between the rituals of the mysteries and the Christian eucharist, and came to the conclusion that the latter had its origin in the former. Further, he decided that the christology of the early church had come into being as a result of the influence exerted by the mystery religions, holding that many Christians had previously been worshippers in the mysteries and had simply transferred their former beliefs about a mystery-god to Jesus, so bringing a theology of Jesus into being.[19]

The discovery of the Mandaean literature in the early part of the twentieth century had a particularly profound effect on the development of the debate. From about 1905 onwards M. Lidzbarski began to publish translations of the texts belonging to this sect, which practised a form of gnosticism. Although the earliest of the manuscripts belonged to the sixteenth century AD, it was held by many that they contained material which was current before the time of Christ.[20] In these texts references were made to the Jordan, to baptism and to John the Baptist. Lidzbarski, supported by R. Reitzenstein, came to the conclusion that the Mandaeans had originated in the baptizing sects of Transjordan. It seemed to some that a vital clue to the development of early Christianity had been found. Of these, the most notable was Rudolf Bultmann (b. 1884).

Even before becoming acquainted with the Mandaean literature, Bultmann had come to believe that a pre-Christian myth of a supra-terrestrial messenger and his message lay at the basis of certain New Testament material and especially of the *Gospel of St John*. In particular, he had already come to the conclusion that the prologue to the gospel was in origin a hymn glorifying the Baptist as the incarnate *logos-sophia* which Christians had turned into an anti-Baptist statement. In 1925 Bultmann found the myth he had already deduced in the Mandaean texts, and followed Reitzenstein and Bousset in seeing this as a development from the ancient Persian myth of the primeval man, Gayomart. He now argued that the author of the Fourth Gospel had made use of Baptist material which had its origin in Persian mythology. This particular theory has been subjected to very severe criticism,[21] but whatever the weaknesses in his handling of the Mandaean evidence, Bultmann must be seen as one of the most outstanding and worthwhile members of the history of religions school, and was in a very real sense its climax.

Talk about myth had often gone on in the past without any
very extensive attempt to define what was meant by it. Bultmann
did attempt to state clearly what he and others in the history of
religions school meant by the term. Unfortunately he was not
altogether successful in this, and the ambiguities inherent in his
definition have led to continual argument. What was clear,
however, was that for Bultmann the pre-existence of Christ, the
virgin birth, the miracles, the resurrection and the ascension
were not statements either about history or about any kind of
metaphysical reality. When Bultmann called these stories
mythical, he clearly meant to deny that they conveyed any
cognitive information.

Bultmann's concept of myth was therefore so negative in
character that he was led ultimately to put forward his programme of demythologization. Myth was for him dispensable.
What had to be kept was simply the religious content of the
myth. He found an alternative and non-mythological way of
stating this content in the existentialism he derived from M.
Heidegger. By translating the myth into existentialist terms,
Bultmann was able to by-pass the possible historical and ontological elements in the mythical presentation. It seemed, therefore, to his opponents that he had reduced the Christian story
to a timeless statement of subjective truth, a suspicion which his
continued assertion of the fundamental historicity of Christ did
little to allay.

All the work we have so far considered caused alarm and
indignation to varying degrees in orthodox Christian circles.
Many reacted in a manner similar to that of F. C. Spurr who,
faced with Robertson's exposition of the Christ-myth theory,
gave forth an impassioned plea to scholars to make an answer
before the educated youth of the day was led astray.[22] The types
of defence which were raised in answer may be broadly considered to fall into two categories, the historical and the
theological.

Because many of the early scholars who spoke of myth in
relation to the New Testament meant simply that all or part of
it was unhistorical, their opponents not unnaturally responded
by marshalling evidence for the historicity of Christ. In the
early years of the debate they were prepared to go so far as to
defend the historicity of every item in the gospel story. T. J.

Thorburn, for example, was convinced that the gospels provided the most intimate and detailed historical records of Jesus. Frequently the arguments advanced were of an *a priori* kind. Gore contrasted the vagueness of mythical stories with the clarity of the gospels and found this to be a basis for accepting gospel historicity.[23] This was a not uncommon appeal to the inherent credibility of the Christian narratives. Wright made use of the popular but dubious argument that movements of thought always have their origin in specific, historic personalities.[24] With the development of critical studies, the maintenance of total historicity was clearly seen to be untenable. Thus, although Wright also assembled a historical defence against Couchoud's arguments, he recognized that both extremes in the Christ-myth debate were at fault because they assumed that the nature of all the gospel material was homogeneous, that it was all either fact or fiction, whereas he held that it was far more likely that the material contained not only fact but also the influence of prophecy and folk-lore.[25] Wright made no effort in his article, however, to define with any precision what he meant by myth, and the question of the relationship between myth and history has remained problematic for scholars down to the present time.

Another form of the historical defence was to show the untenability of theories of dependence on the grounds that the sources posited had not been shown to have had any direct influence upon primitive Christianity, either because they were geographically and culturally too far removed from it or because they were later in date than Christianity itself.[26] It was not difficult to show that hypotheses of dependence had been built on the slenderest of evidence, so that such theorizing tended eventually to come into disrepute.[27] This defence has been so successful with regard to the mystery religions that J. R. Hinnells has recently had to argue that the evidence cannot be ignored, and that in the case of Mithraism at least we have a mystery religion which was in the right place, Syria and Palestine, at the right time, the first century BC, to have been in a position to influence Christianity, although that this actually happened has still to be proved.[28]

The most overt form of the defence based on theological argument relied upon the concept of special revelation. The

relevance of comparisons between the biblical and pagan
mythical material was ruled out on the grounds that the one
came from God while the other did not. The credibility of the
gospel narratives was even asserted on this ground, it being
argued that while pagan myths were inconceivable, the Christian story was perfectly acceptable on the presupposition that it
described a direct act of God. This, however, seemed to be so
obvious a case of begging the question that upholders of special
revelation invariably felt the need to support their thesis with an
appeal to obvious differences.

Gore castigated the mysteries by saying that they were 'at
bottom barbarous and obscene', using the argument of moral
difference which was repeatedly put forward.[29] It often developed into a simple assertion of qualitative difference. Thus
Gore went on to contrast the egotistic concern with personal
salvation in the mysteries with the Christian desire for world
redemption.[30] This often seems to have reflected no more than
a feeling of superiority which we find in many of the early
writers on the history of religion. Lang spoke, like many others
at the time, most disparagingly of anything which was not
Greek. Despite the questionable nature of the form in which
such arguments were expressed, however, most would have to
agree with J. G. Bishop when he summarizes the differences by
pointing to the absolute monotheism, lofty moralism and
exclusive cultus of the Jews.[31]

The claim that Hebrews and Christians had to a large extent
transcended pagan myth could be based on sound historical
evidence. It has been repeatedly asserted, therefore, that the
Old Testament shows a people turning away from myth.[32] The
prophetic movement in Israel clearly fought the mythological
religion which surrounded the nation in their time. The
Deuteronomic reform attempted to put an end to Canaanite
paganism within Israel. Further, the antipathy to pagan
mythology on the part of rabbinic Judaism and early Christianity is well documented in history. Yet despite this evidence
it must be allowed that myth is absent neither from the Old
Testament nor from the New. The polytheism which was
eradicated from the creation narrative by the priestly writer
appeared at least in an attenuated form in some Hebrew poetry.
Similarly, the men of the New Testament period were unable

to abandon mythological modes of expression, although they were vehicles for what was 'essentially new'.³³ Both these series of facts had to be held in tension with one another. In particular, a place had to be found for both history and myth in the biblical material. If this was to be accomplished, however, some real attempt had to be made to appreciate the true nature of myth. As Van A. Harvey says, the liberal 'rarely, if ever, asked any significant questions about the structure of this mythology, its pattern, form, or "logic" ',³⁴ and this was often equally true of both radical and conservative scholars. In particular, it was necessary to get away from the purely negative view of myth.

As Plato and Plotinus had once had to rescue myth from its treatment at the hands of rhetoricians and sophists, so modern scholars had to retrieve it from the clutches of scientific positivism. This had already begun early in the nineteenth century. F. W. J. Schelling (1775–1854) and the Romantic movement opened up a better understanding of myth with the waning of the rationalist age. Schelling saw myth as at least a necessary stage in the evolution of religion, a 'universal process in which the world itself is apprehended and expressed'.³⁵ In consequence, Schelling was able to insist on both the historical and cosmological 'truth' of myth. N. Berdyaev (1874–1948) continued the search for a positive understanding of myth and held that it symbolized the metaphysical presuppositions on which the spiritual life of man depends.³⁶ Another important contributor to this rehabilitation of myth was W. M. Urban (1873–1952), who argued that myth derived from 'the primary experiences of the race' and that it always retains a place in man's intuiting of reality.³⁷ Particularly important was the recognition he expressed of the difference between myth and science. While science sees the world in mechanical terms, myth apprehends it as organic.

The work of these and other scholars, such as E. Cassirer in the field of philosophy and M. Eliade in the history of religion, have made it possible to re-assess the role of myth in the Bible. Even Strauss recognized that pagan mythology was often done less than justice and that the argument for moral difference sometimes rested on a lack of understanding of the original meaning of the pagan examples cited. Armed with the results of recent research, therefore, many would be more willing with

G. Aulén to accept that myth is prominently present in the Bible, especially in its talk of beginnings, of the end and of the Christ drama.[38] Before we can undertake a consideration of the way myth may have been used in the compilation of the gospels, however, we must give our attention to the problems which have troubled writers in the past.

One of the most pressing problems has been to see what significance lies in the fact that the Bible contains material similar to that found elsewhere. The relation of myth to history must also be of crucial importance to the biblical scholar. Finally, we need to understand the real nature of myth, particularly in relation to scientific speculation, and to see for what purposes it came into existence. It is with these questions that we shall be concerned in the remainder of this introduction.

THE PROBLEM OF SIMILARITY

When the breadth of man's knowledge of cultures other than his own was enlarged, he was struck not only by the differences but also by the similarities.[39] Stories, cultic acts and even architectural features were found in a number of religions or cultures to have such a degree of resemblance that it seemed unlikely to be the result of coincidence. In consequence, three types of theory arose to account for it, based respectively on evolution, psychology and diffusion.

Cultural evolutionism. The latter part of the nineteenth century was dominated by the controversy concerning the evolutionary hypothesis. It appeared as an attractive, new tool with which to work intellectual miracles. In anthropological circles it was quickly applied to religion. E. B. Tylor (1832–1917), for example, a patriarchal figure in the discipline, accepted it as a basis for his thinking and argued that there were laws which regulated the development of religion. The thesis appeared acceptable to a number of scholars and has been a recurring feature of anthropological studies since that time. It has been revived recently by L. A. White.[40] Important for our study is the fact that in cultural evolutionism myth was usually seen as a feature of primitive thinking.

Schelling had attempted a praiseworthy effort to raise the value placed upon myth after the unpoetic scientism of the rationalist age, insisting on its place as a medium of truth. Nevertheless, Schelling had seen myth as merely a stage in the evolution of religion and dissolved into the superiority of metaphysics. Less romantically, August Comte (1798–1857) had equated myth with religion and then argued that this was superseded first by philosophy which retained myth in part, and subsequently by science which had transcended and eradicated myth from man's thinking. When Tylor took up the theme in 1865, although he argued that magic and religion decreased as science increased, he perceptively noted the fact that all three elements were present throughout the process.[41] Lewis H. Morgan simplified the sequence into savagery-barbarism-civilization,[42] and Frazer into magic-religion-science. In such a simplification neither ancient science nor modern magic was allowed for, and Frazer earned the rebukes of subsequent workers in the field for his unscientific selection of evidence. L. Lévy-Bruhl went so far as to suggest that primitive man possessed a mystical mentality for which everything was permeated with forces, and therefore that myth represented a pre-logical thinking of earlier times which was superseded by the development of rationality.

In the last few decades many anthropologists have been severely critical of cultural evolutionism. The attack was led in Britain by B. Malinowski (1884–1942) and A. R. Radcliffe-Brown (1881–1955), who argued that to treat myth and ritual as a chapter of universal history was an attempt to make the evidence fit into a preconceived theory derived from metaphysical speculation. In America Franz Boas (1858–1942) led the revolt against cultural evolutionism, dubbing it a premature philosophical theory. In the field of comparative religion we find E. O. James rejecting the notion of a special kind of mythopœic mind and of a mythological age, arguing that what seems odd to us was quite rational and logical, provided that we grant the premises from which primitive man worked,[43] while, in the field of philosophy, Karl Jaspers has pointed out that myth is found in every epoch and is not uncommon in our own day.[44]

The psychological explanation. A second way in which the similarities between religious and especially mythological traditions could be accounted for was suggested by psychology.

Tylor had assumed that the human mind worked according to fixed laws, so that it reacted in a like way under like conditions. Lang argued that the similarities could be explained by the fact that human minds in a 'similar stage of fancy and ignorance' have been confronted by similar phenomena.[45] Similarly, Otto Rank derived the general unanimity of mythical thinking from the presence of constant traits present in the human psyche. Sometimes the psychological explanation was allied to that of cultural evolutionism as in Tylor, and at others used by those who opposed it. Lang, for example, argued against evolutionism in religion on the ground that the high-god concept which evolutionists regarded as a late development was also found among very primitive peoples.

This thesis was given a scientific form in the work of Sigmund Freud (1856–1939) and his followers. On the basis of this work, C. Lévi-Strauss was able to put forward the idea that we can perceive universal structures underlying a variety of forms among both savage and civilized peoples. Contrary, therefore, to evolutionism, Lévi-Strauss's theory of structuralism asserts that fundamentally modern man shares the same kind of mind with the primitive. In consequence he set out deliberately to discover the recurring traits which this view led him to expect. The idea was further developed by C. G. Jung (1875–1961), who found that significant comparisons were possible between the dreams and artistic creations of men in the modern world and the myths of the ancient world. From this he argued that there were certain archetypal figures or ideas which constantly recurred. Hans Schaer, following Jung, therefore finds the answer to the problem of similarity in the common subconscious. This, he believes, is a kind of collective memory of a common past. On the basis of the observed similarities in primitive materials, it is certainly possible to argue that a common psychology produced a common mythological tradition in ancient times.[46]

Diffusionism. A third approach to the problem of similarity was the historical or diffusionist theory. This school of thought explained resemblances by arguing that they were caused by the influence of one culture upon another. It is an approach which has the merit of not relying upon philosophical metaphysics or pre-conceived psychological theories, but is open to scientifically-controlled historical investigation. A mythical element can be traced through a number of cultures with the aid of documentary evidence and archaeological findings. Most scholars in this field, however, have tended to overrate the importance of the cultural tradition with which they are most acquainted and to assume its widespread diffusion on the basis of resemblances which are sometimes somewhat obscure. As a result we find that a number of ancient societies have been regarded as the cradle of mythology for a widespread area.

About 1900, an increased knowledge of Mesopotamian culture caused the rise of the Pan-Babylonian school, which held that Babylon had a developed mythology as early as 3000 BC which subsequently exerted its influence over much of the ancient world, including Egypt, Israel, Greece and Rome. It is often referred to as the German astral school, because there was a tendency within it to see solar or lunar myths as the fundamental basis of Babylonian religion and its derivatives, giving rise to the astrological belief that the celestial bodies were models for life upon earth and revelations of deity. In contrast to the cultural evolutionists, this school believed that there had been a steady deterioration evident in the historical process they posited. The hypothesis had an important influence on the history of religions school, as we have already seen.[47]

Egypt was also a contender. Solar mythology was as much in evidence there as in Babylonia, and the widespread use of pyramidal structures inevitably suggested an Egyptian origin for many features. The thesis was put forward by G. Elliott Smith and by W. J. Perry, who argued that from the fifth dynasty onwards Egyptian culture spread as far afield as India, Indonesia, Oceania and North America.

The myth and ritual school led in England by S. H. Hooke and in Scandinavia by S. Mowinckel, I. Engnell and G. Widengren asserted that a common pattern of culture and religion could be seen throughout the ancient Near East, thus bringing Babylon and Egypt together as part of one basic cultural entity.[48] The school relied much on the diffusionist

theory, but some were influenced by the evolutionary hypothesis.[49] The thesis was criticized by H. Frankfort, but has been
defended recently by Eliade, who argues that the school was
right to compare religious phenomena which were 'historically
related and structurally analogous'.[50]

Another important contender was ancient Indo-European
culture. This was a hypothetical construction derived from the
belief that the Indo-European languages all pointed to a
common basis, which F. Max Müller (1823–1900) called Proto-
Aryan and which was the vehicle for a common mythology. A
similar view was held by George Dumézil, who found the origins
of Celtic, Italic, Iranian and Vedic religion in a proto-Indo-
Europeanism, to which he attributed a well-articulated
mythology.[51] The heavy reliance placed upon the argument
that diffusion took place primarily through the spread of
language was subjected to severe criticism when anthropologists were able to point to myths similar to those in Indo-
European cultures in non-Aryan languages. The attractiveness
of finding one source for widespread cultures and the ease with
which philological evidence can be manipulated to this end,
however, seems to be irresistible. Allegro appears to find the
source of all Indo-European and Semitic cultures in ancient
Sumeria, and does so very largely on the basis of hypothetical
Sumerian roots for words in a wide variety of languages.[52] The
greatest weakness in theories of diffusion is expressed by Schaer
in a criticism of Pan-Babylonianism when he says: 'It is not so
easy for a people really to be influenced in its religion by that of
a foreign people.'[53]

The diffusion hypothesis relies very heavily on the thesis that
similarity indicates dependence, but there are a number of
objections to this procedure.[54]

1. The similarity may be only superficial. A formal parallel
is not sufficient evidence on which to base an assertion of
dependence.[55] The outward form may embody an entirely
different notion. Urban, for example, points out that although
'as the result of modern research it seems necessary to say that
there is scarcely a single element of Christian imagery and
symbol for which a parallel in heathen mythology cannot be
found', this does not mean that the incarnation can be identified
with any of the other traditions cited.[56]

2. The use of verbal and cultic structures resembling those of others may be deliberate, in order to assimilate a prevalent and acceptable motif to an entirely different basis. The use which early Christianity made of the symbolism of the contemporary pagan world provides an obvious example of this. The symbols were appropriated, but given new meaning. The same process is evidenced in the work of E. R. Goodenough on Judaism in the Graeco-Roman period.

3. Some similarities would inevitably have occurred, such as laments for the dead, the use of swaddling clothes and the like, because they were universally present in human custom. As M. Dibelius pointed out, many similarities would derive from the '*law of biographical analogy*',[57] a natural tendency for biography to interest itself in certain matters. A useful criterion upon which judgment can partly be based in such instances is provided by noting whether the element in question was significant for the cultic or social structure. On this basis Thorburn was able to point out that Robertson's citation of the lamentation of the women in the gospel did not offer a parallel to the dying-god cult, because it did not feature in Christian ritual.[58]

4. The argument from language is notoriously difficult. The existence of a similar word does not necessitate belief in dependence, still less does it follow that a borrowed word is being used with its original or even a closely related meaning. When dependence is made to follow from alliterative assonance, the argument is even weaker. The relationship suggested by Robertson between Mary-Myrrha-Maia-Maya, for example, was easily demolished, as Thorburn pointed out when the underlying etymology was followed up.[59]

Finally, we must note that frequently those who wish to see a relationship between two different traditions create a resemblance, deliberately or unconsciously, by their descriptions of them. Gore took Frazer and A. Loisy to task for this,[60] and his point might often be made in this context.

The excess of theorizing in the three approaches we have considered led in anthropology to a reaction against attempts at grand syntheses. Under the influence of Malinowski, anthropology began to concentrate on particular cultures and to determine the nature of their myths by observing their function in society. Attention was turned away from myth as the carrier of belief, and it was seen rather in sociological terms. In this the work of E. Durkheim was clearly bearing fruit, and anthropology was reminding itself of its status as a science and the need to restrict itself to the empirical method. With Malinowski a functionalist school of thought came into being.

Further, Malinowski, here aided by Radcliffe-Brown, was responsible for what is known as particularism: i.e., a culture was to be seen as a unit in itself, 'a functioning and integrated whole analogous to an organism'.[61] In consequence, Malinowski held that we should not attempt to understand the meaning of a particular trait by tracing its history or by noting superficial similarities between one culture and another, but should see it in the context of the particular culture to which it belonged.[62]

The functionalist particularism of Malinowski, however, was a most restricting approach, and subsequently his outlook was modified. E. E. Evans-Pritchard pointed out that although much that Malinowski had said was true, it was nevertheless helpful to know something of the history of a trait. Boas, Malinowski's American counterpart, similarly combined particularism with a degree of historical concern. The conclusions which he drew from a deep study of the Tsimshians, an Indian tribe on the coast of British Columbia, combined the two approaches in a way of some importance for our purpose. He found that similarities with other cultures were indeed to be explained by borrowing, but noted that a tribe did not take over a whole cultural complex when it borrowed one of its elements, nor even the whole story or myth when it made use of incidents within it. Moreover, when these traits had been adopted, a total character was imposed upon them so that they became truly their own distinctive possession.[63]

The particularism of Malinowski was modified in yet another way. Radcliffe-Brown and A. van Gennep were prepared to pass from the particular to the general, and it was hoped that depth studies of particular societies would yield information which would be valuable in the interpretation of other cultures and would even establish certain universal characteristics. Hence it was realized that the truth in particularism does not mean that we cannot gain insight by the comparative method provided Boas' stricture is observed, that we must allow for a new and different use by the adopting society. The comparative method was thereby in part rehabilitated, and it was seen that it could still yield valuable information if based upon studies in depth and handled with care. It can, for example, yield what Paul Bohannan calls a co-ordinating myth. By this he means a generalization which is derived from the study of a number of related cultures. The co-ordinating myth as such is the construction of the observer, and only variants of it can actually be found. It provides a kind of map or model with which the researcher can begin. Its value, however, lies as much in the way in which it enables the differences from a hypothetical norm to be appreciated as in anything else. Ultimately it must be subordinate to and be discarded in favour of the knowledge gained from the study of the particular.[64]

This somewhat lengthy description of developments in anthropological method has been undertaken because it has enabled us to stand aside briefly in order to appreciate the kind of theorizing which often lies behind discussion of the relationship of the gospels to the myths of other cults. We have seen some of the strengths and weaknesses of particular procedures, and can now tackle with greater awareness the problem of similarity with regard to the gospel story. We shall, moreover, find that we have been given some valuable pointers for the evaluation of the New Testament's place in relation to other cultures.

First, we must dispose of the assumption that there was at one time a certain kind of mythological mind which can be dubbed pre-logical. The thesis has been severely criticized with regard to ancient and archaic man. It is even less tenable to attribute such a mental state to the people of the Graeco-Roman world. This was attempted among others by Conybeare, who wrote that in the New Testament age 'there was a general inability to distinguish between subjective and objective experience, between dreams and waking reality'.[65] Consequently, subjective experiences were accepted as revelations from another world and apparitions of the dead Jesus taken as evidence for a resurrection. The thesis so expressed hardly needs to be contraverted, for it conjures up such an absurd picture of the day-to-day activities of the Roman administration and Jewish labourers that we can hardly take the suggestion seriously. Worthy of more serious consideration is the suggestion that in a period when myths are being created, those participating in the process do not think of their creations as myth. This point is made by a number of scholars from differing points of view. John Macquarrie sees the distinction between mythological and non-mythological thinking as the unconscious and conscious use of symbolism respectively.[66] H. J. D. Astley infers a similar distinction when he defines metaphor as 'broken-down myth-ology'.[67] Eliade also implies this in speaking of the early Christians as unconscious of the fact that they were myth-making.[68] This form of the concept, however, can only be accepted with an important qualification.

Mythological thinking is not the working of a certain kind of mind, but a certain manner of apprehending the world through symbols. To distinguish myth from history by asserting that the first is fiction and the latter fact is an arbitrary judgment deriv-ing from modern positivistic assumptions. These assumptions were not made by those who created myths, nor by our New Testament writers.[69] They accepted the reality of the world of the spirit, and so for them the acts which took place within it were as real as those which are acceptable as historical fact to empirical observation. They could express their belief that the reality of these was in every respect equivalent to that of history by narrating them as such. The imposition of our modern, scientifically derived metaphysics on the thinking of the early Christians is therefore entirely unwarranted, because it attempts to understand them by the use of categories which were not only unknown to them but antithetical to their beliefs. It is on this ground that much of Bultmann's treatment must be regarded as fundamentally wrong in approach. To demythologize their myths is to assert that their content was unreal in the sense that they intended it. Such a denial is acceptable as a point of view, but we should not be led to thinking that we are thus doing justice to their beliefs. We must conclude, therefore, that the mind of our evangelists was not unlike our own, but that their manner of writing was determined by a belief in the reality of the spiritual world and that they attempted to state its impinge-ment upon them in their own experience by the use of a language appropriate to it, i.e. symbolic and mythological.

Views about the mythological character of the New Testa-ment are frequently bound up with evolutionist theories which assume a steady progress by mankind away from mythology. Some writers, and Conybeare in particular, have thought of the New Testament as part of a mythological culture which we have now abandoned.[70] Others have held that the New Testament represents the period of transition out of myth. G. V. Jones, for example, argues that it is fundamentally post-mythological but that some mythology has survived into it.[71] Bultmann seems to hold the same opinion. E. Crawley, after examining the parallels between the New Testament and ancient mythologies and characterizing 'the loan-hypothesis' as 'a scientific myth', decided that all religion is the direct outcome of 'elemental human nature', but that in Christianity the grosser elements had been refined away.[72] Crawley's predilection for the evolutionary hypothesis was mitigated by his recognition that savage and civilized men are not so different as many would like to make out.[73] For many the New Testament is clearly post-mythological because, as we have already seen, there are those for whom both the Old and New Testaments have rejected all mythologizing.

Apart from the dubiety attaching to the general theory of evolutionary progress which has been amply stated in recent times, we must note that the New Testament cannot be made to fit within its simple scheme. There can be no doubt now that the early Christians were the heirs of a faith which had attempted a process of demythologization, while on the other hand the creative mythologizing evident in the book of Revelation and in the post-canonical books shows that the age of myth was far from past. A pointer to the solution of the problem is perhaps suggested by noting what happened elsewhere.

When we turn to other cultures, we find that mythology can be followed by a period of demythologization and followed again by remythologization. Thus the *Rig Veda* and the *Brahmanas* are fully mythological. The *Upanishads* represent a subsequent demythologization of Hinduism, while in the even later *Mahabharata* mythology appears again. The cycle repeats itself once more with regard to Krishna, whose mythological character in the *Mahabharata* disappears in the demythologizing *Bhagavad Gita*, only to re-appear in the *Bhagavata Purana*. A similar development appears in the history of Greek religion, in which the Olympic mythology was destroyed by the philosophers and sceptics, only to be replaced by the mythology of the mysteries. We must allow, therefore, for the possibility that a similar process took place in the Hebraic-Christian tradition. According to A. Bentzen, anti-Canaanitism led to demythologization in the Old Testament period as monotheism took firm hold. Later Judaism re-accepted mythology in a new eschatological form. Jesus was part of this last process in that he 'reunites all aspects of the idea of the Primeval Man and Primeval King in His own person, and so the entire mythology of the Ancient East is reinstated'.[74] Bentzen has surely seen how the New Testament might present a dual appearance with regard to myth. He seems, however, to have gone too far in saying that the ancient mythology was reinstated. Surely the resurgence of mythological thinking, if such there was, must have been due to the arrival of something dramatically new. Moreover, as Eliade has remarked, the Christian myth was a living thing, and this was why early Christians saw no similarity between it and the dead and desacralized mythology of paganism.[75] Another view is therefore to be preferred, which sees Christianity launching a vital and new myth on the world. This has been eloquently expressed by Amos N. Wilder. He urges that 'full recognition be given to the operation of the "mythical mentality", in all its creative and quasi-magical power' in the New Testament, because in the Baptist, in Jesus and in Paul 'we can recognize original and fresh mythological vision' and 'primal image-making power associated by students of early cultures with epiphany-phenomena and the genesis of myth and ritual and the naming of things'.[76] Profound insight had been given creative mythological expression by Jesus, and only later would come the schematization, rationalization and literalization which would again eventually lead to a loss of the primal vision and a renewed process of demythologization which accompanies the death of religion.[77]

We must conclude, therefore, that mythology is constantly in a state of disintegration and reintegration and, if we accept that myth is a means whereby the meaning and spiritual reality of the world can be expressed, we shall be inclined at this point to believe that myth has received a new impetus in the New Testament period under the impact of a fresh revelation in the person of Jesus.

If this was so, however, we must face the arguments of those who assert the dependence of the New Testament on the mythology of the past on the basis of certain similarities. For this purpose a number of cultures have been cited.

The frequent arguments advanced at one time for dependence on Hindu and Buddhist narratives carry less weight today in view of the fact that the parallels are usually found with material which is not only later than Christianity, but may even have been influenced by it.[78] There has been a similar tendency to reject the influence of the mystery religions on the same ground, as we have already seen. There remain, however, certain possible sources for the creation of New Testament mythology which remain strongly arguable.

The most obvious of these has been at the centre of the debate for a long time. Schelling, Strauss and Goguel represent a strain of thought which has held that the similarities between certain parts of the gospel story and Old Testament narratives are so close that we must assume that the one has been created out of the other. Strauss, for example, derived the story of the call of the disciples from that of Elisha by Elijah and the cleansing of the lepers from the Naaman episode.[79] Goguel thought that the Bethlehem tradition was derived from Micah 5.1 and the Egyptian interlude in the nativity stories from the saying, 'Out of Egypt have I called my son'.[80] But we have to note with Schweitzer, who criticized Strauss on this ground, that this theory accounts only for the form and not for the origin of the stories.[81] If the evangelists saw that the significance of the events which they had to relate could be made clear by assimilating their form to Old Testament types, this does not indicate that those events had been created out of them. On the contrary, it would seem that the old forms had been given a quite new content.

An even more difficult question is raised by the recurrence of motifs in the New Testament which appear in ancient Babylonian, Egyptian and Canaanite mythology. Much here turns upon the extent to which it is held that the Hebrews had successfully resisted foreign cultic influences. For some this resistance had been totally successful. Most, however, would have to admit with L. I. J. Stadelmann that the 'distinctive

covenant faith' had not completely overthrown 'the cosmological ideas taken over from other peoples' and therefore that
'vestiges of mythological idioms appear in the Bible'.[82] This
position, however, does not account for the resemblances which
have been noted. The Judaism represented by the canonical
literature does not contain sufficient of the old mythology to
account for the continuance of these motifs down to New
Testament times. It can therefore be argued that the Deuteronomic process of demythologization was not entirely successful,
and that pagan mythology lived on outside mainstream
Judaism.[83] J. Sturdy contends, for example, that the pagan
myth of the dying and rising god, the Sumerian Dumuzi,
Babylonian Tammuz and Canaanite Baal (Adonis) has flowed
into and helped to shape the Christian story, as also has the
ancient king-cult.[84] Christianity then would be the heir of an
Israelite-Canaanite religion which was far from the orthodoxy
which characterized the Deuteronomic reform. As Sturdy
admits, however, this would only constitute a partial explanation. While the similarities are undeniable, the differences are
equally evident.

Another manner in which apparently non-Hebraic ideas have
found their way into the New Testament has been more generally
accepted. A large number of scholars have granted that the
religion of Iran has influenced late Jewish apocalyptic literature
and through it early Christianity. The parallels are, however,
superficial even here, and we must accept the fact that early
Christian literature is fundamentally different from any pagan
Near Eastern material which we know.[85]

If we bear in mind the work of Boas, we may be able to see
why scholars have experienced such difficulty in attempting to
find the origin and meaning of the gospel material in the
mythology of earlier times and of other peoples. It will be
remembered that Boas found that although the Tsimshians took
over elements from other peoples, they integrated these into a
distinctive cultural entity of their own. Surely we must grant the
probability that, if any borrowing did take place in early
Christianity, it was done in this way.[86] Indeed, all the evidence
would point to such a conclusion, for while writers have had no
difficulty in finding parallels for isolated elements, stories and
motifs, no one has been able to delineate a cultural unit which

bears any resemblance at all to early Christianity as a whole. We must therefore conclude that in being part of a new integration of mythological ideas, the evangelists stamped them with the image of God seen in Jesus Christ. Urban argues that myth, although fundamentally different in his view from religion, develops into it and furnishes its symbolism. He makes the very important point that it is improper to judge 'the later in terms of the earlier'. The love symbolism of mysticism may derive from the fertility myths, but cannot be evaluated on the basis of the earlier material.[87]

In view of this, it would seem that further dabbling in comparisons would be pointless. This, however, is not so. Despite the unique character of early Christianity, it would nevertheless be part, even though a distinctive part, of a cultural complex which is now only known to us through the medium of a comparatively sparse collection of documents and archaeological finds. In this situation we have to admit the value of what Bohannan calls a co-ordinating myth. By assembling such a myth from the totality of our knowledge of ancient culture and of the Near Eastern complex in particular, we can provide ourselves at least with a starting point, a model from which to appreciate the divergences exhibited by the Christian tradition. In this way, too, we can relearn the possible values of those symbols which constituted the bricks out of which myths were made and the understanding of which we have largely lost. Frequently we shall find that the gospel usage has departed from the norm we have set up, but our understanding will be all the greater for our appreciation of this fact.

It is also particularly necessary for us to assemble a knowledge of the mythological concepts which had been retained down to the time of Jesus. Only then shall we be able to appreciate the anti-mythological thrust in the gospel story, to understand the play upon the old as the new came to destroy it. The creation of a new mythology always meant the destruction of the old, even if elements were retained, and an adequate understanding of the gospel message is only possible if we see something of the building which was being demolished.

Finally, in view of our conclusion that primitive Christianity would inevitably be a mythological complex held together by its own distinctive forces, we see that it must be its own primary

guide to the interpretation of itself. When making comparisons
with other cultural units, we have noted that the form may be
similar while the content is quite different. Now we must
appreciate that the forms may be different but embody the
same fundamental content when they are found together within
a particular complex. A modified form of the procedure used by
Lévi-Strauss is particularly appropriate here. Lévi-Strauss has
argued that if we look beyond the outward forms, we find that
the same structures underlie them. A number of symbols can be
used for the same things, and different groups of symbols can
demonstrate the same relationship. Each individual story can
constitute a *syntagma* of the whole system. Now Lévi-Strauss is
prepared to use this method over a wide range of cultures,
which seems to ignore the distinctiveness which we have noted
belongs to any one complex. If we restrict ourselves to one
cultural entity, however, it would seem reasonable to apply his
method. By doing so we find, provided we have grasped the
basic structure and its distinctive character in Christianity, that
we can see the whole in the part, the fundamental motif played
out again and again, and so interpret one sequence with the aid
of our knowledge of the others.

In conclusion we may say that a study of the similarities can
be of considerable help, provided the differences are given equal
weight and the distinctive character of the Christian material
maintained, so that we look ultimately for an explication of
gospel material from within the tradition to which it belongs.

MYTH AND HISTORY

At the centre of the debate on the presence of myth in the gospels
has been the belief that myth and history are two mutually
exclusive categories.[88] This has been assumed by protagonists
on both sides. Those who have found myth in the gospel story
have usually been sceptical as to its historical value. Strauss did
not deny the historicity of Jesus, but labelled much of his story
mythological with the express intention of denying empirical
truth to the parts so described. Bultmann's proposal to demythologize the gospel was accompanied by radical scepticism
with regard to its historical worth, and L. Malevez is able to
assert with some truth that he has turned the stories of Jesus into

'scarcely more than fictions'.[89] Drews and others of the Christ-myth school have gone further. Not only are the gospel stories held to be imaginative fictions, but their central character is denied all historicity. Those who have rejected the presence of myth in the gospels have usually done so in order to safeguard their historicity and so have worked on the same premise.[90] They have believed that they could demonstrate the absence of myth from the gospels by defending their historical value.

This opposition between myth and history is, however, an over-simplification. It is true that myth as such does not tell of historical events. The stories it tells are usually located in pre-history and in a world other than that in which men live out their time.[91] Nevertheless, these stories do have an integral relationship with ordinary empirical history and with the life of man. The events of myth are understood to present to the reader the divine order underlying all things. They are arche-typal to history in that they set out in dramatic form the divinely ordained pattern which is working itself out in man's time. They act, therefore, as a guide in two primary respects. On the one hand, they enable men and women to see in the apparent meaninglessness of particular events the divine purpose which rules all history. On the other, they indicate the manner of life which the children of Adam and Eve are called upon to live.[92] There was, therefore, in the ancient world 'a quite elementary correlation between myth and the world of concrete experi-ence'[93] which makes any simple opposition between myth and history invalid.

In the Old Testament there can be no doubt that myth and history are brought into close relationship with one another. The great events of Israel's history are often described in mythological imagery. Particular events are seen as fulfilments of mythological archetypes. This is particularly notable in the treatment of the Exodus tradition, where the Sea of Reeds is seen as the great deep overcome at the time of creation. The nation of Egypt is also given a mythological character, being understood as a historical manifestation of the monster slain at the foundation of the world. Because Israel saw her history in this way, she was always able to perceive the hand of God in it. Because the myth declared the victory of Yahweh over the forces of chaos and destruction, Israel could believe that she would

always be safe from them when loyal to her God. Myth thus
enabled the Hebrews to see beyond the empirical facts of
history to the underlying purpose of God which was being
worked out on the stage of time.[94]

The relationship between myth and history in the Old Testament has, of course, been the subject of considerable debate.
Some scholars wish to stress the importance of Israel's consciousness of history and regard this as incompatible with a continuing
use of myth. They would wish, therefore, to say that the Hebrews
succeeded in historicizing myth. Some would even go so far as
to claim that Israel succeeded in demythologizing its ancient
traditions.[95] But while there is some truth in these claims, they
can be pressed too far in an effort to preserve the undoubted
uniqueness of Israel's faith. Demythologization can only be said
properly to have taken place when myth is no longer meaningful or necessary. This can hardly be said to have been the case
while myth was continuing to perform its function as the
explicator of history and remained significant for the interpretation of human life. This it did to varying degrees throughout
the nation's history. There is ample evidence of the persistence
of myth at the popular level. It also appears in the writings of
the prophets and finds a place in all strata of the Pentateuch.
In apocalyptic literature there is a marked resurgence of
mythological imagery,[96] and while this may have been furthered
by foreign influence, it is fundamentally no more than a legitimate development of motifs already present in the Hebraic
tradition.

It is not really necessary, however, to oppose the historicization of myth to the mythicization of history. These two processes
were complementary to one another. Historicization made
myth relevant while the mythicization made history meaningful.

What the Hebrews did with their national history, the
Christians appear to have done with the fact of Jesus.[97] On the
one hand they mythicized the history of Jesus in order to bring
out its transcendental meaning, while on the other they saw in
Jesus the actualization of the hopes embodied in their mythology.

The writers of our gospels were confronted by the task of
witnessing to the occurrence of certain events in their time and
of explaining the significance of those events to their readers. In

order to accomplish this they had to fuse history and myth together. The historical facts had to be given a mythological dimension in order to bring out their eternal significance. Only in this way could it be shown that these events were more than the accidents of history. By mythologizing them, the evangelists declared that they had the validity appertaining to the primordial will of God.

At the same time they saw in these events a fulfilment of the hopes previously expressed in the language of myth. Their mythology asserted the victory of God over all evil and destruction. In Jesus they believed that God's victory was manifested on the plane of ordinary human history. What the myth spoke of in cosmic terms, they understood to have taken place in the land of Palestine in their day. They inherited from Judaism the belief that history would come to a climax with the renewal of the world envisaged in terms of the myth of creation. In Jesus they believed that this eschatological hope had already been fulfilled.[98] They also saw in his life a performance on the stage of history of those dramatic representations of mythological ideas which were performed in ritual.[99] Jesus was the lamb slaughtered from the foundation of the world. For the evangelists, therefore, Jesus was understood to have constituted an irruption of the eternal into the temporal, of the primordial into the present and of God's world into man's. In order to show this, the evangelists punctuate their historical story with timeless events and bring mythological into geographical space. At certain points in the gospel story, time is eliminated. In both the temptation and the transfiguration, 'there is a characteristic irruption of the timeless into time, of the sort that normally gives rise to a fresh myth, but the transfiguration is of a historical person speaking to historical people'.[100] Similarly, at certain points we lose touch with geography and find ourselves in an other-worldly location, in the demonic wasteland, in the midst of the primeval sea or on the sacred mountain of God.

If these conclusions have any validity, we may note at this point that they have some importance for the work which must be done in the realm of gospel studies. For a long time the primary task of the exegete was seen as that of distinguishing between the historical facts in the gospels and the interpretative elements which were embodied in it. For many decades the New

Testament scholar was concerned to build up a set of criteria for
distinguishing between these two elements. Once this was done,
it was believed possible to strip off the accretions of early church
thought and to get back to the historical truth concerning the
life and words of Jesus. While the scholar's work was dominated
by this perspective, the evangelistic interpretation of the Jesus-
event was regarded as largely dispensable in the sense that it was
a hindrance to the object being pursued. This meant, however,
that those following this path usually ended up with very little
indeed. The search for the historical Jesus has led continually to
the elimination of most of the gospel narrative. Because scholars
of this persuasion wished to eliminate everything which might
conceivably be evangelistic comment, Jesus himself was reduced
to minute proportions. A concentration upon historical research
had produced results not dissimilar from those arrived at by
writers whose object it had been to reduce the stature of Jesus as
the Christ by searching in the gospels for the presence of
unacceptable mythology. The Jesus uncovered by the methods
of historical empiricism may have been granted historical
status, but he was a man whose value for faith must be problematic. Because historical fact is constantly conveyed in the
gospels through the medium of interpretative narrative, a
method which relies primarily on the elimination of the latter
must necessarily end by destroying the former. Nothing could
make it clearer that the scientifico-historical approach, while
having a legitimacy apart from the concerns of faith, cannot
do justice to the work of the evangelists in handing on to us,
in a manner relevant to faith, the story of Jesus of Nazareth.

In very recent times the importance of the work done by each
of the gospel writers has been given greater recognition.
Redaction criticism has attempted to do justice to their editorial
creativity. As a result we can now understand something of the
theology which lay behind each of our four gospels. The stature
of the evangelists has grown, and with it our admiration for the
skill with which they contrived to write up the life of Jesus. Yet
this movement, too, may lead us in the wrong direction, in that
the attempt is still being made to see a clear separation between
Jesus and his biographers, between his history and their theological comment. The work of breaking down these elements is
one which the evangelists themselves would surely have regarded

as improper. Indeed, they would have felt that if it could be done, their work was invalid.

The evangelists did not see themselves as creators. On the contrary, they saw themselves as doing no more than bringing out that which was already present in the life and work of Jesus himself. By the power of the pen they attempted to make up to the reader for the fact that he was unable to see the glint in the eye of the master or perceive the glory of God shining in his smile. Unless we are prepared to regard them as charlatans, therefore, we have to recognize a continuity between what Jesus was and what the evangelists portray. We must accept that their work was controlled throughout by two factors. They had to be true both to the empirical facts of which they bore witness and to the perception of transcendental reality which transformed the life of many of those who experienced them.

With regard to the first of these points, it has to be noted that no known mythological pattern appears in the gospels without being twisted into an entirely new shape by the stubborn facts of history. Of the second it must be admitted that the evangelists certainly claimed more for Jesus than he claimed for himself, but they were nevertheless controlled by Jesus' own self-understanding. They only made explicit what was implicit in his own sense of divine vocation.

We shall appreciate the gospels best, therefore, when we see them as a whole and recognize that in them historical fact and mythological interpretation are indivisibly complementary.[101] There is no pure history, because it would have been meaningless without mythological interpretation. There is no pure myth because history lies at the root of all the events.[102]

STORIES OF THE GODS

Another judgment which has inhibited discussion as to the presence of myth in the biblical material is that which asserts that a myth is a story of the gods (or at least of supernatural beings). This popular definition of myth has obtained wide currency, and in works on mythology, anthropology and the history of religions it is often assumed to need no defence.[103] When the validity of the definition is accepted in the field of biblical studies, it leads to certain virtually inevitable conclusions. When scholars are concerned to highlight the unique character of the Hebraic tradition, myth appears to be an entirely inappropriate category in which to place anything stemming from the mainstream of prophetic Judaism. The Hebrew tradition is rightly seen to be dominated by a radical monotheism which is inimical to the use of stories which tell of many gods. It is on the basis of this definition, for example, that John Bright, following Gunkel, holds that Israel's monotheism freed her from the mythology of paganism.[104] If myth is a story about gods, then the leaders of Hebrew thought had no use for it. What mythological elements remain must derive from pre-prophetic Israel or be the result of later pagan influence.

The acceptance of this definition also has important results for the treatment of the New Testament. Strauss accepted it, and agreed that on this basis, it must be said that the Old Testament did not contain any mythology. He also saw, however, that this must mean that the New Testament did contain mythology in so far as Christ is treated as a divine being.[105] Dibelius thought along the same lines. He also argued that Jesus is treated as a mythological being in some parts of the New Testament. This took place when Jesus was represented as a divine or supernatural being. On the basis of this definition, therefore, Dibelius found in Paul's letters 'a Christ mythology', which did not need the tradition concerning Jesus' earthly life to support it. In it, Christ was the Son of God who descended from heaven, died and returned to his exalted state.[106] On the same grounds, Dibelius contended that John's gospel was also mythological in that it spoke of a pre-existent, supernatural being. Indeed he went so far as to say of John's gospel that 'here everything is mythological'.[107] Logically enough, Dibelius found only a partial use of mythology in the synoptic gospels, for here there was held to be no descent to earth, no entry into hell and no description of the resurrection. Myth was here restricted to some parts of the birth narratives, the story of Jesus' baptism, his temptation, the transfiguration, Matt. 11.25–30 and the post-resurrection narratives.[108] So while Dibelius recognized that there were other identifiable characteristics of myth such as otherworldliness, theogamy, miraculous incarnation, connection with ritual, cosmogony, processes of nature and human fate after death, it is clear that his form-critical analysis of the gospels was primarily determined by the definition of myths as 'stories *which in some fashion tell of many-sided doings of the gods*'.[109]

A particular variant of this definition has also been of some importance in the debate. At one time it was held by a number of scholars that the gods of myth were exclusively personifications of natural forces. Myths were then held to be in reality dramatic representations of the sequences observed in nature. This notion was often allied to the argument that myth was 'a disease of language'. G. W. Cox, for example, argued that descriptive names given to natural phenomena developed into gods about whom stories were told when the original meaning of these names was forgotten. Müller was the most notable exponent of one branch of this school of thought which saw all myth as primarily descriptive of solar phenomena. Müller also argued that language which was originally metaphorical came to be taken literally and the symbols to be regarded as gods.[110] This view of the mythological gods led scholars to deny the presence of myth in the Bible with even more emphasis. Accepting the gods of myth as personifications of nature, Karl Adam had no difficulty in drawing a strict contrast between the saviours of Hellenistic myth and Christ. Against the '*mythological* fabrications, *without* any historical basis', who were merely 'radiations of the one mother, nature', he was able to set the historicity of Jesus.[111]

It is, however, unsound to deny the presence of mythology in the Hebraic-Christian tradition on the basis of these definitions. The theories of the nature-myth school have long been discredited, though L. Mair probably goes too far when she asserts that 'nobody now supposes that the personages of myth personify' the 'entities and processes' of nature.[112] The absence of nature-gods from the gospel story, therefore, does not mean that there is no mythology contained in it, and the fact that Yahweh was not for the Hebrews a personification of nature may not be taken as sufficient to show that mythology played no part in their scriptures.

The more general definition of myth as a story of the gods has fared little better. G. S. Kirk has had little difficulty in showing that material commonly accepted as mythological from ancient Greece is not primarily concerned with gods.[113] The definition does not do justice to numerous stories which are undoubtedly to be reckoned mythological. It would seem, therefore, that talk of gods and their doings may be properly taken as indicative of the presence of myth, but that the absence of this does not necessarily mean that the material is not mythological. While a story which did not presume the existence of a divine world could hardly be reckoned mythological, the lack of divine heroes in a tale does not indicate that it is devoid of mythological content.

We may come nearer to establishing a better understanding of the nature of the characters to be found in myth by taking note of the way in which those who accept myths as stories of the gods are forced to create other labels for material which is evidently akin to myth. Cyrus H. Gordon, for example, speaks of certain stories as epics because they tell of men as well as gods and because they are located in this world, though at some remote period of past history.[114] Gordon has been forced to recognize that there are stories which are similar in many respects to myths but in which one or more of the principal actors are often men. There is, however, no reason to reject the label of myth for these on the basis of a definition which is arbitrarily narrow. It is, as T. H. Gaster argues, wrong in any case to define myth in terms of its form, just as it would be to define prayer in terms of litany or music in terms of score and scale.[115] Given the presence of certain other characteristics, these 'epics' must be accepted as myths. We must probably go further, in fact, and be prepared to accept as myths stories in which no divine characters play an on-stage role. In many myths the central character is a man. In some, a man and a woman are the principal actors. Their stories are clearly mythological, however, because they themselves are representative creatures, standing for the human race or epitomizing certain general characteristics of humanity. Their actions are described because they are regarded as archetypal, setting out the pattern of human behaviour in the world. For this reason their doings are usually said to have taken place at the dawn of history, either cosmic or tribal. A story may, therefore, be a myth although it contains no gods or other supernatural beings, provided the events portrayed are regarded as being determinative for man's understanding of his life in the world.

Once we dispense with the idea that myths are always stories of nature-gods, the question of the presence of myth in the biblical literature must certainly be reopened. There are no adequate grounds for rejecting the label of myth for the first three chapters of Genesis because only one God is spoken of or because the principal characters are the patriarchal pair. The eradication of polytheism has not destroyed the mythological character of these stories, as will become increasingly clear throughout our study. Similarly, the presence of myth in a gospel story cannot be denied merely on the grounds that there are no supernatural beings mentioned. There are many other indicators of mythological portrayal which must be recognized.

MYTH, MIRACLE AND WORLD-VIEW

We have now considered two particularly important elements commonly used in defining the nature of myth. We have seen that while myth proper is normally located at the beginning of history or in pre-history, it nevertheless has integral connections with ordinary history, so that it is not irrelevant when considering a primarily historical document. We have also seen that the definition of myth as a story of the gods is too restrictive, and similarly may not be used to exclude the biblical material from our consideration. We must now turn to another outstanding characterization of myth which has caused great difficulty, especially in recent decades. It is that view of myth which sees it primarily as a primitive and pre-scientific mode of viewing the world, as one which accepts the reality of miraculous events and sees the world in a way other than that which we can now accept.

Strauss appears to have seen myth wherever miracle was to be found in the gospels. Myth was that which told of events which were not consistent with the known and universal laws discovered by science.[116] Mair makes the same point but notes that those who relate the events of myth do not expect such things to happen again. 'They belong to a distant "age of miracles", when things were different.'[117] From this simple observation it can be concluded that those who use myth are not attempting thereby to describe the world in which we live. Myth is not taken as a substitute for scientific observation. It belongs to quite another category of thought.

The appearance of miracle in myth might almost be regarded as an accidental product. It does not seem to belong to the essence of myth, but arises out of the structure of mythological composition. Miracle finds a place in mythological stories for a number of reasons, but all of them are dependent on the fundamental character of myth-making.

Few if any entities or events in myth can be taken for what they seem. Even if there is an intention that they should be connected with actual things and actions, it is also clear that these are symbolic, representative of other things, people and events. The philological theorizing of the nature-myth school had some justification in that the character of a myth is often a symbol of a natural phenomenon. And when the dawn and the sun are personified, the rise of the latter may well come to be told as the conception of Shamash from the virgin womb of Aurora. Miracle also intrudes upon myth because it has to represent macrocosmic space and time within the small compass of its own domestic stage. In this way the total history of man's life, and even of cosmic development, may be seen writ small. But this portrayal of the macrocosmic in the microcosmic form of myth inevitably gives rise to the appearance of miracle, as space and time are apparently ignored. How much trouble has been caused by the seven days of Genesis 1 because its symbolic and dramatic presentation of the creation has been taken at its face value? Finally, miracle must also find a place when that which is unseen is portrayed in terms of the seen. The events of the life of the spirit cannot be adequately represented on the stage of our time and space. In their new and improper context they take on the appearance of miracle.

Certain miraculous narratives found in the Judaeo-Christian tradition have arisen on a mythological base in this manner. This is certainly the case in some rabbinic haggada, as for example when Adam loses his extraordinary physical stature as a result of his disobedience. In scripture, however, the connection with history is usually so close that there are few examples of purely mythological miracles. In most cases there is reason to believe that an actual event has been seen in mythological terms, with a resultant heightening of the miraculous element in the story. Whether this has been the case with some of the stories in the gospels must await consideration

at the appropriate place in our study. When mythological
motifs have been discovered to have played a part, however,
this must not be taken as precluding the possibility of historicity
attaching to the core of a particular narrative. On the other
hand, the absence of miracle cannot be taken as evidence of the
lack of a mythical presence. The influence of myth may be
indicated in other ways, especially by the use of a symbolic
cosmography the nature of which has often been misunder-
stood.

The work of Bultmann has been largely instrumental in
maintaining the popular idea that myth consists to a considerable extent of pseudo-scientific speculation. He appreciated the
fact that the pictures of the world found in myth were not
originally intended to be taken as scientific cosmography, but he
perpetuated the fallacy because he also spoke of the later
literalistic understanding of these pictures as mythological.
When he argued that one of the most important tasks of the
modern Christian theologian was the eradication of the out-
dated mythological world-view from the preaching of the gospel,
he thus set up the notion of a quite unjustifiable equation
between myth and pseudo-science.

Myth does share with science a desire to explain, but differs
in its ultimate purpose for doing this. The difference in aims may
be seen basically to be that whereas science attempts to arrive
at an objective description of the world, myth is only concerned
to portray the world in terms relevant to human experience.
Myth is always, therefore, of deep personal concern, and never
operates in a detached and impartial manner. It wishes to see
how man and his society may be integrated into the totality of
things.[118] In order to achieve this aim the statements of myth,
like those of science, must be true. They have to be informative
statements about the way things are. But the kind of truth which
they attempt to portray is not identical with that of science.
Myth asserts that there is a reality beyond the observable and
beyond human existence.[119] Further, it teaches that this divine
reality is the ground of order for the world in which man must
live.[120] Such truth is not demonstrable by scientific methods,
but is held to be vouched for by the interior, subjective experience of mankind. In order to portray this kind of truth, myth
may make statements which are not acceptable in a historical

or cosmological sense and yet nevertheless may be true in that
they convey a proper understanding of human existence.[121]

Myth and science share certain forms of presentation, but
their choice of these and their use of them are characteristically
different. Both speak of beginnings or causes, but whereas
science attempts to explain everything in physical terms, myth
seeks to go beyond the phenomenal to the personal dimension
which it believes to lie beyond the physical. For this reason
myths are often peopled by gods and angels. Events within the
physical world are thus seen as the outworking of personal will.
Mythical events are characteristically set at the beginning of
history, but this is not intended to give a physical aetiology. The
accurate description of initial physical events is of little or no
concern to the maker of myths. His sole aim is to set out the
nature of things so that men may orientate themselves correctly
within a cosmic environment which is believed to be at root
spiritual in nature.[122] For this purpose, an accurate cosmogony
in a physical sense is unnecessary. The mythical story of the
beginnings may be entirely symbolic in character because it is
concerned only to set out the spiritual reality of things as they
are by means of a dramatic description of how they came to be.

Both approaches to the universe also make use of analogical
models. Myth as much as science is aware that it cannot
describe the world precisely as it is, but must continually make
use of comparisons. Only certain aspects of these analogies are
called into play, for no one of them can fit exactly. It is often
assumed that the scientist is aware of this but that the myth-
maker is not. Bultmann has again been largely responsible for
the popular idea that mythology in the New Testament period
invariably thought of the universe as a three-storied building
consisting of earth, heaven and hell, and that this was regarded
as a statement of literal fact. However, the myth-maker is aware
of the limitations of the models which he uses. It is therefore, as
Aulen says, 'more than doubtful' if the early Christians took the
story of the ascension in a material or literal way.[123]

It is also necessary to question the assumption that the idea of
the world as a three-decker building was the only one of any
importance in New Testament times. The multi-tiered universe
certainly appears in the New Testament, especially in Paul and
John, but there are also traces of another and much older model

which embodied a unilinear concept of the universe, in which the concept of the sacred mountain played a dominant role. This will be seen to have played a not inconsiderable part in the language of the Old Testament and to have made its presence felt in the New. It is indeed the model which lies behind much of the controversy between the emergent Christian church and Judaism. Attention will also be paid to another very ancient analogy which spoke of the world as a living body. The use of these models in the gospels is of particular importance to us, because they are often the most prominent survivals of earlier mythological thinking. They help us to understand the forms which certain gospel stories took and to appreciate the mythological concepts embodied in them.

THE PURPOSE OF MYTH AND THE GOSPELS

From what has already been said, we may come to certain conclusions as to the purposes which myth can serve and have some indication of why it might be used in the gospels.

(i) Little argument is needed to show that the first Christians were faced by certain historical events connected with Jesus of Nazareth which transformed their attitudes towards the world and their own lives within it. Harvey makes the valid point that such events take on the function of myth when a pattern is abstracted from the events and used to interpret human experience.[124] Initially at least, however, this could only happen if the events themselves could be related to a pattern already known and seen as relevant to the circumstances. Just such a pattern would be available in the mythology of Judaism. By its means the evangelists would be able to set forth their belief that the life and work of Jesus was of ultimate significance to mankind. It would be endowed with the quality attaching to mythological event. That is to say, it would be shown as determinative for man's understanding of the world and of the divine will.

We are likely to find myth playing a part in the gospels, therefore, when the history of which they tell is related to the archetypal events of the Hebrew creation story. The redemptive work of Christ, for example, is seen against the background of the fall myth.[125]

(ii) Myth provided the means whereby this could be set forth. By speaking of Jesus as Son of God, the evangelists could portray the idea that in him the divine order was present among them in the flesh.[126] By indicating that he was no ordinary man but the second Adam, the Son of Man, they could set him forth as the firstborn of a new creation. By the use of myth, therefore, the person of Jesus could be given a dimension commensurate with the first Christians' faith in his saving power. The story of Jesus always moves on two levels, one human and historical, the other divine and mythological. But only the eye of faith can discern the latter and so see in Jesus the presence of mythological primordiality.

(iii) In the gospels, the other-worldly or mythological character attributed to Jesus by the evangelists is most obvious in those episodes which have a miraculous element. In these the eternal is seen to touch the temporal, the other-worldly to meet with the this-worldly. In these events the bounds of earth are demonstrably broken. For a moment the mundane takes on the character of the celestial. They are the signs, says John, which can lead men to recognize who it is that walks among them.

(iv) Finally, we can already recognize that ancient models are likely to be used again in the service of the new mythology. How can the evangelists portray the relationship between God, Jesus and man without resorting to the analogical language of myth? How else can Jesus be said to have come from God or to have become the new centre of human life? Only by their use can the evangelists avoid the fallacy entertained in some quarters today that Jesus only had existential significance. The models of mythology could help to show that the power of Jesus to work within human experience derived from his very nature. Or, as later philosophical thought would have expressed it, myth and its models enabled the first Christians to express the ontological status of Jesus as the Christ who was of one substance with the Father.

In addition to these primary purposes, myth is likely to find a place for two other by no means insignificant reasons.

(v) The role of myth in validating claims in social relations has long been recognized.[127] In Judaism mythology, as we shall see, was used to assert the political and spiritual superiority of

Israel. This was a use which comes under heavy attack in John's gospel. The story of Peter took on the character of validating myth for the Christian church of later ages. On the basis of things said to Peter in the gospel story, his successors claimed pre-eminence in ecclesiastical affairs. In the gospels, however, this use of myth comes into play primarily in connection with the authority of Jesus himself. He is thus shown as the true king of Israel and of mankind.

(vi) The relationship between myth and ritual has been a much more difficult one to assess. Creuzer's theory that myths were invented to explain ritual has been repeated recently by Wells,[128] but has very little support.[129] Indeed, it has been shown that some myths have little or no connection with ritual.[130] On the other hand, most rituals are probably grounded in myth. By means of ritual, mythical events are believed to become effective in the present, allowing men to participate in them.[131] This is the really important fact for our purpose. In Israel the Exodus took on mythological value, and the ritual connected with it was designed to enable the Hebrew of subsequent ages to experience that event cultically.[132] In this way the Hebrew worshipper was made one with those who had experienced the historical event and derived from the covenant relationship brought into being at that time between Yahweh and his people the benefits which he believed would come. In the Christian church there have been two outstanding rituals practised, and one of these, the eucharist, is declaredly associated with an episode in the story of Jesus. There can therefore be little doubt that the narratives of the last supper and the crucifixion in the gospels have performed the function of myth in relation to the central rite of Christendom. That rite has been celebrated for the express purpose of enabling the worshipper to enter into the effects of the events which it portrays. According to the evangelists at the last supper, Jesus gave a new historical foundation for the sacred meal eaten in Judaism. But that history was only effective as the basis for the ritual in so far as it was believed that it had a mythological quality such as that with which the Exodus had once been credited. The connection between the baptism of Christ and that of believers is more problematic, but if the ritual is not connected with this incident, it certainly is with another. In baptism the believer, says Paul, dies and rises with Christ. From this perspective alone, therefore, it is possible to see why the story of the passion plays so large a part in the gospel story. It was an event in history which had taken on the character of myth, and was thus capable of being originative for the performance of ritual.

It would appear, therefore, that we have every reason to expect to find mythological elements in the gospel story, and that the discovery of them would be of immense value in appreciating the teaching it contains. It has been argued that myth is no longer a form understandable by modern man, and that it is necessary, therefore, to translate mythological statements into some more acceptable language. But even if this is true, we must first appreciate what the myth was trying to say. Too often demythologization has not been a process of translation, but replacement of one set of ideas by another. Many, however, would argue that it is impossible to demythologize, but that one myth may only be interpreted by another[133] and that myth is the necessary language of religion.[134] The attempt must be made, therefore, to get inside the mythological·language of the gospels. Only then may we recapture something of the impact which they had on their first readers and come to a greater understanding of the faith in Jesus as the Christ which they proclaimed.

NOTES

1. F. C. Conybeare, *Magic, Myth and Morals*, Watts 1909, p. xii.
2. Conybeare, op. cit., p.282.
3. Conybeare, op. cit., pp.287ff.
4. J. G. Frazer, *The Golden Bough*, Macmillan 1911.
5. Frazer, op. cit., Vol. IX, ³1913, pp.412–23.
6. R. Angus Downie, *Frazer and the Golden Bough*, Gollancz 1970, pp.21f., 54.
7. C. J. Wright, 'The Problem of Jesus in France', *Modern Churchman* XVII, 1927/8, p.35.
8. J. M. Robertson, *Pagan Christs*, Watts 1903, pp.101–207.
9. J. M. Robertson, *History of Free Thought*, Watts 1929, pp.64f.
10. See the reply of M. Goguel, *Jesus the Nazarene – Myth or History?* T. Fisher Unwin 1926, p.61; A. Deissmann, 'The Name "Jesus" ', *Mysterium Christi*, ed. G. K. A. Bell and D. A. Deissmann, Longmans Green 1930, pp.3–27.

11. A. Drews, *The Christ Myth*, T. Fisher Unwin [3]1910, pp.66f.,75; see Goguel, op. cit., pp.4–68.

12. See C. Clemen, *Primitive Christianity and its Non-Jewish Sources*, T. and T. Clark 1912, pp.267–87, for a description and criticism of Jensen's views.

13. Wright, op. cit., p.36.

14. G. A. Wells, *The Jesus of the Early Christians*, Pemberton Books 1971: evidence for the concept of a suffering Messiah is found in *Sanhedrin* 93b and 98b; cf. S. Mowinckel, *He that Cometh*, Blackwell 1959, pp.327–30.

15. J. M. Allegro, *The Sacred Mushroom and the Cross*, Hodder and Stoughton 1970.

16. O. Pfleiderer, *The Early Christian Conception of Christ*, Williams and Norgate 1905, pp.152ff.

17. See G. Widengren, 'Early Hebrew Myths and their Interpretation', *Myth, Ritual and Kingship*, ed. S. H. Hooke, Clarendon Press 1958, pp. 149f.

18. T. K. Cheyne, *Bible Problems*, Williams and Norgate 1904, p.128.

19. See C. Gore, *The Reconstruction of Belief*, John Murray 1926, pp.335f., 395.

20. W. F. Albright, *From the Stone Age to Christianity*, Johns Hopkins Press 1957, p.365, remarks that Lidzbarski 'inaugurated a period of exaggerated respect for the antiquity of Mandaean literature'.

21. See further W. Manson, *Jesus the Messiah*, Hodder and Stoughton 1943, pp.17–19, 174–90; W. G. Kümmel, *Introduction to the New Testament*, SCM Press 1966, pp.154–61; R. H. Fuller, *The Foundations of New Testament Christology*, Lutterworth Press 1965, pp.93ff; and pp.156f.

22. F. C. Spurr, 'Christianity and Mythology', *Expository Times* XX, 1909, p.229.

23. Gore, op. cit., pp.707f.

24. Wright, op. cit., pp.37f.

25. Wright, op. cit., p.47.

26. Fuller, op. cit., pp.89–93.

27. F. G. Downing, *The Church and Jesus*, SCM Press 1968, p.78.

28. J. R. Hinnells, 'Christianity and the Mystery Cults', *Theology* LXXI, 1968, pp.20–5.

29. Gore, op. cit., p.699, cf. pp.709f.

30. Gore, op. cit., pp.708f.

31. J. G. Bishop, 'The Value of Myths, Images, Types and History for Apologetic', *Church Quarterly* CLXIV, 1963, pp.272f.

32. E.g. R. C. Zaehner, *Concordant Discord*, Clarendon Press 1970, p.24.

33. P. Lobstein, *The Virgin Birth of Christ*, Williams and Norgate 1903, p.161.

34. Van A. Harvey, *The Historian and the Believer*, SCM Press 1967, p.25.

35. W. M. Urban, *Humanity and Deity*, Allen and Unwin 1951, p.85.

36. N. Berdyaev, *Freedom and the Spirit*, Scribners 1935, ch.2.

37. Urban, op. cit., pp.81,86.

38. G. Aulén, *The Drama and the Symbols*, SPCK 1970, pp.126ff., 149f.

39. See as an example of this enthusiasm, T. W. Doane, *Bible Myths*, The Truth Seeker Co. 1882.

40. L. A. White, *The Evolution of Culture*, McGraw-Hill 1959.

41. E. B. Tylor, *Primitive Culture*, Estes and Lauriat 1874.

42. L. H. Morgan, *Ancient Society*, H. Holt 1877.

43. E. O. James, *Myth and Ritual in the Ancient Near East*, Thames and Hudson 1958, pp.28off.

44. K. Jaspers, 'Myth and Religion', *Kerygma and Myth* II, ed. H. W. Bartsch, SPCK 1962, p.135.

45. A. Lang, *Custom and Myth*, Longmans Green 1898, p.51.

46. M. Eliade, *The Quest*, University of Chicago Press 1969, p. 36.

47. For a description and criticism of pan-Babylonianism, see H. W. Schmidt, *The Origin and Growth of Religion*, Methuen 1931, pp.97–102.

48. James, op. cit., pp.40f., found this pattern in the gospels.

49. See the discussion by S. G. F. Brandon, 'The Myth and Ritual Position Critically Considered', *Myth, Ritual and Kingship*, ed. S. H. Hooke, pp.261–91.

50. Eliade, op. cit., p.31.

51. Eliade, op. cit., p.33 defends him.

52. Allegro, op. cit., esp. p. 18.

53. H. Schaer, *Religion and the Cure of Souls in Jung's Psychology*, Routledge and Kegan Paul 1951, p.67.

54. Cf. T. Boslooper, *The Virgin Birth*, SCM Press 1962, pp.135f.; L. I. J. Stadelmann, *The Hebrew Conception of the World*, Biblical Institute Press 1970, p.10.

55. Clemen, op. cit., p.17.

56. Urban, op. cit., p.93.

57. M. Dibelius, *From Tradition to Gospel*, Ivor Nicholson and Watson 1934, pp.108,127,130.

58. T. J. Thorburn, *Jesus the Christ, Historical or Mythical?*, T. and T. Clark 1912, p. 210.

59. Thorburn, op. cit., pp.207ff.

60. Gore, op. cit., p. 700; cf. J. G. Machen, *The Virgin Birth of Christ*, Marshall, Morgan and Scott 1930, p.336; Fuller, op. cit., p.90.

61. R. L. Beals and H. Hoijer, *An Introduction to Anthropology*, Macmillan [3]1965, p.724.

62. Cf. G. Lienhardt, *Social Anthropology*, Oxford University Press[2] 1966, pp.119f.

63. See Beals and Hoijer, op. cit., pp.713ff.

64. P. Bohannan, *Social Anthropology*, Holt, Rinehart and Winston 1963, pp.336f.

65. Conybeare, op. cit., p.289.

66. John Macquarrie, *Principles of Christian Theology*, SCM Press 1966, p.122.

67. H. J. D. Astley, *Biblical Anthropology*, Oxford University Press 1929, p.86.

68. M. Eliade, *Myth and Reality*, Harper 1963, p.168.

69. Cf. O. Cullmann, *Christ and Time*, SCM Press 1951, pp.94ff.

70. Cf. Astley, op. cit., pp.226–34.

71. G. V. Jones, *Christology and Myth in the New Testament*, Allen and Unwin 1956, p. 250.

72. E. Crawley, *The Tree of Life*, Hutchinson 1905, pp.119,261f.

73. Crawley, op. cit., p.200.

74. A. Bentzen, *King and Messiah*, Blackwell, rev. ed. 1970, pp.74ff.,79.

75. Eliade, *Myth and Reality*, p.168.

76. A. N. Wilder, 'Eschatological Imagery and Earthly Circumstance', *New Testament Studies* V, 1958/9, pp.230,234.

77. Zaehner, op. cit., p. 156.

78. See Clemen, op. cit., pp.34–9; cf. G. Parrinder, *Avatar and Incarnation*, Faber 1970, p.241.

79. D. F. Strauss, *A New Life of Jesus*, Williams and Norgate 1865, Vol. II, pp.128,173ff.

80. Goguel, op. cit., pp.156–78.

81. A. Schweitzer, *The Quest of the Historical Jesus*, A. and C. Black 1910, p. 84.

82. Stadelmann, op. cit., pp.4,6.

83. See O. S. Rankin, *Israel's Wisdom Literature*, T. and T. Clark 1954, pp.209f.; Widengren, op. cit., p.158.

84. J. Sturdy, 'Jesus, Tammuz, and the Deuteronomist', *Church Quarterly* II, 1969/70, pp.330–4.

85. Cf. Albright, op. cit., pp.397ff.

86. Cf. Manson, op. cit., p.18.

87. Urban, op. cit., p.94; cf. pp.87ff.,90f.

88. G. Kittel, 'The Jesus of History', *Mysterium Christi*, ed. Bell and Deissmann, pp.36–8.

89. L. Malevez, *The Christian Message and Myth*, SCM Press 1958, p.167.

90. Cf. Bishop, op. cit.

91. H. Schlier, *The Relevance of the New Testament*, Burns and Oates 1968, p.84.

92. See W. Künneth, *The Theology of the Resurrection*, SCM Press 1965, pp.47–62.

93. E. Stauffer, *New Testament Theology*, SCM Press 1963, pp.278f. n. 293.

94. W. Johnstone, 'The Mythologizing of History in the Old Testament', *Scottish Journal of Theology* XXIV, 1971, pp. 201 17; cf. J. Bowker, *Problems of Suffering in Religions of the World*, Cambridge University Press 1970, p.6; K. Grayston, 'The Darkness of the Cosmic Sea, A Study in St Mark's Narrative of the Crucifixion', *Theology* LV, 1952, pp.126f.; Schlier, op. cit., pp.91ff.; G. S. Spinks, *The Fundamentals of Religious Belief*, Hodder and Stoughton 1961, pp.122ff.

95. O. Cullmann, *Salvation in History*, SCM Press 1967, p.139; B. W. Anderson, 'Exodus Typology in Second Isaiah', *Israel's Prophetic Heritage*, ed. B. W. Anderson and W. Harrelson, SCM Press 1962, p.193.

96. See E. Jacob, *Theology of the Old Testament*, Hodder and Stoughton 1958, p.201.

97. See E. O. James, op. cit., pp.17ff.; A. Loisy, *The Birth of the Christian Religion*, Allen and Unwin 1948, pp.11,69.

98. G. Hebert, *The Christ of Faith and the Jesus of History*, SCM Press 1962, pp.95f.

99. Cf. Spinks, op. cit., p.126.

100. G. Every, *Christian Mythology*, Paul Hamlyn 1970, p.18.

101. Cf. J. Daniélou, *The Infancy Narratives*, Burns and Oates 1968, pp.7ff.

102. Cf. Johnstone's remarks on the Old Testament, op. cit., p.217. For attempts to distinguish different types of mythological material in accordance with its relationship to history, see G. V. Jones, op. cit., pp.29f.; B. H. Throckmorton, *The New Testament and Mythology*, Darton, Longman and Todd 1960, pp.115f.

103. See L. Spence, *An Introduction to Mythology*, Harrap 1921, pp.12f.; Beals and Hoijer, op. cit., pp.668f.

104. John Bright, *The Authority of the Old Testament*, SCM Press 1967, p.129.

105. Cf. N. Micklem, 'A Modern Approach to Christology', *Mysterium Christi*, ed. Bell and Deissmann, pp.148f.

106. Dibelius, op. cit., pp.267f.

107. Dibelius, op. cit., p.285.

108. Dibelius, op. cit., pp.269–84; id., *Gospel Criticism and Christology*, Ivor Nicholson and Watson 1935, p.25.

109. Dibelius, *From Tradition to Gospel*, p.266.

110. F. M. Müller, *The Origin and Growth of Religion*, Longmans Green 1880.

111. K. Adam, *The Christ of Faith*, Burns and Oates 1957, pp.84ff.

112. L. Mair, *An Introduction to Social Anthropology*, Clarendon Press 1965, p.229; cf. Lang, op. cit., p.57.

113. G. S. Kirk, *Myth. Its Meaning and Functions in Ancient and Other Cultures*, Cambridge University Press 1970, pp.9f.

114. C. H. Gordon, *Before the Bible*, Collins 1962, p.170.

115. T. H. Gaster, *Thespis*, Harper 1966, p.25.

116. See E. and M-L. Keller, *Miracles in Dispute*, SCM Press 1968, pp.80–91; cf. Schweitzer, op. cit., pp.68–120.

117. Mair, op. cit., p.227.

118. Cf. Lienhardt, op. cit., p.137; L. Spence, op. cit., p.12.

119. See Macquarrie, op. cit., pp.121f.

120. Mair, op. cit., p.229.

121. Harvey, op. cit., pp.280f.

122. Cf. Beals and Hoijer, op. cit., pp.601f.,669.

123. Aulen, op. cit., p.129; cf. Gore, op. cit., p.617.

124. Harvey, op. cit., p.257.

125. Bowker, op. cit., p.82.

126. Cf. Macquarrie, op. cit., p.256.

127. See Lienhardt, op. cit., pp.70–3.

128. Wells, op. cit., pp.234f.; see also E. R. Dodds, *Bacchae*, Clarendon Press ²1960, p.xiv.

129. Gaster, op. cit., pp.24f.

130. Mair, op. cit., p.229.
131. Cf. Gordon, op. cit., p.90.
132. See S. Mowinckel, *The Psalms in Israel's Worship*, Blackwell 1962, pp.166f.; cf. E. Voegelin, *Israel and Revelation*, Louisiana State University Press 1956, p.294.
133. Jaspers, op. cit., p.144.
134. A. N. Wilder, *New Testament Faith for Today*, SCM Press 1956.

PART ONE

Creation Mythology and the Gospels

I   The Old and the New Creation

The starting point for any study of the relationship of the gospel story with mythology is of fundamental importance, because it determines the perspective of the whole. A rather long introduction which has concerned itself primarily with discovering the approaches used in the past and determining the nature of the material which is to be looked for has at least enabled us to choose our way into the subject with care. In particular, it has suggested the importance of two basic factors which indicate fairly decisively the route which we must take.

In the first flush of comparative mythology, scholars looked with enthusiasm in the religious traditions of the ancient East for traits similar to those found in the New Testament. The source of the Christian myth was consequently found in a variety of pagan mythologies. Some looked to the mystery cults or the gnosticizing sects of the Hellenistic world, others to the countries with which Israel had been in intimate contact, Canaan, Persia, Egypt and Babylonia, while others went further afield for their supposed sources in the stories of the Buddha and of Krishna. Now while these claims cannot simply be ruled out as irrelevant because a comparison with other traditions can be a useful check on interpretation, it would seem to be more reasonable to assume that any mythological symbolism used would be dominated by that which was current in the Judaism from which Christianity emerged. The river of religious thought and practice we know as the Hebraic-Christian tradition may well have been fed by a number of tributaries, but they would certainly be swallowed up in the river itself and be conformed to its ways. We look primarily, therefore, to the Hebraic heritage for the source of any gospel mythology there might be.

Further, we have discovered that mythology is largely concerned with the theme of creation, and around this with a cluster of related elements. The mythological complex centred on the creation event generally includes stories of the divine agencies of creation, tales of the first human pair and the use of cosmological models with which to describe the world inhabited by men and gods. There must therefore be a presumption that the presence of mythology in the gospel story would be indicated by the appearance of such elements and in particular by the use of the theme of creation. That early Christian thought did reflect such a corpus of ideas is apparent from the fact that the New Testament tells us of the creative *logos*, reminds us several times of the first man, Adam, and speaks of the Christ event against the background of a cosmography in which Jerusalem has more than a geographical significance. Most of all, however, a clue is given to us in Col. 1.16, where Paul tells his readers that the whole cosmos was created in, through and by Christ.[1] This must lead us to question whether the idea of Christ as creator has played any part in the gospel story, and whether a number of mythological elements do not find their explanation within the context of a Christian use of the creation theme.

On the basis of these two factors it would seem, therefore, to be appropriate that we should look for the origin of any gospel mythology in Hebraic traditions about the creation event. Our line of investigation would be further justified if it can be shown that there was a basis in that tradition for the idea of a new creation such as Christ might have been held to bring about. In order to discover this, however, we must examine, if only briefly, the nature of the Hebraic material concerning creation and its relationship with myth. Only then shall we be able to determine whether any case can be made out for the argument that there are elements present in the gospels which centre upon a Judaic mythology of creation.

THE PERSISTENCE OF A HEBREW MYTHOLOGY OF CREATION

The idea that the creation narrative of Genesis might be mythological in character did not carry any real weight until certain ancient Babylonian texts, particularly the *Enuma Elish*, were discovered which had a degree of similarity with it. The argument for dependence on a Mesopotamian source for the creation story can, of course, easily be challenged. As W. G. Lambert points out, earlier scholars failed to distinguish between the different cultural strata denoted by 'Babylonian', failed to give sufficient weight to the similarities found elsewhere, and most of all did not allow for the considerable differences which existed between the Hebraic and the Babylonian traditions.[2] The archaeological finds at Ugarit opened up an important new phase in the debate, for there seemed to be much more obvious connections with this culture with which the Hebrews had been in prolonged contact. This thesis could also be criticized, for the differences again were considerable, especially with the first chapter of Genesis. Despite the valid arguments which could be advanced against theories of dependence on Babylonia or Canaan, however, it had become clear that there was a link between the Israelite culture and the mythology of the ancient Near East, about which knowledge was continually growing. The problem was to determine the nature of this link.

Even the earliest and most enthusiastic supporters of Babylonian dependence had to admit that in taking over foreign material, the Hebrews had drastically altered it.[3] In particular, it was clear that although a trace had been left in the use of the name Elohim, the polytheism of the supposed originals had been eliminated. Now for many, a myth was by definition a story of gods. The eradication of polytheism, therefore, seemed to indicate that Genesis 1 could not be termed mythological at all. Thus G. Pidoux argues that it is not myth because 'the elements have lost the personality which they possessed in the old myths. They are no longer gods but things.'[4] The personifications of natural forces which were the gods of the old myths had disappeared. In the Priestly version of creation there was but one God, and this was a God who stood behind and beyond all phenomena. The mythical gods had been degraded to the level of things created. They could no longer function as aboriginal sources of creation.

This reaction against the polytheism of the old myths appears to have been the most characteristic feature of the major thrust in Hebraic thinking. In it we can see the effects of the prophetic movement and the Deuteronomic reform. There is reason, nevertheless, to question to what extent this movement was successful in eliminating mythological features, and even whether it was able entirely to rid Israel of remnants of poly-theistic thought. Despite the efforts of canonical Judaism, as we may call it, mythology appears to have survived, although in a somewhat attenuated form, especially in religious poetry and liturgical practice. There are hints of the old myths even in the prophets who, as Hooke pointed out, continued to make use of old poetic forms concerning the Tammuz myth which they adapted to their own religious experience.[5] Moreover, quite apart from any conscious use of ancient mythological motifs by the prophets, there was almost certainly a survival of mythical thinking in Israel. Mythology died hard in the folk-consciousness and remained to provide the basis for future development. As elsewhere, we perceive that a period of demythologization created by the Hebrew prophets was followed by a remytholo-gization which drew its strength from the mythology retained in the popular mind. This ebb and flow of mythological thinking can be seen most aptly for our purpose by noting how Hebrew thought and practice developed with regard to a key feature of mythology, the renewal of creation.

EXPECTATIONS OF RENEWAL IN ISRAEL

The myths of creation speak of creative events which took place in primordial time. Precisely because they are located outside history, however, it was possible to see them as archetypal descriptions of events which were continually taking place within history. In mythological cultures, therefore, the world is frequently seen as running down, coming to an end and being re-created, hence the cyclic view of time which we find in Babylonia, India, Greece and elsewhere.[6] Linked with this concept are rituals whereby man is enabled to participate in the cyclic re-creation, so identifying himself and his society with the cosmic rhythm. Not unnaturally, these periods of creative renewal were frequently associated with the vegetative year, with the movements of the sun and with the lunar cycle. Embedded in the ritual year were times when the creation myth was understood, therefore, to be particularly significant because it gave meaning to what was happening to the cosmos as a whole and especially to crops, cattle and men.

There would be every reason to suppose that the ancient Hebrews had once participated in such rituals. The extent to which these practices were continued in the Old Testament era has, however, been much disputed. The religious revolution achieved by the prophets and priests of Israel was so successful in eliminating these ideas from the sacred writings that the thesis can be roundly denied.[7] Nevertheless, a number of scholars have suggested that creation ceremonies did take place in Israel and, moreover, were potent influences on Jewish thought down to New Testament times. N. A. Dahl gives a moderate summary of this view when he says that 'in the common worship the creation was commemorated and re-enacted, and the future renewal for which Israel hoped, was pre-figured', especially in the festivals.[8] The resemblance between 'part of the creation story in Genesis and Ps. civ with its unmistakable liturgical background' suggests to Widengren that the Genesis narrative may have formed the basis for this cultic renewal of creation.[9] It may have been linked in particular with the feast of Tabernacles or Booths. A number of connections have been seen, of which the most obvious is that both last for a period of seven days. In consequence scholars have held that this feast, held in the autumnal new year, was directed towards 'securing a new world order'.[10] If this was the case, then Israel maintained the mythologically based concept of ritual renewal, more especially in connection with a festival which seems to have provided a significant background to part of the gospel story, certainly in the Gospel of John.

In the Hebrew consciousness as represented by canonical Judaism, however, another factor somewhat foreign to mythology had intruded. The Hebrews were conscious of the significance of history in a way which we seldom, if ever, find in mythological societies. Consequently they saw the really important creative moment in historical rather than in cosmological terms. For them creation was virtually identified with their emergence as a nation in the escape from Egypt. Their experience of the Exodus and their idea of creation mutually influenced each other.[11] In their practices of cultic renewal, therefore, they did not merely celebrate the cosmological creation but also their birth as a nation and its accompanying covenant, always seeing the one in terms of the other. This historical understanding of their existence meant that the Hebrews tended to think not only of recurrent, cultic renewal, but also of moments of a decisive and irreversible nature in history, the two concepts probably existing side by side. On the one hand they celebrated the renewal of the creation and the covenant as an annual, monthly, weekly and even daily event, and on the other hand, they saw history as a line on which specifically new events took place.

Because the Hebrews retained the concept of renewal along with their distinctive idea of linear history, it was perhaps inevitable that they should have developed the idea of an eschatological re-creation. In this the two apparently opposed elements coalesced. As an occurrence at the end of history it was a once-for-all event, and yet as a renewal of creation it was clearly influenced by the ancient mythological concept of periodic re-creation. The emergence of eschatology may have been precipitated, as Bentzen suggested, by the collapse of the historical hope in Israel when the two kingdoms had fallen,[12] but this was only possible because it was a logical development from the peculiar combination of ideas achieved in Israel's view of time. Eschatology was, as A. J. Wensinck declared, 'a cosmogony of the future',[13] the hope for another creative moment such as there had not been since the time of the original creation.[14] Later writers developed the connection between the two creations explicitly. The end would be a return to the beginning,[15] as in Babylonian and Greek thought.[16] Speculation about the nature of the new creation was diverse, as Dahl takes pains to show. Sometimes it was seen as a sudden event[17] and sometimes as a gradual transformation,[18] but always as a renewal of creation, a return to the beginnings.[19]

When speaking of this future event, the Hebrew could hardly avoid the language connected with the primordial creation and hence also its mythological images.[20] When the ideas embedded in prophetic eschatology were developed by the apocalyptic writers of later Judaism, the use of mythological language flourished even more. Consequently we find that the apocalyptic writings of later Judaism must play an important part in our study, because in them we have evidence of the way in which

the Hebrew mythology of creation was understood and applied
to the future in the New Testament period. Another important
source of information is found in the rabbinic writings. Apocalyptic and rabbinic thought provided Jews of Christian
times with the concept of two ages. The present age was that of
the old creation, the coming age would be a new creation, which
would be free from the moral degradation of the old and its
bondage to evil powers. The new age would be eternal, sharing
in the timelessness of God himself.[21]

We have, therefore, a sound basis in contemporary Judaic
tradition for thinking that the gospel story may reflect a
developed and renewed understanding of the Hebraic mythology of creation.

EXPECTATIONS OF RENEWAL INHERITED AND FULFILLED IN CHRISTIANITY

When we turn from the writings of late Judaism to those in the
New Testament we find indeed that many of these ideas have
been taken over. The doctrine of the two ages is certainly
present in Paul and must be linked with his concept of Christ
as creator. The gospels, of course, do not usually handle the
subject in the discursive manner of a Paul. A narrative form
does not lend itself to the same kind of explicit statement.
Rather, the evangelists must indicate their theology by the way
in which they place the events of Jesus' life in a significant
framework. Only in the discourses attributed to Christ can
explicit statements be made. Now in one of these at least Jesus
is represented as sharing the contemporary Jewish beliefs about
the future which we have sketched. In Mark 13.24f. a future is
predicted in which the cosmos will return to its primeval state,
to the darkness and chaos of the beginning as the stars fall and
the powers in the heavens are shaken. These cosmological dis-
placements are clearly intended to indicate the destruction of
the old world.[22] The early Christians certainly, and perhaps
Jesus himself, inherited the apocalyptic hope of a new creation.
The followers of Christ, however, differed in one very important
respect from their contemporaries. Alongside the typical
prophecies of a new age to come, they placed the clearest of
assertions that it had already begun in Jesus. This was the

distinctive element in their thinking. It formed part of the
earliest proclamation,[23] was given eloquent expression by
Paul,[24] and there must be a likelihood that it determined to
some extent the symbolic framework provided by the evangelists. The apocalyptic visions of the future were believed to have
already become fact in the life of Jesus. The work of Jesus himself is destructive of the demonic forces which have taken
control of the world, and with the mission of his seventy
disciples Satan falls as lightning out of heaven.[25] With his death
the world returns to primeval darkness as its sun is blotted out.[26]

A BASIS FOR THE CLAIM TO FULFILMENT IN THE TEACHING OF JESUS

There may well have been a basis for this belief in the teaching
of Jesus himself.

In the hard core of the historical tradition about Jesus a
central place is occupied by his criticisms of the Judaism of his
day. It is not only the sins of contemporary scribalism which are
brought under judgment, but the very best of Jewish religion.
Judaism needs to be cleansed of its corruptions like the temple
which represented it,[27] but further, the Pharisees come under
the severest denunciations although they represented the high
point of the old faith. The rich young man fulfils all the require-
ments of the law but does not by this means attain to salvation.[28] On the other hand, Jesus does not come to destroy the
old but to fulfil it.[29] This appears to represent a gross contradic-
tion in Jesus' attitude until we see that the paradox is reconciled
in the concept of a new creation. Jesus calls for a return to a
beginning which antedates not merely the covenant of Sinai but
even that of Noah. He appeals directly to the primordial
intention of God the creator, to the source behind all elabora-
tions in law. This is most evident in his teaching on divorce, in
which he appeals beyond the Mosaic prescriptions to the
archetypal myth of Eden and so to the original intention of
the creator.[30] Thus both the aberrations of Judaism and the
highest expressions of its faith are brought before the bar of the
divine will as represented in the order established at creation.

The idea that with Jesus there is a revelation of things hidden
from the foundation of the world appears also in Matt. 13.35

and 25.34. The parabolic teaching of Jesus is declared to be a revelation of mysteries unknown since that time,[31] and the kingdom to be inherited by his disciples is one which was prepared then. Now while Jesus may never have made such an explicit claim for himself, the evangelist probably did no more than draw out what was implicit in Jesus' assumption of authority. If this was so, then Jesus may well have felt that he was the instrument of 'a new *emanation of the Divine revelation*' which 'always corresponds to a new age'[32] and so to have believed that he was God's agent in the formation of a new cosmogony.

That criticism of moral and ritual practice should be thought of in cosmological terms may seem less strange if we appreciate that for the Jew the destruction of Judaism was the end of the world, because it meant the passing of the world which he knew and apprehended. For the Jews at Thessalonica the gospel of Paul turned the world upside down.[33] Consequently we find cosmological statements which are not concerned simply with the material world, as they would appear to be, but are, in the manner of myth, dramatic symbolizations of the total unity which is man and the world or the cosmos as received in the human consciousness. The passing of the old Israel could be spoken of as the passing away of the world itself. Hence in the teaching of Jesus we seem to hear an echo of the words of II Bar. 85.10f.:

> For the youth of the world is past,
> And the strength of the creation already exhausted.

For Jesus the wine of Judaism had lost its flavour and its cloth was past repair.[34] The reference to the old garment may be particularly significant in this connection, for in the history of religion we find that a garment was often a symbol for the cosmos, and so investiture with a new garment could represent the coming of a new age or creation.[35] This idea seems to have been present also in Israel. A garment was used as a metaphor for the surface of the earth,[36] and more particularly for the land of Israel.[37] In view of this it would seem that, in referring to the worn-out garment, Jesus would not unnaturally be taken as speaking both of the obsolescence of the old Judaism and of the time of the old world having run out.[38]

THE CREATION THEME IN THE WORK OF THE EVANGELISTS

The isolation of the authentic Jesus tradition is not, of course, the purpose of this work, and so we must be content with these few pointers to the possibility that Jesus by his words and actions suggested an interpretation of his person and work in terms of the idea of a new age and a new creation. We are on much safer ground when we turn our attention to the evangelists.

Jesus is clearly held to have brought a new teaching, commandment and covenant[39] so that in him the old things have passed away and the new have come.[40] This belief could be given symbolic form and may provide the clue to the interpretation of two somewhat peculiar references. We are told that Jesus rides into Jerusalem on an unused donkey[41] and is buried in a tomb in which no one had previously been laid.[42] G. B. Caird argued that these things were thus 'fit for sacred use',[43] but such an interpretation perpetuates the ritual concept of holiness which is directly contrary to Jesus' denial of this outlook.[44] Rather, therefore, we should see in these references the idea that only a world of new things is appropriate to one who renounced the wine of the old world so that he might drink it new in the kingdom of God.[45] In this symbolism, Jesus by anticipation already moves in the world of new things which his religious, ethical, social and cultic revolution was bringing into being. The previously unused grave is particularly appropriate for 'the firstborn of all creation', the beginning of a new race.[46] The same idea may be echoed in the story of his birth of a virgin.

Fortunately the evangelists' use of symbolism is not always so obscure, and it becomes reasonably evident that in Jesus they see the creation myth enacted again.[47] In his work of salvation, Jesus not only gives a new covenant but a new creation, which is intimately connected with the original creative act and seen in its terms.[48] In view of the fact that the fall of man from grace had been portrayed within the context of a mythology of the primeval age, it was appropriate that the coming of salvation to fallen man should be described in terms of a second Adam and a new creation. Before proceeding to a study of this, however, we must note the paradoxical character of the relationship posited of Christ to this creation.

THE SABBATH FULFILMENT AND THE FIRST DAY

As Jesus was understood to have both fulfilled and replaced the old Israel, so on the one hand he was the climax and goal of the creation, while on the other with him the old creation is destroyed and the new begun. This is most apparent in the use made by the early Christians of the symbolism of the sabbatarian cycle.

In representing the newness brought by Christ, the early Christians appear to have made use of the symbolism of the seven-day week, and in so doing to have expressed the Christ-event within the framework suggested by the narrative of Genesis 1. The Hebrews may originally have taken the idea of the sabbatical cycle from the Canaanites, as it appears in Ugaritic mythology,[49] but at all events it was given an individualistic character in the priestly account of creation. With Judaism, the sabbatarian cycle was given significance in a number of ways. Each week was understood as a recapitulation as it were of the creative sequence. At the very basis of the Hebrew cultus lay the idea that each week was a ritual re-enactment of the Genesis myth, with the Jew resting on each sabbath as Yahweh had once rested from his work of creation.[50] Thus the Hebrew exhibited the typical parallelism found in ancient culture between cultic act and mythical narrative. The Deuteronomist links sabbath observance with the Exodus from Egypt[51] because the creative act of Yahweh was, as we have seen, constantly linked with the historical creation of Israel. The seven-day cycle may well have influenced the portrayal of this event, and certainly the entry into Canaan was eventually to be seen as entry into the sabbath rest.[52]

In Jewish apocalyptic writings the idea of the world-week was developed. The whole of historical time was divided up into periods represented by the days of the sabbatarian week, each one of which could stand for a thousand years.[53] In this scheme the last day stood for the period of rest and fulfilment, for the reign of the Messiah and the fulfilment of Judaism.[54] In rabbinic writings, therefore, the sabbath rest could be seen as a foretaste of the world to come.[55]

Sometimes, on the other hand, the Jew looked beyond the week of this world. There then emerged the idea of a further period of time in which the world would be renewed and over which the Messiah would reign.[56]

We must now consider what part these ideas have played in the presentation of Christ in the New Testament.

The most obvious fact in the gospels is the prominence given to the fact that Jesus worked on the sabbath. For the evangelists this was evidence that the Messianic age had come. The old order had been destroyed and the sabbath abrogated. Mark 2.23–28 already anticipates the argument used in John 5.16–18 that the sabbath is overruled by the presence of one who is greater than the sabbath, i.e. the Messiah.[57] The idea is also present in MS D of Luke 6.5, which seems to mean that working on the sabbath is not blameworthy if done in the knowledge that the Messianic age has come.[58] The sabbath is not to be a day of rest but of the Father's work. Again we see a mythologically-based cultic idea being abrogated.

On the other hand, the symbolism of the week is retained. In Hebrews 3.7—4.11 the symbolism of the sabbath rest as connected with the Exodus is given a new Christian meaning. The point is made that the Hebrews had not entered into the promised rest by entering Canaan, but that it was still to come. That rest is now available for men to enter through Jesus Christ. In II Thess. 1.6–7, in a Christian use of the typical Jewish idea of the eschatological and Messianic sabbath, that rest is said to come when the Lord is revealed from heaven. Finally, in Rev. 14.13 we note that there is a rest for the blessed dead from their labours.

That some use of the symbolism of the week is made in the gospels appears reasonably clear, but specific interpretation on the other hand is difficult. Matthew's genealogy may represent a synoptic use of the idea that the sabbatarian age is inaugurated by Christ,[59] which is further elaborated by the fourth evangelist. Thus John Marsh notes that there are 'seven momentous days at the commencement of John's narrative',[60] and J. Estlin Carpenter suggests that the passing of six days since the Baptist's first announcement of Jesus and before the wedding of Cana may well indicate that 'in the gathering of the first disciples the new spiritual creation has begun, and the marriage at Cana falls upon the seventh day'.[61] This interpretation may be supported by the fact that reference is made within the story of the marriage at Cana to six water-pots whose contents are transformed. This could well suggest that the old dispensation, represented by the water used for Jewish purificatory rituals, was replaced by the wine of the sabbath dispensation. But it is possible to reject the presence of any symbolism here as J. H. Bernard did on the grounds that it is simply the record of eye-witnesses.[62] In view of the total context, however, and the presence of other symbols of the Messianic dispensation such as wine and wedding, an interpretation in terms of a sabbath fulfilment is quite possible.

The other use of the world-week concept, i.e. in terms of a new week of creation, also seems to have played a part in the New Testament, for we continually have the paradox of fulfilment and replacement repeated. For Paul the resurrection of Christ constituted a new act of creation,[63] and the persistent assertion that it took place on the first day of the week may well have been intended to make this point.[64] The distinctively Christian act of cultic renewal came to take place on this day and eventually replaced the Jewish sabbath. With the empty grave, the old world had been vacated and the new brought into being.[65] This will be even clearer as we go on to examine the way in which the role of Jesus was related to these events.

This first day could be referred to as the eighth day of the old week. Thus in John 20.26 it is eight days after Thomas' expression of doubt that Jesus appears to him, i.e. on the following Sunday. Now this may be a symbolic way of suggesting that the Christian day is beyond the sabbatarian cycle. The same thought may also lie behind the reference in Luke 9.28 to the transfiguration taking place about eight days after Peter's confession. The transfiguration story is notoriously difficult, and perhaps the principal reason for this is that its meaning is not monolithic but multivalent. In Mark 9.2 we are told that it took place after six days had passed. Now the Markan and the Lukan references to six and eight days respectively may be due to a variation in symbolic usage with regard to the transfiguration. It is possible that Mark intends us to see the event as the sabbatarian fulfilment of the Hebraic week, i.e. as the eschatological epiphany of the Messiahship of Jesus, while Luke on the other hand follows that other tradition we have noted which

thinks of the Christ event as the beginning of a new creation
on the eighth day or on the first day of a new world-week.

THE FIRSTBORN AND LORD OF THE NEW CREATION

In addition to the paradox of fulfilment and replacement the
evangelists present us with another. Jesus is himself shown as
part of the new creation, its beginning and its immanent power,
but also he is transcendent to it and creator of it. This is a fundamental paradox which lies at the root of many problems in
New Testament christology. It is perhaps epitomized by the
presence of the two primary elements in the Son of Man tradition. In the one, the Son of Man is within the world, perhaps its
ideal representative, and suffers with it the agonies of its demise.
In the other, the Son of Man is a glorious and transcendent
figure who comes in power and judgment to the world. Two
usages also appear in talk of the resurrection. On the one hand
we are presented with language which stresses the passive role
of Christ – he is raised by God from the dead. On the other
hand there are passages in which Jesus is not the passive recipient
of divine action, but rather possessed of an immanent power
whereby he rises from the dead. Such diversity of usage probably owes much to the presence of traditions formulated at
different times in the development of the early church's
christology, but we must not ignore the fact that the presence
of paradox is entirely proper within the logic of mythological
symbolism. Thus Jesus is both the son of the Father who
renders an obedience in the garden which Adam did not, but
also himself the creative force remaking the world as Spirit,
Wisdom and *Logos*. As the rabbis identified the Messiah with
the Spirit of God which moved on the face of the waters of
creation,[66] so the prologue to John's gospel implies a similar
equation of Jesus with the creative word. In this connection
R. H. Fuller's suggestion that *logos*, *sophia* and the first or
heavenly Man all derive from a common mythology[67] perhaps
points to the integrating factor in the paradox. The road to
Calvary also has its two paradoxical traditions. In the one it is
the road to the cross, humiliation and destruction. In the other
it is to victory and judgment over the world. In the first, again,

Jesus is the passive recipient, though this time of the world's cruelty of decadence, while in the second he marches towards Jerusalem, whose destruction he predicts as one who brings fire to the earth.

Because the evangelists were concerned to show the total involvement of Jesus with the world whose fate lay in his very person, they could hardly avoid making use of the most characteristic feature of mythological symbolism.

In myth, creation is invariably a cosmogony. The world is not so much made as born. This imagery is preferred because it conveys the mythological apprehension of the world as a living thing. Now whatever demythologization had taken place in Israel, the perception of the world as a living reality appears to have remained.[68] The early Christians appear to have inherited this mythological manner of thinking,[69] and so when Matt. 19.28 speaks of the coming of the Son of Man in the 'rebirth', we must suspect that the language has been influenced by the cosmogonic imagery of myth. The term used by Matthew was a technical one among the Stoics, in the mysteries and in Philo, and Matthew may well have been deliberately turning it to Christian use. In doing so the evangelist is probably concerned to emphasize that in the Hebraic-Christian view a rebirth is not other-worldly, but returns to a proper mythological usage by making it refer to 'the new world'.[70] There was an ancient precedent for speaking of the world as a woman in travail in connection with the day of the Lord,[71] and this imagery was retained by the rabbis, who made use of it with reference to the coming age, speaking of 'the birth pangs of the Messiah', which may well have been an accepted figure in the time of Christ.[72] For the evangelists, too, the new age is born of travail.[73]

Such an outlook on the part of the evangelists could hardly fail to influence their symbolic presentation of the Christ story. It has been pointed out by Astley that the gospel preserves traces of primitive animism.[74] To attempt to dispose of this usage by placing it within a neat category derived from a theory of religious evolutionary development, however, is inept. It does not denote the retention of an unscientific mode of thought but simply of an appropriate symbolism. By its means the evangelists could relate Christ to the totality of the world, with important results for our understanding of their narratives. Jesus is certainly still a historical character who moves on the surface of the earth, but he is also one with whose coming and being the whole of the cosmos is involved and in whom its fate is determined. In consequence the significant moments in his life are marked by cosmic events, by a star which points to the place of his birth and by the rending of the earth at his death.

A recognition that the gospel writers sometimes make use of a cosmic symbolism in which the whole world of objects can be given a kind of personal value will be seen to throw light on much of the narrative. In particular, it enables us to see the way in which the Genesis creation narrative and the material related to it in Judaic culture has formed the basis for some of the gospel events in which the ultimate significance of Christ is shown forth. If this was so, we should expect the prominence given in both Genesis and later Jewish thought to the themes of light and water to be reflected in the gospel narratives, and to these we must now turn.

NOTES

1. Cf. John 1; Eph 2.10; Col. 3.10.
2. W. G. Lambert, 'A New Look at the Babylonian Background of Genesis', *Journal of Theological Studies* XVI, 1965, pp.285–300.
3. E.g. A. Jeremias, *The Old Testament in the Light of the Ancient East*, Williams and Norgate 1911, Vol. I, p.197.
4. G. Pidoux, 'Creation', *Vocabulary of the Bible*, ed. J-J. von Allmen, Lutterworth Press 1958, p.71.
5. S. H. Hooke, *Babylonian and Assyrian Religion*, Blackwell 1962, pp.31f.
6. See S. G. F. Brandon, *Time and Mankind*, Hutchinson 1951.
7. Particularly when connected with sacral kingship, see T. C. Vriezen, *An Outline of Old Testament Theology*, Blackwell 1962, p.182.
8. N. A. Dahl, 'Christ, Creation and Church', *The Background of the New Testament and its Eschatology*, 1964, ed. W. D. Davies and D. Daube, Cambridge University Press, p.424, cf. p.431.
9. Widengren, op. cit., p.175.
10. R. E. Clements, *God and Temple*, Blackwell 1965, p.69.
11. Dahl, op. cit., p.424f. See e.g. Exod. 15.1ff. and Isa. 51.9–11.
12. Bentzen, op. cit., p.73; see Isa. 65.17; 66.22 and cf. D. S. Russell, *The Method and Message of Jewish Apocalyptic*, SCM Press 1964, pp.28off.
13. Quoted E. Voegelin, op. cit., p.302; cf. Eliade, *Myth and Reality*, pp. 54–74.
14. See Isa. 11.6; 65.25.

15. II (4) Esd. 6.1–6; 7.30; II Bar. 3.7.

16. See Dahl, op. cit., p.425.

17. II (4) Esd. 7.75; I Enoch 91.16; II Bar. 32.6.

18. Jub. 1.29.

19. Cf. Barnabas 6.13.

20. Macquarrie, op. cit., p.163.

21. Cf. Cullmann, *Christ and Time*, p.47.

22. Cf. Isa. 13.10; Jer. 4.23ff.

23. As distinct from the concept of Jesus as the second Adam according to W. D. Davies, *Paul and Rabbinic Judaism*, SPCK 1958, p.44.

24. Gal. 6.15.

25. Luke 10.18.

26. Mark 15.33. For a contrary view see J. Estlin Carpenter, *The Johannine Writings*, Constable 1927, p.243.

27. Mark 11.17.

28. Mark 10.17–22.

29. Matt. 5.17.

30. Mark 10.6–9.

31. Cf. Rom. 16.25; Eph. 3.9; Titus 1.2.

32. A. Jeremias, op. cit., Vol. I, p.89.

33. Acts 17.6.

34. Mark 2.21f.

35. See J. Jeremias, *Rediscovering the Parables*, SCM Press 1969, p.103.

36. Job 38.13; Ps. 48.11; Philo, *De Fug. et Inv.* 110–12; *De Specialibus Legibus* I, 84–96; *De Vita Mosis* 117–35.

37. Isa. 26.15; see Stadelmann, op. cit., p.134.

38. J. Jeremias, *Rediscovering the Parables*, pp.91f.; cf. Heb. 1.11f.

39. Matt. 26.28; Mark 1.27; John 13.34.

40. II Cor. 5.17.

41. Luke 19.30.

42. Matt. 27.60; Luke 23.53; John 19.41.

43. G. B. Caird, *Saint Luke*, Penguin Books 1963, p.254; W. Manson, *The Gospel of Luke*, Hodder and Stoughton 1930, p.216.

44. E.g. Mark 7.1–23.

45. Mark 14.25; see further N. Alexander, 'The United Character of the New Testament Witness of the Christ-Event', *The New Testament in Historical and Contemporary Perspective*, ed. H. Anderson and W. Barclay, Blackwell 1965, pp. 16–25.

46. Col. 1.15,18.

47. G. Cavaliero, 'Christology and Creation', *Theology* LXII, 1959, pp.136–41.

48. Cf. C. F. Burney, *The Aramaic Origin of the Fourth Gospel*, Oxford University Press 1922, p.43.

49. C. H. Gordon, op. cit., pp.17of.

50. Gen. 2.2f.; Exod. 20.11.

51. Deut. 5.12ff.

52. Deut. 3.20; 12.9; Josh. 1.13–15; Ps. 95.11. When the land was lost, the future restoration of Israel came to be understood as an entry into the

rest of the Lord, see Isa. 14.3; II (4) Esd. 8.52; E. C. Hoskyns, 'Jesus the Messiah', *Mysterium Christi*, ed. Bell and Deissmann, pp.67–89.

53. G. H. Box, 'IV Ezra', *The Apocrypha and Pseudepigrapha of the Old Testament*, ed. R. H. Charles, Vol. II, p.567; see also Ps. 90.4; Jub. 4.30; II Enoch 32f.

54. II (4) Esd. 6.35–59; 8.52; Life of Adam and Eve 51.2; *Gen. R.* 20.1, *Ex. R.* 25.3,12 etc.; see Every, op. cit., pp.58f.; M. D. Hooker, *The Son of Man in Mark*, SPCK 1967, pp.99f.

55. *Gen. R.* 17.5; 44.17; *Ruth R.* 3.3; *Berakoth* 57b; *Mid. Tel. Ps.* 92.2; cf. *Rosh ha-Shanah* 31a; *Sanhedrin* 97a.

56. *Sanhedrin* 97b speaks of the renewal of the world after seven thousand years, and I Enoch 91.12–17; 93 says that seven of the ten weeks of history have passed and that the eighth week sees the establishment of the Messianic kingdom; cf. II (4) Esd. 14.12.

57. R. H. Lightfoot, *St John's Gospel*, Clarendon Press 1956, p.139; cf. Matt. 12.1–8.

58. C. F. Evans, 'Sabbath', *A Theological Wordbook of the Bible*, ed. Alan Richardson, SCM Press 1950, pp.205f. See also Hooker, op. cit., p.101, who points out that in Matthew the incident in the cornfields follows immediately on Jesus' offer of rest to his disciples, see Matt. 11.28–30; cf. Ecclus. 51.

59. Daniélou, op. cit., p.14.

60. John Marsh, *Saint John*, Penguin Books 1968, p.143; see John 1.28,35, 41,43; 2.1.

61. Carpenter, op. cit., p.377.

62. J. H. Bernard, *St John*, T. & T. Clark 1928, Vol. I, p.83.

63. Rom. 4.17.

64. Mark 16.2,9; John 20.1,19; etc.

65. Cf. Ignatius, *Magn.* 9; Barnabas 15.8f.; Justin, *Dial.* 138.

66. *Gen. R.* 2.4.

67. Fuller, op. cit., p.78.

68. I Chron. 16.31; Ps. 96.11; Isa. 49.13; Jer. 15.18; *Eccles. R.* 1.4; *Mid. Tel. Ps.* 19.1; cf. Stadelmann, op. cit., pp.7f.; A. S. Rappoport, *Myth and Legend of Ancient Israel*, Gresham 1928, p.9.

69. Rom. 8.22ff.

70. J. C. Fenton, *Saint Matthew*, Penguin Books 1963, pp.316f.

71. Isa. 13.8,9.

72. See A. Cohen, *Everyman's Talmud*, Dent 1932, p.370.

73. Matt. 24.8; cf. Mark 13.8.

74. Astley, op. cit., pp.226f.; cf. Matt. 3.9; Luke 19.40.

2   *Light in the Darkness*

Because mythological man attempted to understand his world
by means of his immediate observation of nature, the alterna-
tion of light and darkness suggested to him that the cosmos
constantly underwent a cyclic pattern of renewal. With each
morning the world came alive, and each evening it sank into the
oblivion of darkness. Out of this basic experience and evaluation, archaic man derived the symbols from which he fashioned
his myth of creation. The primeval situation was envisaged as
one wrapped in darkness and creation as the rise and triumph
of light. It is this basic pattern which appears in the book of
Genesis, where the first creation of Yahweh is that of light to
illumine the vast darkness of the primeval deep.[1]

Yet while the Hebrews took over this common mythological
pattern, it was appropriated in a way distinctive to themselves.
Whereas in many ancient cultures the symbols of the creation
myth were raised to the rank of deity, the Hebrew was careful to
preserve the distinction between the symbol and that to which
it pointed. The natural elements which served a symbolic
purpose in the myth were never confused with deity itself.

Light was a symbol of life-giving power and darkness of its
demise. But while this association of ideas remained a per-
manent feature throughout the literature of Judaism, light was
never credited with being in itself the source of life.[2] This was
the prerogative of Yahweh. He alone was the one who made
alive.

In Babylonian myth, the god Marduk is virtually identified
with light, so that the account contains no mention of its
creation. In Genesis, on the other hand, light is specifically said
to have been the creation of Yahweh, and while the psalmist

was prepared to say that 'God is light', he was never to say that 'light is God'.[3]

It was natural that the sun should become a symbol of the creative light which it appeared to embody to a very large extent. In many ancient mythologies, however, the sun also ceased to be a symbol and was itself identified with the source of life. An elaborate solar mythology came into being in which the sun was raised to the rank of deity and its fortunes held to mirror the rise and fall of universal life. This was a concept which the Hebrews entirely rejected. Yahweh was raised above the ebb and flow of cosmic life and believed to be the one permanence in a sea of change. To ensure this, all traces of solar deity are removed. The sun is nothing more than a thing created by the transcendent God.

What the Hebrew did with the sun, he also did with the rest of the natural elements. In the kind of thinking which produced the solar myth, deity was totally fragmented. The sun was clearly not the only power in the universe, and so other gods came into being, producing a riot of pluralism. The response of the Hebrew priestly writer to such polytheistic thinking was that of a radical monotheist. Yahweh is declared to be Lord of all phenomena. All cosmological entities are made to surrender their deity so that Yahweh alone may be supreme as Lord of creation.

The eradication of cosmic pluralism appears to have been carried out completely in the priestly creation myth, but the fundamental duality of mythological symbolism is not quite removed. In Gen. 1 the primeval ocean of darkness retains something of its archaic autonomy. It is not said to have been created by Yahweh. Rather, 'both sea and darkness stand as symbols of the chaos out of which the universe was created'.[4] On the other hand, they are given no divine status, and are entirely passive before the overruling will of Yahweh.

Having ensured in this way that there should be no confusion between deity and light, the Hebrew was then free to use the symbol with some freedom. In particular it provided an apt imagery in which to speak of that illumination which Yahweh had vouchsafed to the Hebrew in his law.[5] The revelation of God's will embodied in the law could be seen as the means whereby the Hebrew could walk safely through the darkness of other men's moral uncertainty. He could see himself as a missionary spreading the light of God's path among the peoples of the world.[6] He could safely ascribe ultimate primordiality to such a light.[7] This mythological device was aptly used to denote his belief that the Torah was one with the archetypal law of the universe. It was not a product of historical circumstance but a revelation of the eternal will of the creator. As the very foundation of the moral order by which the cosmos was governed, the law was appropriately included among the seven things held to have been pre-existent to creation.[8]

When the Jew spoke of the heavenly light of God, therefore, he was usually thinking of something other than the rays of the sun. He was speaking of Yahweh's moral majesty and of the beatitude which it could confer upon the lives of men. In consequence it was possible for him to develop a myth indigenous to his own culture, which expressed his understanding of human history in ethical terms. What at one time had largely been symbolism intended to portray the cyclic evolution of the cosmos was used as the material out of which to fashion a myth which told how the primordial light of God had been given to man as part of his creative bounty, how it was lost through sin and how it would eventually be regained.

The opening of the new myth in its rabbinic form may be taken from *Gen. R.* 3.4, which says that in the beginning God wrapped himself in light 'as in a robe and irradiated with the lustre of His majesty the whole world from one end to the other'.[9] The whole earth was thus initially illumined by the glory of God's light, and although one variant asserts that it was concealed from man in anticipation of his wickedness,[10] it is more generally held that Adam originally had the benefit of the primordial light in Eden. Because of its continuous illumination Adam was not subject to the cycle of day and night, and was able by it to see throughout the whole world.[11] He was even able to participate to some measure in its glory. Adam himself shone brighter than the sun.[12] God clothed him with his light and his face shone with its wonder.[13]

Adam's possession of the heavenly light was, however, a condition of his state of innocence. Although the fact is not mentioned in Genesis, it was concluded, therefore, that mankind had lost the benefit of this light as a result of the fall. There is a hint of the idea already in Job 38.15, which speaks of light being withheld from the wicked in the context of talk about creation. In rabbinic writing the forfeiture of the divine light is explicitly connected with the sin of Adam. At his fall, the father of mankind was said to have lost the perpetual light of God's glory and his own shining appearance along with the other privileges which he had enjoyed in Eden.[14] From that point on mankind had been cut off from the light kept hidden by God in the garden, and the solar symbol of the divine light was appropriately said to have become temporarily dark at this moment of human transgression and loss.[15]

As the primordial light had been lost by Adam's sin, the subsequent history of the human race was said to have been acted out in a world of darkness and death.[16] In the present age man had to make do with the light of sun, moon and stars. Only in the law did he have something of the light of God to act as a lamp to guide him through its darkness. Eventually, however, even the little light he now possessed would come to an end. The world would return to its primeval situation of inpenetrable darkness.[17]

Following the destruction of the world, however, there would come its renewal and the restoration of the primordial light of the new creation.[18] Then mankind would return to the conditions enjoyed by Adam in Eden. Night would be destroyed,[19] for endless light would be among them.[20] Once again the light of God's presence would be among his people.[21]

The coming Messiah is often seen in the context of this new light myth. The light of God will shine upon him. Like that of the first Adam, 'the raiment with which God will clothe the Messiah will shine from one end of the world to the other'.[22] He will appear as lightning flashing across the breadth of the earth.[23] Whereas the sun mourned the sin of Adam, the Messiah can be compared to the solar image of the divine light.

> And his star shall rise in heaven as of a king,
> Lighting up the light of knowledge **as the sun the day,**
> And he shall be magnified in the world.
> He shall shine forth as the sun on the earth,
> And shall remove all darkness from under heaven.[24]

So characteristic was light of the character and role of the Messiah that it became one of his titles.[25]

Finally, the new myth gave expression to one of the deepest hopes of the Judaic faith, that one day the glory of God might be again enjoyed as in the days of Adam. Now he might glimpse something of its splendour in vision or in the Torah, but the Jew looked forward to the time in the world to come or in the seventh heaven when he would be dazzled by its power and beauty.[26] He waited, therefore, for death in the knowledge that as one of the just he would exchange his burial clothes for garments of glory and be clad in shining light.[27] He would be one of the faithful to whom the portals of heaven would be opened, that they might see the divine light and themselves shine 'as the lights of heaven'.[28] He would be one of those of whom II Baruch declared that 'their splendour shall be glorified in changes, and the form of their face shall be turned into the light of their beauty, that they may be able to acquire and receive the world which does not die'.[29]

ALLUSIONS TO THE LIGHT MYTH IN THE GOSPELS

Although much of the material used in order to reconstruct the light myth as it developed in late Judaism may be later than the gospels, the evangelists themselves are evidence of the existence of such a myth in its broad outlines in their day. While they have no cause to delineate the myth in detail, the gospel writers appear to assume knowledge of its basic features. Nothing is said of its primordial stages, of the creation of light and its loss, but the description of the present age and of that to come are couched in terms which necessitate the assumption that some such scheme of thought was familiar to them.

It is constantly assumed that men are now living in an age of darkness. It is an age characterized by the night-time in which men may be found asleep when the eschaton breaks.[30] It is midnight when the bridegroom comes.[31] As wanderers in the night of the world, men walk as though they were blind and are led by blind guides.[32] But even the darkness of the present time does not equal the blackness which is to come. Sun and moon will cease to give any light and the creation will sink back into the primeval darkness out of which it arose.[33]

Mt 5:16

light
hidden
under
bushel

In the present dark age, the only light in the world is that shining forth from the righteous. The world is lost, therefore, if the light that men have in themselves is hidden under a bushel.[34] Jesus' disciples are to let their light shine before men that men may see their good works and glorify their heavenly Father.[35] They may then look forward with confidence to the day to come when the Son of Man will appear as lightning flashing from one end of the earth to the other,[36] when there shall be no more night, but the constant light of the Lord shining upon them.[37] The righteous will then participate in that light as Adam had once done, so that they will shine forth as the sun in their Father's kingdom.[38]

Mt 22:
11-13

Matthew in particular seems to emphasize the hope of the righteous in a manner typical of the Jewish tradition. The righteous are admitted into a kingdom which is surrounded by the outer darkness into which the unworthy are cast.[39] The first evangelist also uses the imagery of the garment required of and provided for the righteous in his parable of the wedding feast.[40] The garment lacked by one of the guests in the parable has most frequently been taken to symbolize some specifically Christian attribute, but it is more likely that this is also part of the traditional Jewish scheme, so that it is none other than the clothing of righteousness which may become the garment of the heavenly light. This explanation would certainly have suggested itself to those Christians steeped in the Judaic symbolism of the Messianic robe of light.[41] Matthew is not, however, a slave to the accepted tradition. On the contrary, his constant point is that those who thought that their share in the light of the kingdom was guaranteed will frequently find themselves excluded. In their place will come men like the centurion, whose chances of entry were considered to be anything but certain.[42] Nor is this the only change wrought in the pattern of expectation bequeathed by Judaism.

Rev.
3:4,5,18.

The development which dominates the four gospels in their treatment of light-symbolism is centred upon their christology. In Jesus the eschatological hope is held to have been fulfilled. With him the primeval darkness is once again dispelled. This is expressed by a variety of devices embedded in the evangelistic narratives. It is done most directly by the use of metaphor, so that Jesus as the Christ is said to be the bringer of the light or to be himself the light. Most frequently, however, the evangelists are content to be allusive. Reference is made to the time at which certain events take place, so that their meaning might be enriched by the symbolism attached to the night and the day. In certain cases mention is made of extraordinary phenomena accompanying decisive moments of the gospel story. By these means the evangelists try to show that what the Hebrew had hoped for had become a present reality in their lord. By the use of symbolism derived from the ancient myth of creation, the Christ event is shown to bring about its renewal. By isolating certain aspects of the gospel tradition, we can thus discern the appropriation to Christ of the Judaic myth so that he is presented as restorer of the primordial light.[43]

The Christ comes to a world sinking deeper and deeper into the oblivion of the night. What is merely hinted at in Matthew's narrative of the flight into Egypt,[44] that the lord comes to a world ruled by the powers of darkness, is made explicit in John's prologue. Deliberately recalling the opening verses of Genesis, John speaks of the light which comes to shine in the darkness of the world.[45] The conflict between Jesus and the forces opposing him is aptly characterized by the use of these symbols.[46] As the passion approaches, the power of the night increases. The night belongs to Judas and in it he betrays his master and himself.[47] The soldiers come to arrest Jesus under its cover.[48] The disciples flee into the anonymity of the darkness and in the grip of its power. Finally, the very height of day is turned into blackest night at the crucifixion. The sun fails and the world is plunged into the primeval darkness out of which it arose.[49] The darkness is not, however, a power in itself here any more than it was in Genesis. Confronted by the light that bursts upon it, the night is powerless.

The way had already been prepared for John's description of Jesus' coming in terms of light shining in the darkness by Matthew and Luke. The first evangelist saw in the opening of Jesus' ministry the fulfilment of Isa. 9.1f. The people of Galilee of the Gentiles who were in darkness have seen the great light promised by the prophet. To those living in the shadows of death was brought the light of life by the man from Nazareth.[50] According to Luke 2.25–32, Jesus' fulfilment of the prophetic hope that a light should come to the Gentiles had already been

foreseen by Simeon at the time of his presentation in the
temple. The notion is probably a very early one in the history
of the gospel tradition. It already appears in acted symbolism,
where Jesus is shown as one who brings the light of day into the
night of the blind.

That the gift of sight was understood as complementary to
that of light is suggested by a comparison of Matt. 4.13–16 with
Luke 4.16–19. Both passages introduce the character of Jesus'
ministry by the use of quotations from Isaiah. But whereas in
Matthew, Isa. 9 is employed to indicate that it constitutes the
coming of the eschatological light, in Luke, Isa. 61.1f. is used,
which defines Christ's role as the giving of sight to the blind. It
is also possible to see a structured relationship set up by Mark
between the stories of the blind man of Bethsaida, Peter's confession at Caesarea Philippi and the story of the transfiguration.[51] The parallelism between these events may have been
immediately clear to his readers, who knew that Bethsaida was
Peter's home.[52] If this was intended, then the gift of sight at
Bethsaida has its full explication in the revelation of Jesus on the
mount—a revelation which we shall see to have been integrally
concerned with the symbolism of light. The 'opening of the
eyes' was, moreover, a familiar term for the enjoyment of supernatural vision, and particularly appropriate as a designation
for sight of the heavenly light.[53] In John, the connection between
the gift of sight to the blind and of Jesus as the light is made
clear. The healing of the man born blind is an 'efficacious sign
of the truth' that Jesus is the light of the world.[54] As the light of
God, Jesus illuminates man's path with the word of God, so
mediating the action of God himself as portrayed in the Old
Testament. In this he takes over the role previously assigned to
Jerusalem.[55] In Jesus the world receives a new centre from
which the revelation of God is radiated among mankind.

But Jesus could only perform such a function if he were himself blessed with the light of God. He was therefore shown as
one on whom the heavenly light shone, who was enveloped in
the glory of the Lord. This was a notion which was early
incorporated in the evangelistic tradition and was of such
importance that it was constantly developed in subsequent
literature. It naturally assumed particular importance in
connection with crucial points in the evangelistic narrative. Of

outstanding significance were the stories of the nativity, the baptism and the transfiguration.

Matthew and Luke made little use of the symbolism of light in their nativity stories, but provided sufficient basis for the growth of a rich tradition. Luke employed a common Judaic symbolism when he described the angels coming to the shepherds in a blaze of divine glory.[56] Matthew spoke of a star which designated the time and place of Christ's birth.[57] In later Christian literature both of these images were developed. In the *Gospel of the Infancy* and elsewhere, the place of Jesus' birth is filled with theophanous light.[58] In the *Gospel of the Nativity of Mary*, Mary's chamber is filled with light at the appearance of the angel Gabriel. According to the *History of the Blessed Virgin Mary*, Matthew's star turned into a pillar of light.[59] Already in Ignatius the star was said to have outshone all others and to be indescribable,[60] while the gnostic Theodotus said that the star shone 'with a new light that is not of this world'.[61]

Light symbolism quickly found a place in the story of Jesus' baptism. Two MSS of the Itala have for Matt. 3.15: 'Then he consented; and when he was baptized a huge light shone from the water so that all who were near were frightened.'[62] In the *Gospel of the Ebionites*, it is recorded that after the voice had spoken 'immediately a great light shone round about the place'.[63] While no mention is made of the heavenly light in the canonical versions, it is likely that reference to the opening of the heavens provided a foundation for it. Theophany was regularly presented in this way, and it is perhaps significant that Heb. 6.4 and 10.32 speak of the baptized person as one who was enlightened.[64]

In the story of the transfiguration, the synoptists have already made use of light-symbolism and so placed their canonical seal on the imagery already mentioned. On the mount Jesus is seen by the disciples to enjoy that which was promised to the beloved of God. He appears with Moses and Elijah, who have already inherited the glory prepared for the saints. He himself is temporarily transformed so that his face shines like the sun. His clothing is changed so that it shines intensely white. Mark ensures that the reader should understand that this was not brightness of a human kind, while Matthew compares it to that of light.[65] These are clear indications provided to show Jesus as

one who is here already blessed with the light of God and
enrobed in its glory. The promise of the eschatological garment
of light is already anticipated, possessed now by the lord of the
sons of light. [66]

In this developing Christian tradition it is not difficult to
recognize the Judaic myth of the eschatological light. In Jesus
the light forfeited by man through his sin is restored. With him
the light, which once shone at the time of creation, sheds its
light once more, for in him a new creation is taking place. There
can be little doubt that this is how we must understand John's
reference to Jesus as the light in his prologue. He is designated
as the true light which comes into the world, and this light is
undoubtedly seen here as effecting a new creation. In view of
this, Jesus must be seen as the true light in the sense that he is
the heavenly or primordial light of which the earthly light was
but a pale copy, as the fulfilment of the archetypal light of the
Genesis myth. [67] But John has here placed at the beginning of
his gospel an idea which in the synoptists finds its place at
the end.

The darkness of Mark 15.33 'is the beginning of the re-
creation of the world', [68] and the first day after the sabbath
constitutes the beginning of the new creation. This is probably
indicated by all four evangelists in their references to the time
at which the resurrection was discovered. All four agree that it
was early in the morning, but do not agree as to the precise
time. John states that it was still dark. Matthew also suggests
that the sun had not yet risen. Luke, on the other hand, says
that they came as the sun began to rise. Mark has two notes of
time which A. G. Hebert finds 'flagrantly inconsistent'. The
gospel says that they came very early, which suggests sometime
before dawn, while it also states that they came after the sun had
risen. [69] These discrepancies may reflect not so much ignorance
of the facts as a desire to speak of the time involved in such a
way as to make a theological point. The notion that the women
came while it was still dark may well be intended to indicate
existential rather than chronological time. It is still dark for
them, because they do not yet know that Jesus has risen. But in
fact Jesus as the sun had risen. Mark's contradictory timing
therefore may have been the result of attempting to state both
the resurrection fact and the women's ignorance of it. At all

events, it would seem clear that the evangelists were concerned to connect the resurrection of Christ with the dawn of the sun of righteousness,[70] to show him as lord of the new creation.

There is a similar concern for the timing of events in those stories which are connected with the sea of Galilee.

The synoptic account of Jesus walking on the water in Matt. 14.22–33 and Mark 6.45–52 tells of Jesus coming to the disciples in the fourth watch of the night, recalling the motif which appears in some of the parables.[71] The lord comes to men enveloped in the darkness of the present age. In John's account of this incident the point is made with greater force. At 6.17 a connection appears to be made deliberately between the fact that it was still dark and that Jesus had not yet come to them.

Luke 5.5 associates the failure of the disciples to catch fish with the night-time. Again John is more explicit. While the Lukan story assumes that success comes with the day and the presence of Jesus, the Johannine account specifically states that Jesus appears at daybreak to bring success to their efforts. In John 9.5 the teaching which is merely hinted at in the synoptists is made plain. 'In him only the world has its day in which men may walk safely (12.35); in his absence is darkness.'[72]

That the darkness into which Jesus came was associated with the sea in this way should occasion no surprise. When speaking of the return to primeval chaos which would precede the new creation, Luke could substitute 'the roaring of the sea' for the deep darkness referred to in the Markan tradition.[73] These were virtually interchangeable symbols in Hebrew thought because they had been placed together in the creation myth.

NOTES

1. Gen. 1.2f.

2. See Job 38.9; Ps. 88.4–7,10–12; *Deut. R.* 7.3; C. K. Barrett, *The Gospel according to St John*, SPCK 1960, p.131.

3. Ps. 27.1; see W. Cruickshank, 'Light and Darkness', *Encyclopaedia of Religion and Ethics*, ed. James Hastings, T. & T. Clark 1908, Vol. VIII, p.64.

4. Grayston, op. cit., p.126; cf. p.123; Bentzen, op. cit., pp.14f., points out that when Ps. 95.5 speaks of Yahweh making the sea, this is probably to

be understood as referring to 'the sea of the ordered universe after the third day of Creation'.

5. Ps. 119.105; cf. II (4) Esdras 14.20f.; Philo, *De Opificio Mundi*, 31; *Sifre Num.* 6.25,40.

6. Isa. 42.6; 49.6.

7. Prov. 8.22f.

8. *Pesahim* 54a; *Nedarim* 39b; *Mid. Tel.* Ps. 72.6; 90.12; *Pirke de Rabbi Eliezer*, ch. 3; *Gen. R.* 3.1.

9. Cf. Ezek. 1.4ff., 28; 10.4; 43.2; *Mid. Tel.* Pss. 27.1; 104.4.

10. *Gen. R.* 42.3; L. Ginzberg, *Legends of the Bible*, The Jewish Publication Society of America 1956, p.3.

11. *Num. R.* 13.5; cf. Life of Adam and Eve, 12.1.

12. *Lev. R.* 20.2; Rappoport, op. cit., Vol. I, pp.143,146.

13. *Gen. R.* 20.12; *Num. R.* 4.8; cf. Ecclus. 49.16; Mowinckel, *He That Cometh*, pp.374f.

14. *Lev. R.* 11.7; J. Bowker, *The Targums and Rabbinic Literature*, Cambridge University Press 1969, pp.118f.

15. *Hagigah* 12a; *Num. R.* 13.5; Ginzberg, op. cit., p.42.

16. II (4) Esd. 14.20.

17. Jer. 4.23ff.; cf. Isa. 60.2; Joel 2.2; Amos 8.9.

18. II Bar. 48.50; *Hagigah* 12a; *Gen. R.* 3.6; *Ex. R.* 15.21; *Mid. Tel.* Ps. 97.2; C. G. Montefiore and H. Loewe, *A Rabbinic Anthology*, Macmillan 1938, p. 584.

19. Zech. 14.7; Rev. 21.25.

20. II Enoch 65.9B.

21. *Sifre Num.* 6.25,40.

22. *Pes. K.* 149a.

23. II Bar. 53.8ff.; cf. Dan. 7.13.

24. Test. Levi 18.3f.; cf. Isa. 42.6.

25. Barrett, op. cit., p.278.

26. Asc. Isa. 8.25.

27. II Enoch 22.8–10; Book of Noah 108.12; cf. Odes of Solomon 11; Ginzberg, op. cit., p.9.

28. I Enoch 104.2; cf. 38.4; 39.7; 92.4; II (4) Esd. 7.97,125.

29. II Bar.51.3; cf. 51.5.

30. Mark 13.35f.

31. Matt. 25.6.

32. Matt. 15.14; cf. 23.16,24,26; Luke 6.39.

33. Matt. 24.29; Mark 13.24; cf. Acts 2.20.

34. Matt. 5.15.

35. Matt. 5.16.

36. Matt. 24.27; Luke 17.24.

37. Rev. 22.5.

38. Matt. 13.43.

39. Matt. 8.12; 25.30; etc.

40. Matt. 22.11–13.

41. See Rev. 3.4,5,18; 7.9,13f.; V Ezra 2.38–45.

42. Matt. 8.5–13.

43. Cf. R. Bultmann, *The Gospel of John*, Blackwell 1971, p.342 n. 5, who sees in John's gospel a Christian version of the gnostic myth of the light-redeemer.

44. Matt. 2.14.

45. John 1.1–5.

46. Cf. John 3.19–21.

47. John 13.30.

48. Luke 22.53.

49. Matt. 27.45; Mark 15.33; Luke 23.45. The darkness attending the crucifixion has been compared to similar phenomena reported to have accompanied the death of Caesar (Virgil, *Georgics* i, 463) and others, see Conybeare, op. cit., pp. 284f.

50. Matt. 4.16.

51. Mark 8.22–26, 27–30; 9.2–9; cf. R. H. Lightfoot, *History and Interpretation in the Gospels*, Hodder and Stoughton 1935, pp.90ff.

52. John 1.44.

53. Num. 24.3; II Kings 6.17; Isa. 42.6f.; Luke 24.31, cf. 45; E. A. S. Butterworth, *The Tree at the Navel of the Earth*, de Gruyter 1970, p.74.

54. Barrett, op. cit., p.292; John 9.1–7,35–8.

55. Isa. 60.3–5.

56. Luke 2.9.

57. Matt. 2.2,7,9,10.

58. Boslooper, op. cit., pp.71f. Similar phenomena were said to have accompanied the births of Noah and Moses: I Enoch 106.1–2; Qumran fragment in T. H. Gaster, *The Scriptures of the Dead Sea Sect*, Secker and Warburg 1957, p.330; Rappoport, op. cit., Vol. I, p.229.

59. Boslooper, op. cit., pp.72ff.

60. Ignatius, *Eph.* 19.2.

61. Quoted J. Daniélou, *Primitive Christian Symbols*, Burns and Oates 1964, p.114; cf. *Protoevangelium of James* 21.2.

62. Quoted B. H. Throckmorton, *Gospel Parallels*, Nelson [D]1967, p.10.

63. Epiphanius, *Haer.* XXX, 13.7.

64. See further J. Daniélou, *A History of Early Christian Doctrine*, Darton, Longman and Todd 1964, p.230. Cf. Justin, *Apol.* I, 61.12f.; 65.1.

65. Matt. 17.2; Mark 9.3.

66. See II Peter 1.19; cf. Daniélou, *Primitive Christian Symbols*, p.110.

67. John 1.9; cf. I John 2.8; Philo, *De Somniis* I, 75.

68. Grayston, op. cit., p.127.

69. See A. G. Hebert, 'The Resurrection Narrative in St Mark's Gospel', *Scottish Journal of Theology* XV, 1962, pp.66–73.

70. See Luke 1.78; cf. Isa. 60.1; Mal. 4.2.

71. Matt. 24.43,50; 25.6–13; Luke 12.38–40.

72. Barrett, op. cit., p.296.

73. Luke 21.25.

3   *The Sea*

Paired with the primeval darkness in Genesis is the *tehōm* or deep, the vast expanse of water which enveloped all. Only with the parting of this water could the firmament come into being and only with its gathering into one place could dry land appear.[1] This is the first mention in scripture of a motif which appears frequently both within and outside Jewish canonical literature until we read in the Apocalypse that the sea is no more.[2] This leads us to suspect that the references to the sea in the gospels may well be illuminated by a knowledge of this tradition, which we must first consider outside the Hebraic literature.

The symbolic use of the sea or ocean is extensive in the literature of the ancient world. We can, however, note the primary uses to which it was put while restricting ourselves to traditions closely related geographically and temporally to Hebrew culture.

One strand of the ocean tradition is found in the Babylonian epic of creation, the *Enuma Elish*, the Ugaritic mythology of Canaan, in the Heliopolitan *Book of the Dead* and the *Book of Apophis* in Egypt. In these writings the sea is a force which has to be overcome by creative deity. The Babylonian epic tells how the creation was achieved through a struggle with chaos which the great ocean represented. The earth is won from the sea like reclaimed land from flooding, and the sea is overcome in the sense that it is made to keep its place. Its waters are held back so that there could be good earth on which life could flourish. As water was not only around the earth, but also above and below it, as evidenced by rain from above and by springs from below, the *Enuma Elish* speaks of the sea having been split into two parts to form the upper and the lower waters. In both cases we can see the basic idea of a space being created in the waters for life.[3] Similarly, in the Phoenician myths the Lord Baal overcomes Yam, the Canaanite god of the sea, lakes and rivers. Here there is no doubt that the god has to battle with and overcome the sea.

Closely connected with this tradition is the idea of water as a symbol of death. In the *Gilgamesh Epic* the paradise of Utnapishtim is surrounded by the waters of death. In Greek literature the river Styx is that through or over which the dead must pass. The conquest of the sea could also, therefore, be a defeat of death as in the Ugaritic myth, where Baal's conquest of Yam is paralleled by his defeat of Mot, the Lord of Death.

A quite different usage is found in Sumerian, Egyptian and Homeric mythology. The concept of a struggle with the sea is not prominent in this tradition.[4] For the Egyptians water was associated particularly with the Nile and therefore with the source of life. Prominent in Egyptian mythology, therefore, was the idea of the earth as the primeval hill which rose out of the waters of Nun. In Homer, Oceanus is the primeval water which is 'the begetter of us all', the source of all things. In these mythologies water is seen primarily in its good or life-giving aspect, and the concept of a primeval watery chaos is either absent or has receded into the background.

THE TEHŌM IN HEBREW THOUGHT

The significance of the sea motif in the development of the biblical tradition has been the subject of investigation and discussion for some time. It occupied an important place in the work of the writers of the myth and ritual school and has continued to call forth scholarly comment down to the present time. Most commonly the roots of the Hebraic myth have been found in the first of the traditions we have noted, and associated in particular with the Babylonian *Epic of Creation*. The priestly account of creation is then related to the Babylonian new year festival and the water of Gen. 1.2 equated with Tiamat-*Mummu* of the Babylonian epic. This was a popular view for many years in some quarters. The discovery of the Ugaritic literature, however, led to a modification in the theory, so that it was argued that Babylonian influence had been mediated through the Canaanite environment. Indeed, Lambert questions the idea of dependence on Babylonia altogether. He argues that the *Epic of Creation* is late, dating it about 1100 BC, and holds that it was a sectarian product and does not represent the norm of Babylonian tradition. Consequently he holds that the allusions to Yahweh's battle with Leviathan and the *tannīn* found in the Old Testament derive from Canaanite Baal myths and 'show no signs of dependence on Mesopotamian sources'.[5] The pursuit of similarities between the Hebraic and the Babylonian or Canaanite traditions in the interests of historical reconstruction can, however, tend to neglect the singularity of Hebrew thought with regard to the primeval sea. Certainly we must now note that the Hebrews appear to have developed their own distinctive view, although related to elements found elsewhere, and that in this the sea had a positive as well as a negative character.

The Hebrew word *tehōm* used in Genesis 1 may be related to the Akkadian word Tiamat, but there are dangers in pressing this relationship too closely. Tiamat was a female personification of the sea of salt water, *tamtu*, as distinct from Apsu, the male representation of the cosmic river of fresh water. It would seem, however, that the Hebrews did not always preserve the distinction between the salt sea of chaos and the fresh water of life.[6] Nevertheless, there was a special relationship between *tehōm* and the Tiamat-*tamtu* concept, which becomes clear as the different usages of *tehōm* are delineated.

Tehōm is first used in Scripture in Genesis 1 of the waters which were parted, the upper from the lower, and which were kept back so that the earth might appear. This was a fundamental idea among the Hebrews and was maintained down to rabbinic times.[7] It is reminiscent of the Babylonian myth which spoke of Tiamat being split into two parts, but on the other hand that the primeval water was evil in any sense is not apparent in Genesis 1. It is merely there, and no suggestion is made of a battle with it.

The word was also used for the deep beneath the cosmic ocean.[8] It then designated the source of all the waters of the earth, 'the primordial abyss' and 'the great reservoir of subterranean waters'.[9] The manifestation of these waters on the surface of the earth could take a benevolent or a hostile form, for when the *tehōm* impinged upon human life it took on a particular character in so far as it promoted or inhibited human life.

Rivers, wells and springs had their origin in the *tehōm*. These were among the blessings which the *tehōm* gave to man.[10] In this way it made Canaan a good land and suitable as a gift from Yahweh to his people.[11] The *tehōm* nourished the land and enabled its cedars to grow tall.[12] It was the source also of the waters of the sea out of which God brought forth abundant life.[13]

On the other hand, the *tehōm* was the source of the flood waters which devastated the crops and threatened the whole human race.[14] It was, then, the proper home of the flooding waters. Jubilees 5.29 and 6.26 speak of the Noachian flood waters receding into the mouths of the abysses and descending into the deep below. The *Assumption of Moses* reflects this usage when it looks forward to a time when 'the sea shall retire into the abyss'.[15] In this aspect the *tehōm* appears to retain, in some parts of Scripture, something of the character which Tiamat had. Traces of the conflict motif appear in some of the psalms,[16] suggesting that the priestly demythologization had not succeeded in eradicating the mythological concept of the *tehōm* as a force which Yahweh had to overcome.

But while *tehōm* normally designated the subterranean deep from which issued waters for good and ill, it could also be used for these waters themselves, probably when the intention was to stress their depth. So in Ps. 104.6–9 the flood water is called *tehōm*, while in Job 28.14 and 38.16 the abyss or deep is placed in parallel with the sea, *yam*, when it is desired to duplicate the expression of unfathomable depth.

Finally, we must note that the negative value attaching to the word *tehōm* is given clear expression when it is connected with the pit of death. Here again the association of *tehōm* with great depth is plain. 'At the bottom of the abyss is found the entrance to the kingdom of the dead.'[17]

The complexities of Hebrew usage which we have just noted suggest that a number of influences may have played their part in Israel in connection with this theme, but there is nevertheless a general coherence which we may attribute to the fact that the Hebrews integrated various concepts into a whole peculiar to themselves. In this the *tehōm* is a symbol whose richness is

evident in its multivalence. When we speculate, therefore, on
the possible meaning of the miniature sea in the temple of
Solomon, we may note with W. F. Albright that the Akkadian
Apsu could be used both for the fresh-water ocean and the
basin of water in the temple,[18] but not allow our understanding
to be finally determined by such facts. In view of our discussion
it is likely that the bronze sea possessed a diversity of meaning
and almost certain that any strong personification of it tended
to be eliminated by the prophetic and priestly development of a
radical monotheism in Israel. This statement with regard to
Solomon's bronze sea may serve as a broad conclusion to our
study of the sea in the Hebrew tradition and also point the way
in which we must approach the references in the gospels to the
sea of Galilee.

THE SYMBOLISM OF THE GALILEAN SEA IN THE GOSPELS

While the ocean can hardly be said to figure in the gospels,
several stories centre on the sea of Galilee. This sea is the scene
for a number of events in which symbolism would appear to
have been used. The historical connection which Jesus undoubtedly had with Galilee appears to have become the basis
upon which the evangelists could develop a symbolism of the
sea in order to illuminate their message about the Christ.
Following our train of thought up to this point, it is moreover
easy enough to see that the stories connected with the sea of
Galilee fall into two primary categories. In one, wind and storm
turn it into a threat to human existence; in the other, it is the
source of abundance for the fishermen of Jesus. The sea of
Galilee in the gospels, therefore, would seem to have functioned
as an instance of the cosmic sea, setting forth both its aspects as
understood in Hebrew thought.

Galilee was in fact an inland lake, but it was dignified by the
evangelists as a sea. This is hardly an instance of Galilean pride
but rather an apt descriptive name. The configuration of the
surrounding land was such that it was subject to squalls which
could be as disastrous to a fisherman as any storm on the ocean.
In this lay its suitability as a symbol of the primeval ocean in its
negative and sinister character. This appears most obviously in

the twin stories of the stilling of the storm and the Gadarene demoniac.[19]

That these two episodes should be treated together because they are closely related in thought and structure has been recognized by a number of scholars.[20] The interrelation of the two narratives becomes plain as we discover the traces of mythological symbolism contained within them.

If we consider the two stories in the context of creation mythology, their complementary character becomes immediately apparent and, moreover, points to the symbolic value of the references to the sea in them. The watery waste of the Priestly account of creation is paired in Gen. 2.5 by the lifeless desert. The sea and the desert were in fact complementary symbols of the pre-creation state. Now if we place our two gospel stories side by side, these two symbols appear to be set in parallel. In Mark and Matthew the habitation of the demoniac is said to be among the tombs and in the mountains, a description which is clearly intended to represent a desert place apart from ordinary human occupation. Luke 8.29, however, describes the place explicitly as a wilderness. From this parallelism we can reasonably infer that the sea was understood as the primeval waste, the lifeless threat to life, and that Jesus is depicted as the saviour from its enveloping forces of destruction.

The mythological character of the sea in these episodes is also made explicit by Luke's gospel, in which it is referred to at 8.31 as the abyss which translated the Hebrew *tehōm* and was connected in later Greek writings with the depths of original time, with the primeval ocean and with the world of the dead.[21] The sea from which Christ had just saved his disciples becomes the proper place for the destruction of the demonic legion. The forces of destruction return to the symbolic source of negation.

If Austin Farrer's argument that the literary model of the story of the stilling of the storm is to be found in the Old Testament Jonah narrative[22] is sound, we have a further justification for this view. There can be little doubt that the early Christians saw the sea in the Jonah account as a symbol of the cosmic ocean in its sinister aspect, as a figure of death.[23]

Another possible Old Testament allusion points in the same direction. C. E. B. Cranfield notes that *dielthomen*, found in Mark 4.35, normally means 'to pass through', and is used in

I Cor. 10.1 of the passing of the Israelites through the walls of water of the Red Sea.[24] The significance of this for our purpose would lie in the fact that the Red Sea became in the Israelite tradition a historification of the cosmic ocean in its antagonistic aspect.[25] Cranfield's suggestion would be supported, if the parallelism of our two stories is granted, by the argument of C. H. Cave, who sees the Exodus complex lying behind the episode of the Gadarene demoniac.[26] In both, the enemies of the Lord are destroyed in the sea. Exodus 15.5 has a close parallel in Luke 8.31, and in both stories a request to depart out of the country is a significant feature.

Again Luke suggests a mythological interpretation of the stormy sea here. The Lukan version of the apocalyptic discourse adds to other cosmic features of the eschaton, the roaring of waves of the sea.[27] We can see from this that for Luke, at least, the storm on the sea here was symbolic of a return to the state of primeval chaos which heralds the eschatological salvation of God. The stilling of the storm must therefore be seen as a victory by Christ over cosmic evil in which Jesus asserts his authority over chaos, over the *tehōm*, and so re-enacts the moment of creation.[28] The 'clear traces of cosmological mythology' seen here set forth the incarnation as a new creation with Jesus as its Lord.[29] In seeing the event in this way, modern scholars simply recapture the insight into gospel symbolism possessed in the early church.[30]

It will be noted that the interpretation so far offered has not sought to see the gospel story in terms of a battle. Nor has the Tiamat myth been regarded as determinative for exegesis. This has been a deliberate omission because although, as F. H. Borsch points out, there seems to be a connection between Mark 4.35ff. and the battle of the Man figure with the sea such as we find in the *Odes of Solomon* 39,[31] the idea of a conflict in which Jesus finally emerges victorious is absent. At no time in the course of the story is there any suggestion that Jesus might fail or that he has to exert himself in any way in order to achieve his purpose. Quite simply, the Lord is on the side of the disciples and so the waters are unable to overwhelm them.[32] Both the stories are again in parallel in presenting Jesus' action as an exorcism. The sea is addressed using a word which appears in Mark 1.25 as part of an exorcist formula, while the story of the Gadarene is centred on the exorcism of the demonic legion. Both stories, as Farrer remarked, are examples of Jesus overcoming the rebellious 'breath', and are antitypes of the exorcism in the synagogue in Mark 1.24ff.[33] Yet despite this personification of the forces of negation which here threaten man, and which we must consider more closely in the next chapter, there is no battle with them, but rather the all-powerful presence of the Lord of creation.

The image of Jesus as Lord of creation is also presented to us in the gospel story in accordance with that other tradition in which the cosmic ocean is the source of life. The stories which concern us here are found in Luke 5.1–11 and John 21.3–13. In both of these a miracle occurs and the sea gives of its bounty.

The great catches of fish given in the Lukan and Johannine stories are usually taken either as physical prodigies in which Jesus demonstrates his divine power, or as parables of the apostolic task of bringing men and women to Christ. Neither of these approaches, however, seems to do justice to the stories when they are seen in the context of the Hebraic tradition. If they are taken as ordinary historical events, then it must at least be conceded that something more than a mere manifestation of miraculous power was intended. On the other hand, a symbolic interpretation is usually dominated by the reference to the disciples becoming fishers of men in Mark 1.17 and Luke 5.10, and ignores the multivalent quality which true symbols always have. Central to both stories are fishes produced in abundance from the sea and, as S. Maclean Gilmour points out, 'Luke's fish are fish, not Christian converts',[34] while R. H. Strachan notes that the objection to taking John's fish as symbolic of the work of the apostolic church is the fact that the fish are specifically regarded as edible.[35] It is possible, therefore, that the association made with the statement about becoming fishers of men has been misleading and that the primary symbolic emphasis lies elsewhere, although an application to the mission was a legitimate extension of its symbolism.[36]

Luke 5.4 speaks of their putting out into the deep, which he here calls *bathos*. *Abussos* is not used here because its associations, as we have seen, were with death, and it often designated the prison of evil spirits. *Bathos*, on the other hand, could simply refer to physical depth, of water or of soil.[37] In view of the context, however, Luke's choice of vocabulary may have been further influenced by the use of *bathos* to suggest inexhaustible abundance, as in Rom. 11.33. The sea is here not the potential enemy of man, but magnificently fruitful at the command of Christ, as it once was in obedience to the word of the creator.[38]

It was commonly held in rabbinic times that the Messianic age would see a marvellous increase in the productivity of nature.[39] That this fruitfulness should be typified by great draughts of fish is hardly surprising. Fish were commonly understood as symbols of fertility and plenty because of the multitude of eggs produced in a single spawn. It was undoubtedly for this reason that they appear in Canaanite fertility cults. It is likely, therefore, that the great draughts of fishes were intended to indicate the new creativity of the Messianic age. This conclusion is further supported in the case of John's narrative by the links it appears to have with Ezek. 47.

Here Ezekiel speaks of a river which will flow from the temple, becoming a great torrent as it flows down to the Dead Sea. The passage contains a number of elements which are significant for our theme. There are traces of paradisal symbolism. The river has its origin under the threshold of the temple, and in view of the symbolic equation of Zion and its temple with the garden of Eden which we shall note later, Ezekiel would seem to be referring to the river of life.[40] This in fact is made clear, for the waters of the river bring life wherever it flows. Further paradisal symbolism is introduced by the reference to the trees which will grow on the banks of the river. These will produce new fruit every month, and their foliage will be sources of healing. The increased productivity suggests the period of the new creation. The paradisal tree was frequently regarded as having healing properties which are here possessed both by the river and the trees on its banks.

That Ezek. 47 influenced early Christian symbolism is clear from the fact that Rev. 22.1–3 is unmistakably based upon it. It is not surprising, therefore, to find it underlying John's story of the miraculous catch of fishes. John 21 speaks of the disciples being told to cast their net on the right side of the boat and, as Strachan points out, this may be linked with the fact that Ezekiel's river of life flows from the right side of the temple.[41] The feature would only have been repeated in the Johannine

story if it possessed significance. A clue to this meaning probably
lies in the suggestion that the right was the lucky side, for such
superstitions often derive from an earlier symbolism which has
ceased to be understood. Much ancient symbolism was dualistic
in structure in order to represent the conflict between good and
evil, being and non-being, etc. When such dualistic symbolism
made use of the two hands, the right invariably represented the
good or the honourable. Both Ezekiel and John, therefore,
would seem to share the same symbolic usage at this point.
Another link may be seen in John's troublesome reference to the
exact number of fish which were caught. A number of suggestions as to the significance of the number 153 have been
made, among which is one derived from Jerome's commentary
on Ezek. 47.9–12. This refers to a popular belief that there were
153 different species of fish. If this was the significance of the
number, then a link becomes apparent with Ezek. 47.10, which
says that fishermen will spread their nets in the river which
contains the various species of fish in the same way as the great
sea does. The point in both cases then would be the notion of a
new bringing forth of all the species from the sea, an act of
re-creation.[42] Finally, the healing of the lifeless sea appears to
be logically involved in the action of Jesus.[43] The sea which had
been at various times in the gospel narrative a threat to the
disciples is now healed through Christ. It is transformed from
being a manifestation of the *abussos* to become the *bathos* of a
new creation.

Our two narratives, therefore, seem to be concerned to
portray Jesus as the new creator with reference to the sea. In
Luke, the whole ministry is characterized as such by his placing
of the episode near its beginning, while in John it is connected
with the re-creative moment of the resurrection. In both cases
the action of Jesus elicits recognition of his lordship on the part
of Peter,[44] which can only be interpreted as a lordship of a new
creation. The attention of the reader is drawn away from the
sea to Jesus at whose command it becomes productive. There is
here no hint of any personification of the sea which can in no
sense be a life-giving source in itself. This is not strictly true of
the sea in its negative aspect, however, and to this we must now
turn our attention.

NOTES

1. Gen. 1.2,6–10.
2. Rev. 21.1.
3. Stadelmann, op. cit., pp.13,17,21f.
4. Stadelmann, op. cit., pp.14,33 and n. 152.
5. Lambert, op. cit., p.290.
6. Stadelmann, op. cit., p.13 and nn. 78,80.
7. *Mid. Tel.* Ps. 93.5; *Erubin* 22b; *Gen. R.* 4.4.
8. A. R. Johnson, *The Vitality of the Individual in the Thought of Ancient Israel*, University of Wales Press 1949, pp.90ff.
9. E. Dhorme, *Job*, Nelson 1967, p.407.
10. Gen. 49.25; Deut. 33.13.
11. Deut. 8.7.
12. Ezek. 31.4.
13. Gen. 1.20–22.
14. Gen. 7.11.
15. Ass. Mos. 10.6; cf. Sib. Or. III, 84f.; V, 158f.
16. Ps. 46.3; 65.7; 89.9f.; 93; 104.5–9.
17. Dhorme, op. cit., p.583; cf. Ps. 71.20; Job 41.24.
18. I Kings 7.23–26; see W. F. Albright, *Archaeology and the Religion of Israel*, Johns Hopkins Press 1942, pp.148f.; J. Gray, *I and II Kings*, SCM Press 1964, p.177; C. A. Simpson, 'An Inquiry into the Biblical Theology of History', *Journal of Theological Studies* XII, 1961, p.3.
19. Mark 4.35–41; 5.1–20 par.
20. Caird, op. cit., p.121; Davies, op.cit., pp.40f.; Austin Farrer, *A Study in St Mark*, Dacre Press 1951, pp.85ff.,326.
21. Note how Paul substitutes *abyssos* for the *thalassa* of the LXX of Deut. 30.13 in Rom. 10.6f., in order to make a direct reference to Sheol.
22. Farrer, op. cit., pp.326f.
23. Matt. 12.39f.
24. C. E. B. Cranfield, *The Gospel according to St Mark*, Cambridge University Press 1959, p.173.
25. Cf. Ps. 114.3ff.; Isa. 51.9f.
26. C. H. Cave, 'The Obedience of Unclean Spirits', *New Testament Studies* XI, 1965, pp.93–7.
27. Luke 21.25; cf. Caird, op. cit., p.232.
28. Cf. A. Smythe Palmer, *Babylonian Influence on the Bible and Popular Beliefs*, D. Nutt 1897, pp.6of.
29. Davies, op. cit., pp.40f.
30. See Arnobius, *Adv. Gentes* I, 46; P. T. Achterneier, 'Jesus and the Storm-tossed Sea', *Interpretation* CVI, 1962, pp.169–76; Cavaliero, op. cit.; N. L. A. Tidwell, 'A Biblical Concept of Sin', *Church Quarterly* CLXIII, 1962, pp.411–20; G. W. Wade, 'And the sea is no more', *The Interpreter* XIX, 1923, pp.282–7.
31. F. H. Borsch, *The Son of Man in Myth and History*, SCM Press 1967, p.388 nn. 1 and 2.

32. Cf. Ps. 124.1–5.

33. Farrer, op. cit., pp.85ff., 326.

34. S. M. Gilmour, 'The Gospel according to St Luke', *The Interpreter's Bible*, ed. G. A. Buttrick, Abingdon Press 1952, Vol. VIII, p.101.

35. R. H. Strachan, *The Fourth Gospel. Its Significance and Environment*, SCM Press 1941, p.335.

36. See Rev. 22.2, which extends Ezek. 47.12 in this way.

37. Matt. 13.5; Mark 4.5.

38. Gen. 1.20.

39. *Shabbath* 30b; *Ketuboth* 111b.

40. See Austin Farrer, *The Revelation of St John the Divine*, Clarendon Press 1964, p.222.

41. Strachan, op. cit., p. 335; see Ezek. 47.1,2; cf. *Mid. Tel.* Ps. 90.12, where the garden of Eden is located on the right and Gehenna on the left of God.

42. Cf. the reference in Akiba to the spring in the wilderness which brought forth fat fish and which Philo called Wisdom or *logos*: E. R. Goodenough, *Jewish Symbols in the Graeco-Roman Period*, Princeton University Press 1968, Vol. XII, pp.99f.

43. Cf. Ezek. 47.8f.

44. Luke 5.8; John 21.7.

4   The Satanic Serpent

In accordance with the usual manner of myth, the waters were
frequently theriomorphized. Of the forms used for this purpose,
the most prominent were the water-serpent, the crocodile and
the dragon. As the symbol water was multivalent in significance,
so also were the forms given to it in the myths. In general, however, as G. E. Smith found, the dragon was primarily a personification of the life-giving properties of water on the one
hand and of its life-destroying powers on the other.[1]

Both the symbol of water and the association of animal forms
with it appear to have been very widespread, and the various
traditions together form a remarkably homogenous whole. In
South America, one of the best known of the gods, Quetzalcoatl,
or feathered serpent, was associated primarily with water. In
Aztec teaching the dead had to pass over a river of nine waters
and meet a snake and a crocodile. A very similar mythology was
current in ancient Egypt. There the spirit of darkness and of the
storm was the serpent Apep or Apophis, who was overcome and
killed by the sun-god Ra in the Heliopolitan *Book of the Dead*[2]
and the *Book of Apophis*. Egypt also had another serpent-god in
Set. The Greeks recognized their own Typhon in the Egyptian
Set, and also had a myth about the seven- or nine-headed
Hydra which was slain by Heracles. In China and Japan,
dragon deities were regularly associated with water, with rivers,
marshes, lakes, seas and rain. In India the *naga* or serpent kings
or gods were water spirits. The similarity between the Indian,
Chinese and Japanese conceptions was such that Buddhism was
able to assimilate them with one another. There was therefore
a mythological tendency to represent the waters as a dragon or
a serpent over much of the earth.[3]

This motif is also found in the religious traditions most frequently associated with the Hebraic. In Assyria, Tiamat-*Mummu* was a personification of the sea.[4] It has been generally accepted that Tiamat was envisaged as a great monster or dragon. The support for this is not as great as is often supposed, but there is some evidence for it. The texts refer to Tiamat as '*ku-ku*', which may mean monster, and there is some iconographical support provided by archaeology. These hints have been generally a sufficient basis on which to assume that the Assyrian tradition conformed to the widespread pattern. The seven-headed monster also appears in the allied Akkadian and Ugaritic mythologies. The Canaanite *yammu* (sea) and *naharu* (river) were both conceived as dragons.[5] In Persia, the water-serpent Dahaka is taken as an incarnation of Angra Mainyu, the evil spirit springing from heaven in the form of a serpent. Feridan conquers, binds and imprisons it in the mountain Demavend. Later Dahaka breaks loose, but is finally slain by Keresaspa.[6]

The myths were not content, however, merely to give the seas, rivers and lakes an animal form. Having done this, they then often spoke as though the dragon or serpent and that which it symbolized were two different entities. This was perhaps the distinction between the water as such and the power which resided in it. Consequently the dragon or serpent is frequently said to live in the water of whose properties it was a symbol. Two examples may make this clear. In Hindu mythology we read of the demon Kaliya who dwells in a deep pool of the river Jumna, from which it emerges to devastate the surrounding countryside in the time of Krishna. The god, however, defeats him and makes him go and live in the ocean. Here we can see how the idea of the waters having to keep to their proper place was given the narrative form of myth. Strabo provides us with our second example. He tells us that the river Orontes was carved out, according to those living nearby, by a great dragon who then disappeared into the earth at the source of the river.[7] In this tradition we can recognize familiar elements. The waters of the river are likened to a dragon. The cutting of a channel in the earth by the water is seen as its work. The dragon's disappearance into the source of the river both identifies the river with it and indicates that the Orontes has its source in the subterranean ocean or the great dragon.

This mythological manner of speaking could easily cause confusion. When Amos 9.3 speaks of the serpent in the bottom of the sea it is easy to forget that the distinction between the inhabitant and the locale is merely a mythological device.[8] This judgment, of course, is dependent on the extent to which we can hold that the Israelites retained mythological thinking of this type.

PERSONIFICATION OF THE SEA IN ISRAEL

It appears to have been totally eradicated in the Priestly account of creation. The reason for this is simply that Yahweh is here the sole participant in the drama. The chaos is not an obstacle in Yahweh's way, but is his creation.[9] Over against Yahweh there is merely a nothing.[10] The writer has not yet arrived at the abstract concept of creation *ex nihilo* first explicitly stated in II Macc. 7.28, but has certainly moved towards it.[11] The sea has been depersonalized as part of this programme. It does not have to be overcome, for it is no longer a power as in older mythologies.[12]

Elsewhere in Hebrew literature, however, the personifications of mythology do figure, and this enabled the conflict motif to come into play. In some cases it is barely perceptible, as in Ps. 104.6–9, where the personification of the deep and conflict with it is merely implied by the fact that it can be rebuked.[13] In others it is clearly stated, as in Isa. 27.1, where not only is the sea personified, but the mythological character of the passage is heightened by the picture of Yahweh as the warrior who wields a sword against Leviathan.[14]

Such passages are an embarrassment to those scholars who wish to assert with O. Eissfeldt that 'real myths are not to be found in the Old Testament'.[15] He has to admit that there is mythological material in the Old Testament,[16] which he thinks the Hebrews have borrowed from elsewhere, but nevertheless holds that in taking it over, Israel had largely destroyed its mythological character, as in the stories of the creation and the flood. For Eissfeldt, the moment of demythologization is that at which the conflict element is removed, for he holds that 'a real myth presupposes at least two gods, the one contesting with the other'.[17] In the de-deification of the nature-gods, therefore, the element of conflict was in principle removed. Yet he has to admit further that it remains, and attempts to save his position by declaring that Old Testament references to divine battles are not really mythical, because in them the one God always triumphs. The argument thus becomes confused and untenable. The nature-deities are completely eradicated in some parts of Scripture, but in others they are merely demoted. They no longer function as autonomous, but as subordinate beings. They cannot be finally triumphant, but in the meantime they can play the part of opponents to Yahweh. These limitations prevent their being gods in the traditional sense, but not the growth of mythical narrative around them. Moreover, these fragments point to the existence of a more truly mythological account of creation, showing that 'primeval conflict between Yahweh and some monster was a well-established belief in Hebrew folklore'.[18]

In this tradition, forces ranged against Yahweh are given a variety of names, many of which clearly indicate mythological beings.

Tehōm is usually devoid of theriomorphization, but a hint of it is contained in the metaphor used in Deut. 33.13. This says that the *tehōm* 'coucheth beneath', i.e. like a crouching beast.[19] This may owe something to the Tiamat tradition.

The figure of Lotan found in the Ugaritic mythology has its counterpart in the Hebrew Leviathan.[20] It was pictured as a great fish or sea serpent 'at the bottom of the sea over the fountain from which the sea gets its water',[21] and so is closely associated symbolically with *tehōm*, as is further suggested by Job 3.8. Here the rousing of Leviathan is equivalent to a return of the earth to primeval chaos. To arouse this monster is to bring an end to the world.[22] Leviathan is probably the Hebrew equivalent of the many-headed hydra found in other traditions.[23]

Rahab appears to have links with Tiamat.[24] Like Tiamat, Rahab had a number of helpers,[25] and again we have personifications of the sea in these venomous, aquatic serpents.[26]

According to D. S. Russell, Behemoth[27] was also equivalent to Tiamat, while Leviathan was parallel to the Babylonian Kingu.[28] He thinks that both were originally sea monsters, but that Behemoth later took on the character of a land monster, i.e. of the wilderness, a symbolic equivalent of the primeval watery chaos. Goodenough equates Behemoth with the great bull and notes that the bull symbol of eternal life associated with a number of Near Eastern gods was borrowed by the Jews and used as a figure on their graves and in their synagogues.[29] The original association, however, is probably with the sea, as is the case with the other figures reviewed.

The connection which each one of these has with the sea and their common serpentine form suggests that they are all symbolic equivalents, personifications of the sea, especially in its treacherous aspect.[30] In some cases the serpent or water-dragon acts at Yahweh's command, while at others it is his enemy. It is this latter role which looms largest in the development of eschatological thought.

The serpent was in the present imprisoned in the depths. This was, of course, a mythological way of saying that the sea was kept within bounds, that evil and death were held in control. Apocalyptic writers developed the idea that it would eventually be released and have to be finally overcome at the end of history.[31] It was this concept which significantly influenced the author of Revelation and which may well lie beneath some passages in the gospels.

SATAN AND HIS DEMONS IN THE GOSPELS

Of the fact that evil is given a clear personal identity in the gospels, there can be no doubt. Satan is here a proper name. Moreover, the subordination of Satan to the role of one of God's agencies[32] in the Old Testament tends to give way to a characterization of Satan as an enemy of God. He is the leader of the demons who are also described as though personal beings. They are credited with a supernatural intelligence, are able to speak and to manipulate the minds and bodies of men and women.

Both Satan and his demons are commonly said to enter and live in a human being, and an exorcism consists of driving out the demon or demons. Now if it is accepted that these are mythological creatures, it becomes very important to remember that such a being is in myth not really distinct from its habitat, an aspect of which it expresses. So in cases of possession, the demon may best be understood as representing some element in the person possessed. This may be moral evil or physical disease.[33] The controversy centred on the question whether Jesus accepted the existence of evil spirits, therefore, is probably often misguided. If Jesus was aware of what we may call the mechanics of mythological language, then the notion of their separate, physical existence would not have occurred to him. That this was the case may be evidenced by the absence on Jesus' part of the use of sympathetic magic or ritual incantations which are usually associated with a literalistic rather than a symbolic understanding of demon possession. References to the power of the name, of a demon and of Jesus,[34] may suggest a magical outlook,[35] but in most cases these are unlikely to have derived from Jesus himself.

A number of influential streams of thought probably came together in the New Testament concept of Satan. Particular importance has often been attached, for example, to the impact of Persian ideas concerning Angra Mainyu. The roots of the concept, however, are probably much more ancient and are to be found in the primary symbols for negation in the creation myths.

There is some evidence to support the argument of W. O. E. Oesterley that the idea of Satan developed from the mythological concept of the *tehōm*,[36] especially as symbolized by Tiamat. Both stand for the ultimate threat to creation which has to be overcome. Satan has his army of demons to help him, just as Tiamat had a brood of serpents. Satan thus came to be identified with the serpent or dragon in Christian apocalyptic.[37] The gospel tradition may well reflect this connection. The synoptists speak of seven spirits as though they constituted a total invasion of the demonic.[38] References to seven spirits occur frequently in the Babylonian texts,[39] and both usages may well derive from the tradition found in Babylon and elsewhere in which the primordial serpent is described as having seven heads. Of more importance is the possibility that the *tehōm* represented by the sea of Galilee in the gospels was intended to be understood as demonic.

Mark narrates the story of the stilling of the storm as though it were an exorcism. The wind is censured and the sea commanded to be silent. The sea at this point is clearly being given a personal value of a demonic character. W. Manson argued that there was a tendency to assimilate all miracles to exorcisms,[40] but this is to some extent misleading. The mythological apprehension of the world which the evangelists seem to have shared would have led them to think of the wind and sea as agencies of personal power. No part of creation would have been for them impersonal, as it has usually become for us. It would be perfectly natural, therefore, for them to understand Jesus' conflict with the wind and sea as being as much a confrontation with demonic personality as when he was dealing with men and women possessed of demons. They did not, therefore, have to assimilate the so-called nature miracles to exorcisms, because the former were properly regarded as such.

TREADING UPON SERPENTS

Although the story in which Jesus walks on the water is not obviously written up as an exorcism,[41] an appreciation of its significance is probably dependent on a recognition that this factor is present. The stilling of the storm and the walking on the water appear to be symbolic equivalents.[42] In both, the disciples are threatened by the violence of the wind on the sea of Galilee and saved from it by Jesus. While the wind ceases in the former story at the command of Jesus, in the latter it does so at the moment when Jesus enters the boat. Here the conquest of the storm is accomplished by the successful walking of Jesus on the sea. This, then, is the feature which requires elucidation.

Attention has been drawn to the fact that Matt. 14.28–33 is similar to a Buddhist story in the Sîlânisainsa Jataka in which a lay brother walks on the river Aciravati. Van den Burgh van Eysinga even suggested that the gospel story was influenced by the Indian.[43] Dibelius points out, however, that there is an important difference between the two stories, each of which reflects the standpoint of the religion in which it appears. Although the lay brother is upheld by the joyful thought of the Buddha, his ability to walk on the water is a miracle of self-help. Peter, on the other hand, is upheld by faith in Christ.[44] Peter's ability is derivative, i.e. from Jesus. An explanation of Peter's accomplishment, therefore, must be dependent on our understanding of Jesus' own ability to walk upon the sea.

Parallels are not difficult to find in pagan mythology.[45] As Robertson pointed out, Poseidon showed his rulership of the sea by striding over it,[46] as also did his son, Euphemus. The Poseidon myth is by no means irrelevant. In particular it shows that mastery of the sea could be expressed by the act of walking in triumph upon it. The background of our story, however, is more likely to be in Hebraic than Greek myth, and there is no need to see in it the addition of non-Christian myth, as Dibelius did.[47] It is more profitable to turn, as did Strauss, to the Old Testament.[48]

In most cases, Strauss noted,[49] Hebrew stories speak of the waters being parted to allow passage on dry land to the other side.[50] Thought of Yahweh's 'way in the sea' and 'paths in the great waters'[51] is dominated by the hold exercised by the Exodus over the Hebrew imagination.[52] In one passage, however, Job 9.8, Yahweh is said to tread upon the waves of the sea, so providing a close parallel with the action attributed to Jesus in Mark 6.48, where the Greek is remarkably similar to that of the Septuagint. In describing Yahweh as trampling upon the waves of the sea, Job clearly intended that the reader should see this as an image of the prostration of the helpers of Rahab, the sea-monsters, under the feet of God.[53] There is therefore a Hebraic precedent for the equation of walking on the water and treading upon the serpent. When we further note that Christ's conquest of evil was expressed in the New Testament in the familiar imagery of treading down,[54] it is not unreasonable to see Mark 6.45–52 as a parallel to Yahweh's crushing of the heads of Leviathan in Psalm 74.13f.[55]

Only once is there specific mention in the gospels of treading upon serpents. In Luke 10.19 this is a power given by Jesus to the disciples as part of their authority over 'all the power of the enemy'. The spurious text of Mark 16.18 would suggest that this was some kind of magical immunity. This, however, is probably the product of a literalistic mind failing to perceive the symbolism of the original saying. The clue to the meaning of Luke 10.19 should rather be found in the story of Matt. 14.28–33. The two passages illuminate one another because they employ parallel although different symbolisms. In stepping out across the water, Peter had begun to assert that spiritual mastery over evil which Jesus bequeathed to his disciples. If it is correct to relate Luke 10.9 to Mark 6.47–51 and Matthew 14.28–33 in this way, we have a further reason for thinking that the sea was taken to be properly represented by the symbol of the serpent.

THE DEMONIC WASTELAND AND THE TEMPTATION STORY

As the desert was a complementary image to that of the sea, so we find that the personification of evil is also connected with the desert. The wilderness was spoken of as the haunt of evil spirits throughout Hebraic literature, both canonical and apocryphal.[56] It appears to have been a standard motif in Near Eastern folklore.[57] The gospels not unnaturally reflect this. Matt. 12.43 speaks of disembodied spirits roaming the waterless places, and Luke 8.29 of a demon driving Legion into the desert. The outstanding example, however, is that provided by the story of Jesus' temptation.

That an understanding of the temptation narratives depends upon an appreciation of their symbolism is generally admitted. There is considerable disagreement, however, as to how this should be done. Some scholars have seen them as descriptions of a period of meditation on the part of Jesus. The story is compared with those in which saints are aided by angels in their fight against evil.[58] Inevitably this approach leads to a comparison with the story of the Buddha's fight with Mara, which is so clearly a symbolic expression of a meditative experience.[59] But there is in the gospel story no suggestion of uncertainty as to his mission on Jesus' part, and it logically requires that the temptation takes place before the baptism, for which there is no warrant.

The extensive use of typology in the gospels has led most scholars today to see in this the clue to a proper interpretation of the evangelists' intention here. This may be attempted without reference to mythological material. The forty days of Jesus' sojourn in the desert can be seen as a recapitulation of the wilderness wanderings of Israel.[60] The principal objection raised to this hypothesis is that while the Hebrews were tested by God, Jesus is here tempted by Satan as an opponent rather than as agent of God. This is not a fatal objection, however, for the provision of an exact correspondence is not a feature of typology. Nevertheless, such an approach cannot be considered adequate. The Israelite understanding of the Exodus event was itself influenced by older motifs which may be playing a renewed role here.

The reasons for which F. W. Beare holds that 'the story is cast in the form of myth', that there are allegorical elements present and that it is historically impossible,[61] may be inaptly stated, but the conclusion is nevertheless accurate. There are undoubtedly mythological features present. Similarities to other material point to this conclusion. The Persian Venidad tells how Zoroaster was offered sovereignty of the worlds if he would renounce Ahura Mazda.[62] In the *Sacred History of Euhemerism* by Ennius,[63] we find Jupiter being led by Pan to the top of a mountain from where he can contemplate the earth. Now while the gospel story can hardly be an ethical adaptation of this latter, as Robertson suggested, for the fundamental idea is different, the parallelism does suggest that we should be aware that mythological forms may be present in the story of the temptation.

The narrative has been seen as a mythological reflection of the type of struggle exemplified in the defeat of the monster by the Babylonian Marduk.[64] This, however, is misleading. The gospel suggests a background in terms of the primeval waterless desert of the Yahwistic creation account[65] rather than of the watery chaos of the Priestly narrative and its Babylonian counterpart. Here and in Gen. 2.5 it is the barren wasteland which represents the world bereft of God's life-giving activity. If the Satan of Christ's temptation is a personification of primeval negation, therefore, it is in association with the symbol of the desert, not the ocean.

The story has also been explained against the background of the Eden myth, particularly in the Markan tradition.[66] The temptation of Jesus is compared with the testing of Adam in the garden. As Adam was offered the prize of deity, so Jesus is offered divine kingship, and in both cases on condition that they follow the methods and exalt the values which are anathema to God. Whereas Adam failed, however, Jesus is victorious, thus reversing the primordial defeat and beginning the restoration of paradise.[67] The particularly telling criticism of this view is that Jesus is not in a garden but in a desert. Once again it is the desert motif which is forced on our attention.

In Mark the desert is elsewhere referred to simply as a place in which Jesus finds or attempts to find peaceful solitude apart from the harrying crowds.[68] It does not follow from this, however, that the desert in Mark 1 is to be understood in the same way. Only here is the desert the location for a confrontation with Satan. Mention of the presence of wild beasts may be taken as reinforcing this. Some commentators have taken the passage to suggest the paradisal harmony between man and beast[69] which would be restored in the Messianic age.[70] D. E. Nineham notes that beasts are subject to the righteous man,[71] but Bultmann points out that 'tempted of Satan' in Mark's narrative is inconsistent with such a picture.[72] It is precisely the mention of Satan which forces the attribution of a demonic character to the beasts here. They emphasize not only the loneliness and horror of the desert situation,[73] but also that it is the domain of Satan. The biblical writers often used wild beasts to represent devastation and desolation.[74] Their symbolic value, therefore, was closely akin to that of the primeval desert. It must be concluded, then, that the collocation of the desert and Satan with the wild beasts means that the latter are to be understood here as having the character given to them in Ezekiel 34. The beasts of the field which preyed upon the flock of God here surround the shepherd.

Over against the wild beasts are the angels which constitute a further mythological feature in the narrative.[75] This appears to reflect an established Hebraic pattern in which wild beasts confront the angels who support the beloved of God. Jesus here alludes to precisely this idea as it appears in Ps. 91.11f. The angels uphold him and keep him from harm. In that strength he can tread upon the lion and the serpent. The temptation narrative seems to fall quite clearly into this symbolic pattern, especially in the form given to it in Test. Napht. 8.4, which says:

> And the devil shall flee from you,
> [And the wild beasts shall fear you],
> And the Lord shall love you,
> [And the angels shall cleave to you].

Jesus has gone out into the desert of Satan and his demons, and is upheld by the love of God and the ministry of his angels.

The real significance of the incident is now clear. In Satan the malevolent character of the desert and the wild beasts is personified in the manner of myth. Satan is present at various points in the gospel story in a number of guises, but here primarily as the embodiment of the wasteland into which man moves when he attempts self-sufficiency. In this must surely lie the reconciliation of the various elements which scholars have seen here. Jesus is an Adamic-like figure at this point, but he is not in a garden. The new Adam is here in the wilderness of the world, into which the old Adam was cast when he attempted to usurp deity to himself. Jesus has 'gone out' into the wilderness of a new Exodus to feel its hunger and to destroy its power, aided by the divine presence, in order that he might ultimately lead men into the plenteous land of the spirit.

The temptation story cannot, therefore, simply be lined up with any one ancient narrative or motif. Rather, it reflects a number of ideas embedded in the Hebrew tradition. These are welded together into a quite new pattern in order to represent the arrival of a situation previously unknown, in which the Son of God is victorious over the alienation represented by the hunger-producing desert, symbolized by the wild beasts and personified as Satan.

In conclusion, therefore, it may be said that our gospels have retained not merely the symbolism of the creation myths but also traces of their ancient personification.

NOTES

1. G. Elliott Smith, *The Evolution of the Dragon*, Manchester University Press 1919, p.1.
2. Stadelmann, op. cit., p.33 n. 152.
3. For further examples see Palmer, op. cit., appendix note A.
4. See Dhorme, op. cit., p.30.
5. Albright, *Archaeology and the Religion of Israel*, pp.148f.; cf. Stadelmann, op. cit., pp.154–60.
6. See F. Max Müller (ed.), *Sacred Books of the East*, Clarendon Press 1880, Vol. V, p.lii; Vol. XVIII, p.110 n. 4.

7. See W. Robertson Smith, *The Religion of the Semites*, A. and C. Black, rev. ed. 1894, p.171.

8. Cf. W. O. E. Oesterley, *The Evolution of the Messianic Idea*, Pitman 1908, pp.47f.

9. Tidwell, op. cit.

10. Vriezen, op. cit., p.181. n. 1, notes that the word *tōhū* used here is in Isa. 40.23 placed in parallel with *'ain*, not to be.

11. Stadelmann, op. cit., p.28; cf. Prov. 8.22ff.

12. Stadelmann, op. cit., p. 14.

13. Cf. Job 38.8–11.

14. See Oesterley, op. cit., p.50.

15. O. Eissfeldt, *The Old Testament: An Introduction*, Blackwell 1966, p.35; cf. Vriezen, op. cit., p.181.

16. E.g. Isa. 14.12–15; Ezek. 28.1–19.

17. Eissfeldt, op. cit., p.35.

18. Stadelmann, op. cit., p.17.

19. Cf. Gen. 49.9.

20. Widengren, op. cit., p.172.

21. Goodenough, op. cit., Vol. XII, p.99.

22. See Dhorme, op. cit., p.31.

23. Ps. 74.14; Rev. 12.3ff.

24. Dhorme, op. cit., p.134; Widengren, op. cit., pp.170f.

25. Job 9.13.

26. See Dhorme, op. cit., pp.30,105.

27. See Job 40.15.

28. Russell, op. cit., pp.123f.

29. Goodenough, op. cit., Vol. XII, p. 133.

30. Cf. Oesterley, op. cit., pp.49ff.; Dhorme, op. cit., p.105.

31. See Test. Asher 7.3; I Enoch 60.7–9; II (4) Esd. 6.49–52; II Bar. 29.4.

32. Job 1f.; cf. Isa. 45.7.

33. Matt. 16.23; Luke 13.16; 22.3; cf. E. Langton, *Essentials of Demonology*, Epworth 1949, p.149, who argues that apocalyptic writing emphasizes the first while the synoptic gospels stress the second.

34. Matt. 7.22; Mark 5.9; 9.38; 16.17; Luke 9.49.

35. Langton, op. cit., p.157.

36. Oesterley, op. cit., pp.175ff.

37. Rev. 12.9; 20.2; cf. Life of Adam and Eve 16.4; and see G. E. Smith, op. cit., pp.137f.

38. Matt. 12.45; Mark 16.9; Luke 8.2; 11.26.

39. See Langton, op. cit., pp.18ff., 150.

40. W. Manson, *Jesus the Messiah*, p.44.

41. Mark 6.47–52; John 6.16–21.

42. Cf. R. Bultmann, *The History of the Synoptic Tradition*, Blackwell 1963, p.216.

43. See H. van der Loos, *The Miracles of Jesus*, Brill 1968, pp.662f.

44. Dibelius, *From Tradition to Gospel*, p.277 n. 2, cf. p.116; Parrinder, op. cit., p.242.

45. Van der Loos, op. cit., pp.655–8.

46. J. M. Robertson, *Christianity and Mythology*, Watts 1900, p.358.
47. Dibelius, *From Tradition to Gospel*, pp.100,277.
48. Strauss, op. cit., pp.245–51.
49. Strauss, op. cit., p.246.
50. Exod. 14.16; Josh. 3.13–17; II Kings 2.14.
51. Ps. 77.19.
52. Cf. Isa. 43.16.
53. See Job 9.13, Dhorme, op. cit., p.134; and cf. Ps. 110.1.
54. E.g. I Cor. 15.25.
55. See E. C. Selwyn, *The Oracles of the New Testament*, Hodder and Stoughton 1911, p.305; cf. Cyril of Jerusalem, *Cat. Lect.* III, 11.
56. Num. 21.6; Deut. 8.15; Isa. 13.22; 30.6; Tobit 8.3; II Bar. 10.8.
57. See Palmer, op. cit., pp.72–6.
58. E.g. Test. Napht. 8.4.
59. Cf. T. O. Ling, *Buddhism and the Mythology of Evil*, Allen and Unwin 1962, pp. 81–95.
60. Cf. I Cor. 10.1–4.
61. F. W. Beare, *The Earliest Records of Jesus*, Blackwell 1962, p.43.
62. Venidad 19.6.
63. See Lactantius, *The Divine Institutes*, Bk. I, ch. 11.
64. Bultmann, *History of the Synoptic Tradition*, p.253.
65. Stadelmann, op. cit., p.12; Vriezen, op. cit., pp.185f.
66. See W. D. Davies, op. cit., pp.42ff.; J. D. G. Dunn, *Baptism in the Holy Spirit*, SCM Press 1970, pp. 30f.; Borsch, op. cit., pp.370f.; C. K. Barrett, *The Holy Spirit and the Gospel Tradition*, SPCK 1958, pp.49f.
67. See J. Jeremias, *New Testament Theology*, Vol. I, SCM Press 1971, Vol. I, pp.69ff.; J. Jeremias, 'Adam', *Theological Dictionary of the New Testament*, ed. G. Kittel and G. Friedrich, Eerdmans 1964, Vol. I, p.141.
68. Mark 1.35,45; 6.31,32,35.
69. Apoc. Moses x-xii; Ps. Gospel Matt. 18–19.
70. Isa. 11.6–9; 65.25; etc.; see Borsch, op. cit., p.370, n. 2.
71. D. E. Nineham, *Saint Mark*, Penguin Books 1963, p.64.
72. Bultmann, *History of the Synoptic Tradition*, pp.253f.
73. R. Leivestad, *Christ the Conqueror*, SPCK 1954, pp.55f.
74. Isa. 13.20f.; 34.14; Jer. 50.39.
75. Dibelius, *From Tradition to Gospel*, p.274.

PART TWO

The Coming of the Son

5 *The Expected One*

When a Jew thought about the age to come, he tended to do so in terms of a figure or type. The prophets and apocalyptists had taught him to think of his own nation not as a collection of individuals but as a total personality. That corporate entity could therefore be represented by such figures as the Servant, the Son of Man, the Elect One or the Messiah. To speak, therefore, of the coming of such a figure was also to speak of the coming of a new community. The representative figure was not, however, always seen as an abstract idealization. The character of the community could be embodied in a particular group or even in an individual. Pictures of the age to come were peopled with certain distinct figures who set forth its character. As they lay in the future and were unknown as yet, they could only be spoken of by the use of analogies drawn from the past. While the future might be a new creation and something far more glorious than anything ever experienced before, the Jew could nevertheless only conceive of it in terms derived from the heights of past Israelite attainment both in a political and in a spiritual sense.

When men were faced by the phenomenon of Jesus of Nazareth, they inevitably attempted to fit what they saw in him into the terms which had already been created. When Jesus asked his disciples who men said that he was,[1] the disciples showed by their answers that people were attempting to place him within some recognizable and meaningful framework. But because these were all drawn ultimately from the past, they had to be rejected as inadequate for that which was to be vitally new.

One framework of thought into which it was perhaps inevitable that the people should have attempted to place Jesus in view of the circumstances of his day was that of the nationalist kingdom. Their scriptures told them how God had raised up saviours for them in times of national adversity. Their sacred history-books told them how first judges and then kings had been brought to the fore by Yahweh to save the people from their enemies. Their royal line had been broken and they were now occupied by a foreign power. Consequently, hopes for a renewal of national prosperity found their way into Judaic expectations of the new age. They looked back to the time of David when their kingdom had reached its greatest geographical extension and political influence. It was for a restoration of these ancient glories that many people looked during a period of foreign oppression. And so they saw in Jesus one who might well be he who would bring back the glories of Davidic rule. They tried to make him king.[2]

It would seem that the disciples shared this hope, at least for a time. But Jesus would have none of this and made it clear that his mission was not a political one. His Messiahship was not to depend upon either military success or Davidic descent.[3] Later, however, the ascription of Davidic descent became an integral part of the Christian message, as we see from the use of the title 'Son of David' in Matthew[4] and from the genealogies supplied by Matthew and Luke. Perhaps it was felt that this could be safely used as a means of authentication once any danger of its being understood in a political sense had passed.

Another framework in which the people could place Jesus was that of prophecy, and this is the one reflected in the answers given by the disciples to Jesus' question at Caesarea Philippi. A more spiritual appreciation of the nature of the coming age saw in it a renewal of the charismatic gift such as Israel had lacked for so many years.[5] The people, therefore, suggested that he was Elijah, Jeremiah, one like Moses or the Baptist.[6]

The gospel narratives constantly show Jesus to us as one who had all the marks of a prophet. He is called by God and given the divine Spirit. He is a recipient of visionary experience and of divine compulsion and torment. He has supernatural knowledge of past, present and future events and can read the thoughts of men's hearts. Not surprisingly, the people accepted him as a prophet.[7]

Even when the gospels were being created, this appreciation

of Jesus was playing an important role. Some of Luke's narratives, for example, suggest that a comparison with Elijah was in view, while Matthew undoubtedly intends that Jesus should recall the law-giving activity of Moses.[8]

Acceptable in many ways as this framework might have been, it was ultimately inadequate. Jesus does not merely reflect Moses but transcends him. In John particularly, the superiority of Jesus to the patriarchal and prophetic figures of Israel's past is declared unmistakably.[9] Here again the analogy of the past broke down, for something quite new had entered the arena of history. What Jesus was could not be grasped in any terms derived from the past. His work could not be authenticated from within history, but only from outside it. The evangelists are pushed into a categorization for which their history provided no parallel. Jesus was declared to have his authenticating origin, not by physical descent nor by prophetic endowment, but by an origin from outside this history and this world. Not as Son of David nor as prophet was he to be understood, but as the Son of the Living God.[10]

THE SON OF GOD

Both the earliest and the latest of our gospels are concerned to stress that to speak of Jesus as the son of Joseph was the result of 'defective understanding'.[11] Mark tells his readers that the people of Nazareth were puzzled by Jesus' wisdom and mighty works because they had at the forefront of their minds the fact that he was born into a family known to them.[12] In John the point is made with even greater emphasis. The Jews could not understand who or what Jesus was, because they judged according to the flesh and thought of his origin only in terms of his human parentage.[13] For both evangelists, the significance of Jesus was only explicable as one who called God his Father and whom God called his son.

The designation of a man as Son of God could, however, be understood in a variety of ways.

Because the Jews regularly used the father-son relationship to indicate likeness of character, the divine sonship of Jesus could point to his fulfilment of the command he laid upon his disciples to become like their Father in heaven.[14] Just as James and John could be termed 'sons of thunder' to point the violence of their character and the Jews 'sons of the devil' because they were filled with his lies,[15] so Jesus may be called Son of God by virtue of his moral similitude. So John sets the moral relationship of Jesus with God over against his physical origin. In John 8 there may be a hint of the slander alluded to by Origen[16] that Jesus was illegitimate, but if this is so, John does not counter it on the level of physical fact, but by directing attention to Jesus' moral rectitude, taking this as evidence of the only parentage which is relevant, i.e. that of God as Father.[17]

In ancient Assyrian usage the title was applied to the king as one who was designated by God to carry out certain functions. As such it was probably used by the kings of ancient Israel.[18] There is some evidence that it was also used as a title of the high priest in a period in which Judaism lacked a monarchy.[19] The discovery of the Dead Sea Scrolls has now made it possible to conclude with Fuller that it was *'just coming into use* as a Messianic title in pre-Christian Judaism'.[20] It was likely, therefore, that it should find a place as a title of function in early Christian vocabulary.

Finally, Son of God could be a metaphysical title, designating what Jesus was in his very being. We find such a use in the Old Testament where angels are named sons of God,[21] and in Hellenistic speculations concerning divine men. This usage had a long history, going back to ancient Egyptian thought concerning the Pharaohs, and it would not be surprising if Christians were driven to it by the realization of the inadequacy of other interpretations. Even this would have to be stretched, however, in order to find a valid place in the Christian complex of thought.[22]

All three concepts are to be found in our gospels, but there they have to be translated into narrative forms and be seen to derive their validity from God himself. The very idea of Christ's sonship involved the notion that what Jesus was came not from within himself but from his Father. So the evangelists had to set forth their understanding of Jesus in terms of a story of origin, of how he came to be what he was by the act of God, and in doing so were pushed inevitably into the use of symbolism and myth.

The character of Jesus is not provided with a miraculous

explanation until much later, when his moral integrity was turned into formal sinlessness. Indeed it may have been seen at first as a prerequisite of his exaltation to sonship.[23] In any case, history could here be allowed to speak for itself, the sublimity of his love and care testifying unmistakably to his divine sonship in the moral sense. The other aspects of his sonship, however, could only be portrayed with the use of symbols, and so they were authenticated with great care by narratives of origin.

Elevation to an exalted function as Son of God was most appropriately seen in terms of a ritual ordination. Over a wide range of history and territory, initiation rites have been performed that men might transcend their ordinary human conditions and come to be related, in a special way, to the gods.[24] In many of these we can see elements which are familiar to us from the gospel story: separation from the mother and initiation into the sacred, metamorphosis, the ordeals of passion followed by resurrection and exaltation. But while we may speculate as to the extent to which the evangelists were consciously making use of many of these motifs, there can be no doubt that they believed that Jesus' baptism and withdrawal into the wilderness constituted a sacramental and existential initiation. Here 'the simple fact . . . has been transposed into a mythico-theological framework'.[25] This moment of Jesus' history is understood to have been charged with originative significance, to have been the historical and ritual point at which something determinative for his role was accomplished. As such it was not merely an earthly event but also a heavenly one. It partook not only of the historical *now* but also of the primordial *then*. And so the story gathered to itself mythological features which could explicate and validate the meaning of the event.

While a rite could be conceived as a means whereby a man was adopted by God and designated for a certain role, it could not, unless a miracle of transubstantiation was assumed, put forward the idea that he was in his very being different from other men by virtue of a special ontological relationship with God. For this purpose, it was necessary to speak of an extraordinary origin for his very existence. In a simple way this might be achieved by attributing mystical significance to Jesus' descent from the Jewish royal line. More tellingly, his birth could be seen as one which was brought about by a special act of God. Matthew and Luke, therefore, have chosen to give Jesus' ontological origin in a way which must raise the question of the mythological nature of their accounts. In John's gospel also, we are given a narrative of a mythological character. The being of Jesus is taken back, not to the action of God in his birth, but to the primordial time in which all myth is properly located.

The variety of methods used in the presentation of Jesus' sonship has not unnaturally suggested to scholars that it reflects a development in early Christian thought. As the Christian community moved out of a Palestinian milieu into a Hellenistic Jewish background and finally had to adapt itself to a thoroughly Gentile environment, changes in thought would have been inevitable. The words used of Jesus would have different meanings and so force Christian thinking into new channels. It was precisely this process which has caused the long arguments as to the origin of the very title with which we are concerned.[26] The impact of different language complexes would tend to bring out the latent possibilities in very early material, which in turn may have derived originally from Jesus' own filial consciousness.[27] Thus John's doctrine of Christ's pre-existence may well owe something to the originally non-ontological motif of God sending his son, which is so prominent a feature of his gospel.[28]

The movement out of Judaism and into Hellenism would in particular have tended to produce a shift from functional to ontological categorizations of Jesus' sonship. While the Jew would think primarily in terms of Jesus being equipped with the Spirit of God, the Hellenist would more readily embrace the concept of a pervasion of his being by the Spirit. It is probably inaccurate, however, to think of a dramatic change from functional to ontological thinking, for the earliest gospel is not without its sense of the uniqueness of Jesus' being, while the latest continually stresses the idea that Jesus' relationship with God in an ontological sense is evidenced by his moral similitude. Rather, the difference is one of approach and particularly of choice in manner of presentation.

Because of the need to ground his sonship more and more securely and in such a way as to cover the totality of his person and ministry, there was also a tendency to locate the sonship at a point even further back in the story, until it found its natural home in the primordial act and intention of the Creator.[29] The oldest tradition may have thought of Jesus' sonship primarily in connection with the resurrection, in view of Acts 13.33.[30] Whatever may have been present earlier in the minds of the disciples, there can be no doubt that the resurrection experience was that in which the sonship of Jesus became a meaningful reality to them. In the four gospels, however, we can see how the crucial moment is pushed back towards the beginning. It may have been connected at one time with the transfiguration.[31] But it is the baptism which is usually singled out as likely to have been the earliest presentation of Jesus' authentication as the Son of God, either as a designation of what was to take place at the resurrection or as itself the moment of the son's birth.[32] Luke's gospel partly anticipates the Matthean development, but still retains the baptism as a decisive moment for Jesus' sonship.[33] In Matthew the momentous character of the baptism is relinquished, the story being remodelled because for this evangelist the nativity story has already dated his sonship from the moment of birth. Finally, in John it is grounded in his being with God before creation.

Yet while we can be certain that development did take place, the caution with which some writers have dealt with it is justified.[34] It is not unusual nor lacking in value that alternative presentations should exist side by side. The church itself recognized this when it canonized all four of our gospels. It will, however, be convenient to use the order which is generally accepted in our arrangement of the material for further consideration.

NOTES

1. Matt. 16.13; Mark 8.27; Luke 9.18.
2. John 6.15.
3. Matt. 4.8–10; Mark 12.35–37; John 18.36.
4. Matt. 1.1; 9.27; etc.
5. I Macc. 9.27; 4.46; 14.41; Josephus, *Contra Apion.* I, 8; H. Danby, op. cit., p.446 and n. 5.
6. Matt. 16.14; Mark 8.28; Luke 9.19.
7. Matt. 21.11,46; 26.68; Mark 1.10ff; 2.8; 7.29; Luke 7.39; 10.18,21; 12.50; 21.6; John 4.16ff.

8. Compare Luke 7.11–16 and I Kings 17.17–24; Luke 24.50–52 and II Kings 2.11; Matt. 5.1 and Exod. 19.25.

9. John 4.12ff.; cf. Mark 10.4ff.

10. Matt. 16.16.

11. J. Weiss, *Christ*, Philip Green 1911, pp.149f.

12. Mark 6.2–4; cf. Matt. 13.54–56.

13. John 6.41f.; 8.19,41.

14. Matt. 5.48; Luke 6.36.

15. Mark 3.17; John 8.44.

16. Origen, *Contra Celsum* I, 32. See H. Chadwick, *Origen: Contra Celsum*, Cambridge University Press 1965, p.31n.

17. John 8.18,29,38,41. In this connection it may be pertinent to note that the suffering righteous man was called son of God in Hellenistic Judaism and that Jesus is referred to as 'the righteous one' in the New Testament: see Wisd. 2.13,16–18; 5.5; Acts 3.14; 7.52; 22.14; cf. I Peter 3.18; I John 2.1; Fuller, *The Foundations of New Testament Christology*, pp.70ff.

18. II Sam. 7.14; Ps. 2.7; 89.26.

19. Mal. 1.6; Test. Levi 4.2; 18.6.

20. Fuller, op. cit., p.32; cf. C. E. B. Cranfield, 'The Baptism of Our Lord – A Study of St Mark 1.9–11', *Scottish Journal of Theology* VIII, 1955, p.62; C. H. Dodd, *The Interpretation of the Fourth Gospel*, Cambridge University Press p.253.

21. Gen. 6.2; Job 38.7.

22. Macquarrie, op. cit., p.258.

23. See Mark 1.11; 15.39; Rom. 1.4.

24. See M. Eliade, *Rites and Symbols of Initiation*, Harper, Torchbook edition 1965, esp. pp.130ff.

25. Macquarrie, op. cit., p.260.

26. See e.g. F. Hahn, *The Titles of Jesus in Christology*, Lutterworth Press 1969, pp.279–346; Fuller, op. cit., pp.164–7.

27. See Cranfield, *The Baptism of Our Lord*, p.63; Fuller, op. cit., p.115.

28. See Hahn, op. cit., p.304 and below ch. 8.

29. Cf. F. C. Grant, *The Earliest Gospel*, Abingdon Press 1943, p.155: 'Step by step, the growing doctrine or theology of the church pressed the *origin* of Jesus' heavenly Messiahship, of his divine nature, back to the very confines of time and place, and then beyond.'

30. Cf. Rom. 1.3f.; H. Conzelmann, *An Outline of the Theology of the New Testament*, SCM Press 1969, p.77. It may also be noted that resurrection at dawn can symbolize birth, see Conybeare, op. cit., p.300; Weiss, op. cit., p.41; Fuller, op. cit., p.167.

31. Conzelmann, op. cit., p.78.

32. See Weiss, op. cit., pp.42f.; Conybeare, op. cit., pp.173ff.; K. Kohler, *The Origins of the Synagogue and the Church*, Macmillan 1929, p.214; Conzelmann, op. cit., p.78; Daniélou, *A History of Christian Doctrine*, Vol. I, pp.224-31.

33. See Hahn, op. cit., pp.305f.

34. See Lobstein, op. cit., pp.65f., 104,126 and n. XIII; Pfleiderer, op. cit., pp.16ff.

6　From the Waters of the Jordan

THE SYMBOLIC AND MYTHOLOGICAL CHARACTER OF THE STORY

The importance which must attach to the story of the baptism of Jesus is out of all proportion to the amount of space devoted to it by the evangelists. It is one of those dramatic events in the gospel history which, like the transfiguration, the last supper and the crucifixion, have always been at the centre of Christian thought and art. That the incident has been so emphasized must derive from its own intrinsic character, from the fact that it has an inherent quality which speaks immediately to the religious consciousness. Christian history witnesses to the enormous wealth of symbolic power which the story possesses.

Dibelius was so struck with the peculiar character of the narrative that he decided that it was one of the very few stories to be categorized as myth in the gospels. For him references to the opening of the heavens, the descent of the Spirit as a dove and the heavenly voice proclaimed its mythological nature. In view of the fact that vital symbolism usually derives its energy from the power of its antecedent myth, Dibelius is likely to be following a right instinct in this. If it is implied, however, that mythological material has been brought into an earthly framework to produce a Christ legend,[1] we must quarrel with his approach on two grounds. Dibelius has clearly determined which elements in the story are mythological by the criterion of non-historicity. This ignores the fact that a firm historical event may also have a mythological significance. In this case, for example, there is no reason to doubt that the waters of the Jordan were historically involved here, yet we shall see that this feature must be considered as fully mythological as the elements to which Dibelius refers. This in turn means that we should not think of a mythical tale being brought into a historical context, but rather that a historical event has been given a transcendental dimension by the use of mythological symbolism. The distinction is important. There is no need or warrant for postulating the intrusion of a formulated myth into the gospel story. Rather, it would seem that out of a crucial moment in the life of Jesus a distinctively new and Christian myth emerged.

The approach of J. M. Robinson is therefore to be preferred. Here the narrative is seen to begin as a purely human story, but to continue with happenings which lie outside the realm of ordinary experience. It begins with a common enough occurrence in the ministry of the Baptist, and then moves on to quite a different level as cosmic symbolism becomes the very substance of the narrative. In the first part Jesus is within the realm of the human and the empirical, while in the second he is the centre of a supernatural and divine drama.[2] Even so, it becomes apparent that any rigid distinction between the two parts of the story is impossible, with the result that Robinson's point of division seems to be an arbitrary one. As Jesus enters the waters we are already within the realm of mythological symbolism, while still firmly within that of the empirical.

It would seem, therefore, that account must be taken of symbolism in the narrative as a whole in any attempt to discover what the significance of this earthly event was for the evangelists and through them for the faith of the church. In pursuing this aim, the very simplicity of the narrative can be misleading. As with so many other matters, scholars have frequently assumed that a choice had to be made between one interpretation and another. But this does not allow for the multivalent significance which naturally adheres to a symbol. The formal analysis of symbolic language therefore supports the contention of G. R. Beasley-Murray that the significance of the baptism is complex, so that the pursuance of restrictive theorizing here does not take account of the riches locked up in the narrative.[3] If it be objected that too much is drawn out of so short a story, it can only be asserted that here again the evangelists were able to rely upon an immediate apprehension of symbolic values such as they could not have done if they had been writing in the twentieth century. For this reason it will be considered appropriate here, as elsewhere, to take note of the way in which later writers, who were nevertheless still within the thought-world of the gospels, gave expression to the meaning embodied in the narrative's symbols and originally allowed to speak for themselves.

THE WATERS OF THE JORDAN

Something of the multivalent symbolism involved in the concept of water has already been noted. With the story of Jesus' baptism, this is enlarged even further. Additional dimensions of water-value can clearly be seen in the variety of meaning which came to be attached to this incident.

Cleansing

The use of water as a cleansing agent in a physical sense led naturally into its use as a sacramental symbol. As the body needed to be washed clean of accumulated filth, so also did the soul. That this was the primary meaning of John's baptism Mark has no doubt. He calls it 'a baptism of repentance for the forgiveness of sins', and so it was accompanied by an act of confession.[4] Matthew and Luke are equally explicit.[5] In John this concept is perhaps implied, but is not explicitly stated.[6] Doubt has been cast on the ascription of such a meaning to John's baptism, particularly because Josephus asserts the contrary.[7] Whatever the truth of this matter, however, it is clear that John's baptism was understood by the evangelists and by subsequent Christian tradition as a cleaning for sin.

This is all the more remarkable in that it appeared to give rise to a theological problem. Why should Jesus as the righteous one have submitted to such a rite? The question is clearly reflected in Matthew, where Jesus overcomes John's attempt to prevent the baptism by arguing that 'it is fitting for us to fulfil all righteousness'.[8] It is brought out even more prominently in the *Gospel according to the Hebrews*.[9] The problem was perhaps not a real one in that the righteousness of Jesus lay precisely in his lack of self-congratulation.[10] For those engaged in the formulation of christological conceptions, however, it was the reality of his sinlessness which mattered, because for them the rite was not a relic of past conventions but a determinative act. They had to think the matter through in another way.

An answer came easily out of the Hebraic background, in which the idea of vicarious action was well known. This must surely be the significance of the fact that John's gospel chooses this context in which to have the Baptist speak of Jesus as 'the Lamb of God, which beareth the sin of the world'.[11] The baptism thus becomes a sacramental enactment of that reality which Jesus achieved in the totality of his life and epitomized in his death. 'The baptism of Jesus is his whole existence in the form of a servant.'[12]

The waters of death

Although a river was usually a symbol of life-giving power, it could also serve, when occasion demanded, as a figure for the serpentine ocean. Consequently descent into and rising out of the water could also represent death and resurrection. Sinking beneath the waves of the ocean was a common enough metaphor in Judaism for death, as the parallelism of a number of passages in the Psalms shows.[13] The imagery inevitably found its way into rites of initiation. In the Mithraic cult, for example, there was a baptism which was understood as a ritual death and resurrection. Mithraism has probably drawn upon a common motif[14] which it shares with early Christianity, which significantly practised baptism by immersion, and with Judaism, in which proselytes were said to have died in baptism and to have been new born as Israelites.

Some scholars have objected to any attempt to interpret the baptism of Christ in the light of what is said about that of believers because only at I John 5.6ff. may this connection actually be made.[15] This reticence, however, is probably to be explained by an unwillingness to compare an originative and vicarious act with baptism, whose sacramental effect was derivative and individual. This does not preclude, therefore, the possibility that the imagery of death and resurrection used of believer's baptism reflected part of early Christian understanding of Jesus' baptism. There are, moreover, hints in the gospels that this was so.

Jesus' reference to the sign of Jonah in Matt. 12.40 brings

together descent into the ocean, within the belly of its theriomorphic monster, and entry into death. In Mark 10.38, a
baptism which Jesus must undergo is paralleled with the cup
which he must drink. From the Old Testament we know that
the cup here must be an image of suffering, death and wrath. In
Luke 12.49f., this baptism is placed alongside the imagery of
fire which was intended to suggest divine judgment.[16] Ps. 11.6
conjoins fire and cup for divine judgment, while Isa. 30.27f.
brings fire and flood into juxtaposition. It would seem, therefore, that Jesus understood baptism in terms of the Old Testament use of water as a symbol of God's judgment, of suffering
and death.

It must, of course, be noted that in these sayings Jesus is
looking forward to his coming passion rather than backwards
to his baptism, but, as J. A. T. Robinson notes, the present
tense is used in Mark 10.38f., and so we must recognize that
Jesus' baptism was an ongoing thing which gathers others into
its orbit at the cross.[17] It can be said, therefore, to have already
begun at the Jordan; at that point he had already entered into
the realm of death. This was certainly how Justin Martyr
understood the matter. For him the fire is already kindled with
Jesus' going down into the water.[18] He has already cast fire on
the earth, has kindled it in the Jordan, and is to undergo its
torment. It is not surprising, therefore, that John's gospel sees
an appropriate connection between baptism, the giving of the
Spirit and death.[19] So for his followers at least Jesus' 'Baptism
in Jordan was a pointer to, or rather an early part of, His
Baptism into death and hades'.[20]

If this was so, that event was a victory. In the gospels themselves we only have this implied by the symbolic events after
the baptism itself. There the heavens opened to greet the *victor
ludorum*. Subsequent Christian writers, however, realized that
this implied that a victory had been won in the waters. If the
heavens were opened above the Messiah in the Jordan, so also
had the abysses opened beneath him.[21] The waters are seen in
their monstrous form and Jesus as the one who breaks 'the head
of the dragon in the water'.[22] So also for Cyril of Jerusalem,
Jesus' baptism was a victory over the oceanic monster. 'When,
then, Jesus must break "the heads of the dragons", he went
down and bound the mighty one in the waters.'[23] In this way

'the Lord had himself baptized, not that he had need of it for himself, but so that he might sanctify all water for those that are regenerated in it'.[24] Again we meet the idea of the restoration to the water of its fallen character, that it might be a source of life to man. Already in his baptism, therefore, Jesus could be thought of as having defeated death and 'rescued us from the fire'.[25]

While subsequent writers went much further than the biblical texts when speaking of what Jesus accomplished at his baptism, it does seem that they were only drawing out what was implicit in their symbolism. Descent into the water suggested death. In his ascent from the Jordan, therefore, Jesus had already anticipated in some measure that victory which was completed at the resurrection and made available to believers in the sacrament of baptism.

Birth from the water

Water was also understood as the source of life. A rising from the waters could therefore be taken as a symbol of new birth. The idea appears to have been a fundamental one in various mythologies, and is certainly a familiar one in the ancient Near East. The classic example is that of the birth of Marduk in the heart of Apsu, the primeval waters, given in the Akkadian epic of creation. The motif was readily applied and appears in connection with such diverse deities as Hathor, Mithras and Aphrodite. Particularly significant for our purpose, however, is the use of this imagery to speak of the emergence of various types of saviour figures. In Northern European myth the rulers of the new world come from the sea.[26] In Persian literature the Saoshyant or Messiah is born of a virgin after she has 'bathed in a lake where Zoroaster's seed had been concealed'.[27] Similarly the gnostic hero of the *Pistis Sophia* and the primal Man of the Mandean literature[28] arise from the water.

In ancient mythology water, like other natural elements, is believed to be instinct with divinity. It was, therefore, divine in itself. This, of course, was a feature of the mythological apprehension of the world in which every element of nature was taken as part of a living whole. There was a danger in this of simply equating deity with the natural elements and thus of neglecting the quality of transcendence. As part of their programme of demythologization, the Hebrews stressed the transcendence of God even to the extent of imperilling the concept of his immanence. In consequence, the water ceased for them to have life in itself. It only became a life-giving force when imbued with the energy of Yahweh. Nevertheless, the contrast must not be pressed too far. We find examples in ancient mythology of precisely the distinction which the Hebrews made. Indeed it becomes clear that the idea of deity fructifying the waters of the primeval ocean was one which the Hebrews shared with their cultural neighbours. So when we read in John 5.4 of water gaining healing properties as a result of angelic action on God's behalf, and find flowing water referred to as living water, we must recognize the continuance into New Testament Judaism of ancient mythological motifs.[29]

II (4) Esd. 13.2f. is particularly instructive of the way in which late Judaism related the motifs found in Gen. 1.2 to the appearance of the eschatological Man. G. H. Box sees in this figure 'the Cosmic Man – the "Urmensch" – who, endowed with supernatural gifts, fights and overcomes the monster of chaos'.[30] But while it is appropriate to see in this passage a reference to the primeval victory, as all emergence out of the waters must signify, the most striking element in II (4) Esd. 13 is the parallelism with Gen. 1.2 used to suggest the emergence of an eschatological figure. The form of a man appears from the sea as a result of a violent wind stirring all its waves. In this it is possible to recognize the ancient motif of the wind as the breath or Spirit of God which causes the primeval ocean to give birth.

It is hardly surprising, therefore, that Christians should have inherited this symbolism and have applied it to both their own rebirth at baptism and to the experience of Jesus at the Jordan. It was a complementary rather than an alternative imagery to that of death and resurrection. The font became both a tomb and a womb. Christians not only rose again to new life in baptism but were also reborn into it.[31] A Syrian liturgy was therefore able to refer to Jesus as living 'in the womb of the baptismal water',[32] and in the *Sibylline Oracles* it is said that 'after he (the Son of God) has received a second birth according to the flesh, being washed in the blue, sluggish stream of Jordan, when he has escaped the fire, he will be the first to see a God coming with good favour by means of the Spirit on the wings of a white dove'.[33]

Whether this was a legitimate interpretation of Jesus' baptism must largely depend upon factors yet to be considered, but the idea was clearly inherent in the symbolism of water and already has some justification from the Gospel of John. In John 3.5 Nicodemus is told that only those born of water and the Spirit can enter the kingdom of God. Now John elsewhere applies to believers what is specifically understood of Christ himself, and we can be reasonably sure that the author intends us to understand that Jesus was so born of water and the Spirit, for this is a description which exactly fits the baptismal narrative. It may therefore be said that John 3.4ff. 'sets forth the ancient conception of birth and rebirth' from the waters which recall and symbolize those of the womb.[34]

THE OPENING OF THE HEAVENS

The opening of the heavens as Jesus rises from the Jordan is an essential ingredient of the story. The brevity of the reference is such, however, that its meaning is not immediately evident.

On the one hand it is suggestive of a spiritual ascent into heaven, of an opening up of the curtain of symbolic cloud which veils the glory of God from mortal man. This is its meaning in a formative Old Testament passage, Ezek. 1.1, and is taken over by the Christian tradition as we see from Acts 7.56.[35] This is the symbolism naturally favoured by those who see the baptism as primarily a visionary experience on the part of Jesus.

The opening of the heavens could, on the other hand, form part of the imagery of descent. In the *Testament of Levi* 18.6 it is said that:

> The heavens shall be opened,
> And from the temple of glory shall come upon him
> sanctification,
> With the Father's voice as from Abraham to Isaac.[36]

This may well be a reflection of the Christian understanding of the baptismal narrative, and we must therefore think of the heavens opening so that the power and glory of the heavenly realm may descend upon Jesus. In that case we have yet another example of a theme constantly employed in the gospels whereby Jesus in his person is endowed and identified with the values of heaven. At his baptism Jesus receives what he will subsequently offer to all, the gifts of paradise.

THE DESCENT OF THE SPIRIT

The descent of the Spirit has also been variously interpreted. Luke 4.16ff., in which Jesus immediately after his baptism goes to Nazareth and announces that the Spirit of the Lord has commissioned him to preach the Messianic message, would support the idea that it designates the gift of prophecy. But while the coming of the Spirit would necessarily include such a gift, it is unlikely that this alone is the idea involved.

Similarly, it is probably inadequate to see in it simply a commissioning out of the sea such as that which the disciples received from Jesus himself.[37] If Jesus is now 'charismatically endowed for the fulfilment of his vocation' as Messiah[38] and in a way which goes beyond prophetic or discipleship calls, it raises him at least to the rank of divinely approved kingship.[39] Again, however, the full significance can only be found in the Hebraic mythology which was antecedent to all applications of its motifs, whether to prophets or kings.

In Gen. 2.7 the reader is told that God formed man from the dust of the ground and breathed into him the breath of life. The gift of the Spirit is therefore an originative act. For this reason Christians saw in the bestowal of God's Spirit evidence of rebirth, and in Acts 10.47 the argument is used that baptism in water cannot be withheld when the spiritual fact which the rite symbolized had already taken place. Jesus, therefore, receives the Spirit as a new creation and this is a 'presage of the gift to be given to Him in the Resurrection of "all flesh" '.[40] In his baptism he is already in a sense the firstborn from the dead, and designated as the one who will himself give the Spirit of the new creation.[41]

THE DOVE

All four gospels refer to the Spirit coming to Jesus at his baptism as a dove, and later writers delight in this feature. It is conceivable that Bernard was correct in retaining the view that this tradition arose from the fact that a dove did actually alight upon Jesus at this time and was understood as indicative of the Spirit's coming.[42] On the other hand, L. E. Keck has recently put forward a strong argument that there was originally nothing more than an adverbial phrase referring to the dove-like motion of the Spirit. He holds that Hellenistic Christianity was later responsible for turning the simile into a phenomenon, abandoning the dove-like motion for a dove-like form and so slipping into the language of mythology.[43] But whether it is based on empirical fact or poetic language, it is necessary to consider the symbolism of the dove in the religious background of the New Testament. Only so can we appreciate the role which the dove has already come to play in our gospel narratives.

Bird symbolism in general and of the dove or pigeon in particular was widespread and varied in the ancient Near East.[44] Its primary uses, however, can be briefly given.

(i) The dove was an 'attribute and hence symbol of the multi-named Eastern goddess' of fertility.[45] Ishtar, for example, was probably associated with a bird[46] which was her theriomorphic form.

(ii) A natural extension of this was to regard the dove 'as a divine messenger and helper', as among the Syrians and Phoenicians.[47]

(iii) Notably in Egypt, but also in Indo-European cultures, the bird was used as an image of the soul. As such it could be envisaged as departing from the body to join the divine world of spirit.[48]

When we turn to the Hebrew tradition, we find that these motifs have largely disappeared. In rabbinic literature the dove is most frequently used as an image for Israel. Despite this, however, some traces of the older mythology remain, and account must be taken of this in coming to grips with the Christian use of the symbol.

While the evidence for the idea of the soul as a bird in the Old Testament is slight, there is reason to believe that it did survive in Judaism and could have been a living motif in New Testament times.[49] Any idea that the baptismal dove represented the divine soul of Jesus must, however, be immediately abandoned as far as the evangelists are concerned. Christian gnosticism later spoke of the begetting of the *aeon* Jesus in the heavenly world and its subsequent descent to Jesus at his baptism, but there is no evidence for the existence of such a view lying behind the gospel narratives or extant in the mainstream of Christian development.

Of far more importance is the continuation of that association of the bird with deity when dealing with a story in which a number of symbols are used to denote the divine presence and approval. While the bird itself was never confused with Yahweh, it remained an acceptable and appropriate metaphor in which to express certain characteristics of divine activity. It is, however, the juxtaposition of the dove and the Spirit in the baptismal narrative which is at once most puzzling and potentially most instructive.

Common acceptance of the dove as a symbol of the Spirit of God has been called into question on the ground that it is only treated in this way in rabbinic literature to a very limited extent.[50] Nevertheless, there is some evidence of such an association which the evangelists may have seen good reason to use.

The dove, the Bath-Qol and the Spirit formed 'a group of associated ideas' for the rabbis.[51] The Bath-Qol was said to moan or chirp like a dove,[52] while *Yebamoth* 46b speaks of coming 'under the wings of the *Shekinah*'. The importance of this lies in the fact that all three motifs appear in the story of Jesus' baptism and seem, therefore, to suggest a threefold symbolism of the divine presence, the dove being one.

This at least is clear from John 1.51. Nathanael is told that he will see the heavens opened and the angels ascending and descending on the Son of Man. The experience of Jacob given in Gen. 28.12 clearly lies behind this, and so the promise to Nathanael must be intended to indicate that he will have a clear assurance that God is present with and in Jesus. Further, we can see that the experience promised to Nathanael is in a parallel relationship with that vouchsafed to the Baptist. In John, the Baptist is enabled to recognize the Lord by the opening of the heavens and the descent of the Spirit as a dove.[53] The dove, therefore, in John's mind at least, may be said to designate Jesus as one with whom God chooses his Spirit to dwell.

If the dove is not to be dismissed as a superfluous parallelism, however, its own special contribution to the total picture must be gauged. The most important pointer to this is probably to be found in the fact that it is here related to the immersion of Jesus in the waters of the Jordan. This conjunction may well have been intended to recall the allusion to the Spirit of God as a bird which may lie behind the use of the verb *merahepheth* in Gen. 1.2.[54] The verb used is very rare, appearing elsewhere in the Old Testament only at Jer. 23.9 and Deut. 32.11, and an exact translation seems to be impossible. Some have taken it to mean 'brooding', which would suggest a background in the idea of the hatching of the cosmic egg, but this translation is difficult to support philologically. Stadelmann argues that it refers to violent rather than gentle action, suggesting that Gen. 1.2 speaks of a wind keeping the primeval water in motion. So Amon, as the wind, moved across the surface of Nun to give it the motion required for it to become creative.[55] A. R. Johnson notes that there is a cognate Ugaritic word used of Anat joining the eagles to hover over Aqhat.[56] Comparative studies would therefore seem to suggest that we are here dealing with a word used to describe the creative act in conjunction with the primeval ocean. Further, however, its use at Deut. 32.11 of an eagle 'teaching her young to fly',[57] together with talk of Yahweh under the imagery of a bird elsewhere, certainly makes it possible that the author of Genesis had Yahweh's creative activity under the simile of a bird in mind. This at least is what two rabbinic writers understood to be the case. Ben Zoma says that '*the spirit of God hovered over the face of the waters* – like a dove which hovers over her young without touching [them]',[58] while Rashi says that: 'The Throne of Glory was suspended in the air and hovered over the face of the waters, sustained by the breath (*ruach*) of God and His command, like a dove hovering over the nest.'[59]

If the reference to the dove in the story of the baptism is correctly seen against this background, then the evangelists may well have seen it as reinforcing the symbolism here of a new creation with Jesus in his baptism being the point of its beginning.

As with so many features familiar to mythology, the Hebrew tradition gave the dove as a divine messenger a curious and distinctive twist in its story of Noah's flood. The possible relevance of this lies in the fact that the dove of the Noah story with its olive branch was a popular image among the Jews of the Graeco-Roman period.[60] Two elements in the Noah story call for mention here. It was on the one hand a story of the world falling back into the abyss of the chaotic waters. The dove, therefore, brings to Noah the news that a new creation has emerged. This association would therefore reinforce the connection of Jesus' baptism with the coming of a new world. Perhaps even more to the point is the role of Noah's dove as one whose olive branch tells a message of the end of divine wrath and the beginning of mercy. Now if Jesus' descent into the waters symbolized in part an entry into the tribulation of men under the wrath of God, then the descent of the dove upon him may be taken as suggesting the coming of God's mercy and peace. This is all the more likely in view of the use of the dove as an image of peacefulness, and would explain why the bird of this creation had to be a dove rather than an eagle.[61]

May a connection not be made, then, with the stress upon Jesus' role as a bringer of peace? As one who rides upon an ass rather than on a horse and offers the peace of God to his disciples,[62] does he not fulfil the prophecy found in the *Testament of Levi* 18.4, that with the coming of the Messiah 'there shall be peace in all the earth'? If Jesus brings division rather than peace in the world's sense, does he not also bring again the primordial peace of God won through his baptism of water, blood and death over the demonic legions of the watery waste?[63]

THE VOICE FROM HEAVEN

The words spoken from heaven at the baptism of Jesus must be regarded as key evidence for the interpretation of the episode. Unfortunately there are difficulties in determining what the original text contained at this point. The text usually given, 'Thou art my beloved Son; in thee I am well pleased', appears in the majority of the mss. This seems to be a conflation of Isa. 42.1 with Ps. 2.7. One important ms, D, some early patristic witness and the *Gospel of the Ebionites*, however, give a text clearly taken from Ps. 2.7 alone, 'Thou art my Son; today I have begotten thee'.

Scholarly judgment is in consequence divided as to whether Isa. 42.1 or Ps. 2.7 was the original basis for the words spoken.[64] Beasley-Murray retains the conflation as it appears in the accepted text.[65] This position is certainly most appropriate for our purpose, in that we are concerned with the meaning of the incident as it was understood by Christians at the time when the gospels were written, and they all agree in giving us this fusion of the two Old Testament texts. By setting it out in this way the evangelists suggest a richness of symbolic potentiality which is merely impaired by attempts to narrow the field of reference.

The use of Isa. 42.1 brings the incident into the context of the servant concept. If the river of Jordan here represents, at least in part, the despair and destruction which men experience bereft of God, then the words of the Bath Qol pronounce a blessing upon the servant who endures these things on behalf of God's people. Yet Jesus is here the servant who is named God's son. His claim to this title is firmly connected with this incident and cannot be avoided, despite the theological difficulties which this seems to involve.

The words here spoken must have been as suggestive of adoption formulae to the men of the first century as they are to many modern scholars.[66] This cannot be rejected simply because it brings with it traces of ancient rites of sacral kingship.[67] They are present here, although put to a use never before envisaged.

However, if the idea of adoption does not do justice to the range of meaning here suggested, nor must the significance of the narrative be determined by attempts to create a systematic theology out of the disparate material of the gospels. It is unacceptable procedure to eradicate the idea of new sonship from the baptismal narrative in Mark because Matthew has carried it back to the time of Jesus' birth, or because John has placed it in the eternity of pre-history with a consequent weakening of the symbolism of birth here in those gospels. Thus while the episode undoubtedly constitutes an epiphany of Jesus as the Son of God[68] and a message of assurance to Jesus himself, the further reality of this incident must not be evaporated by an arbitrary subordination of it to other incidents such as his birth or resurrection, which are deemed to be the point at which his sonship became a fact in the fullest sense. The assertion that Jesus is born of God in his baptism does not exclude an identical meaning being attached to other incidents, and certainly does not entail in symbolic, as it would in propositional language, a denial of that sonship before the baptism. Jesus is constantly born as the Son of God, an idea which eventually found a credal expression. At this point in his life story, it is presented in one set of symbols, while at others it is given in another. We must see in the various forms given to the words of the Bath-Qol at the baptism a reflection of the many facets which this story had.

By declaring his son the beloved and favoured one, God has already proclaimed the victory which he is accomplishing over evil, suffering and death. A divine begetting does not involve here any more than elsewhere the notion of ordinary procreation,[69] but this should not restrict our interpretation of the Markan form to the idea of adoption. Rising from the waters, Jesus is born anew within the context of a symbolism which proclaims him the firstborn of a new creation, into whom God breathes his own Spirit of life, setting before him the task of bringing into being a humanity renewed in the image of God. It is for this reason that the baptism of Jesus became 'the prototype of the Christian sacrament in which rebirth was effected by the union of water and the Spirit'.[70] He is, moreover, able to do this because not only has he received anew the life of God for men, but as the heavens are opened to him there is re-established for and in him that converse between God and man which had not been known since God walked and talked with the parents of mankind in the garden of Eden.

NOTES

1. Dibelius, *From Tradition to Gospel*, pp.271-4.
2. J. M. Robinson, *The Problem of History in Mark*, SCM Press 1957, pp. 26f.
3. G. R. Beasley-Murray, *Baptism in the New Testament*, Macmillan 1962, p.62.
4. Mark 1.4.
5. Matt. 3.2,6,7; Luke 3.3,8.
6. John 1.29.

7. Josephus, *Antt.* XVIII, 5.2; Jeremias, *New Testament Theology*, Vol. I, pp.44f.

8. Matt. 3.15.

9. In Jerome, *Adv. Pelagium*, III, 2.

10. Cf. Beasley-Murray, op. cit., pp.47f.

11. John 1.29 (RV margin); cf. Matt. 8.17.

12. J. A. T. Robinson, *Twelve New Testament Studies*, SCM Press 1962, p. 160; cf. J. Heron, 'The Theology of Baptism', *Scottish Journal of Theology* VIII, 1955, p.42.

13. Pss. 18.4f.; 69.14f.; 88.6f.; see also LXX of Isa. 21.4 which uses 'baptize' of being overwhelmed by lawlessness.

14. See further Borsch, op. cit., pp.83f.

15. See Beasley-Murray, op. cit., p.64 and n. 1.

16. Cf. Matt. 3.11; Luke 3.16; Qumran, *Hymns* III.

17. J. A. T. Robinson, op. cit., p.160; cf. Beasley-Murray, op. cit., pp.73f.

18. Justin, *Dial.* XXX, 13.2.

19. John 7.37–39; 19.34f.; J. A. T. Robinson, op. cit., p.164, cf. p.161.

20. Heron, op. cit., p.42.

21. Odes of Solomon 24.1–3.

22. Test. Asher 7.3.

23. Cyril of Jerusalem, *Cat. Lect.* III, 11.

24. Clem. Alex., *Eclog. Proph.* 7, quoted Daniélou, *A History of Early Christian Doctrine*, p.227.

25. Clem. Alex., *Exc. Theod.* 76.1, quoted Daniélou, *A History of Early Christian Doctrine*, p.228, who remarks that 'the themes of the descent into the Jordan as a struggle against the dragon of the sea, or as a passing through the fire of judgement have a parallel theological significance'. Cf. Sib. Or. VII, 83f.

26. H. R. Ellis Davidson, *Gods and Myths of Northern Europe*, Penguin Books 1964, p.138.

27. Russell, op. cit., p.347; cf. Borsch, op. cit., p.77.

28. Mowinckel, *He That Cometh*, p.392.

29. See Beasley-Murray, op. cit., pp.3f.; cf. John 4.10ff.; 7.38.

30. G. H. Box, 'IV Ezra', *Apocrypha and Pseudepigrapha of the Old Testament*, ed. Charles, Vol. II, p.616.

31. Gal. 3.26f.

32. Eliade, *Rites and Symbols of Initiation*, p.120.

33. Sib. Or. VI, 3–7, quoted Daniélou, *A History of Early Christian Doctrine*, p.228.

34. G. E. Smith, op. cit., p.183.

35. Cf. John 1.51; II Bar. 22.1.

36. Cf. Test. Judah 24.2f.

37. Farrer, *A Study in St Mark*, p.63.

38. E. O. James, *Sacrifice and Sacrament*, Thames and Hudson 1962, p.255.

39. Isa. 11.2.

40. Beasley-Murray, op. cit., p.66.

41. John 20.22; Acts 2.2.

42. Bernard, op. cit., Vol. I, p.49.

43. L. E. Keck, 'The Spirit and the Dove', *New Testament Studies* XVII, 1970, pp.41–67; cf. Jeremias, *New Testament Theology*, Vol. I, p.52.
44. For a concise treatment see H. Greeven, '*Peristera*', *Theological Dictionary of the New Testament*, ed. Kittel and Friedrich, Vol. VI, pp.64ff.
45. Goodenough, op. cit., Vol. XII, p.145.
46. E.g. Cheyne, op. cit., pp.83ff.; Conybeare, op. cit., p.166, but note the caution required here, see Greeven, loc. cit.
47. Barrett, *The Holy Spirit and the Gospel Tradition*, p.35.
48. See Goodenough, op. cit., Vol. XII, p.145.
49. See Greeven, loc. cit.
50. Goodenough, op. cit., Vol. XII, pp.145f.; Keck, op. cit.; cf. Bernard, op. cit., Vol. I, p.49; Greeven, loc. cit.
51. W. F. Flemington, *The New Testament Doctrine of Baptism*, SPCK 1948, p.28.
52. *Berachoth* 3a.
53. John 1.32ff.
54. Dunn, op. cit., p.27; cf. Borsch, op. cit., p.368; Cranfield, *The Baptism of Our Lord*, pp. 53–63.
55. See Stadelmann, op. cit., pp.14f.; B. S. Childs, *Myth and Reality in the Old Testament*, SCM Press ²1962, pp.34f.
56. Johnson, op. cit., pp.32f. n. 8.
57. Childs, op. cit., p. 34 n. 2.
58. *Hagigah* 15a; cf. *Gen. R.* 2.4.
59. Rashi on Gen. 1.2, in A. Cohen (ed.), *Chumash*, Soncino Press 1956, p.1.
60. See Goodenough, op. cit., Vol. I, p.157; Vol. II, pp.119f., 244; Vol. VIII, p.26.
61. Matt. 10.16; Ps. 74.19.
62. Mark 11.1–10; John 20.19.
63. See pp.265f. below.
64. See O. Cullmann, *Baptism in the New Testament*, SCM Press 1950, pp.16ff.; Jeremias, *New Testament Theology*, Vol. I, pp.53ff.; Cranfield, *The Baptism of Our Lord*, p.60; E. Schweizer, *The Good News according to Mark*, SPCK 1971, pp.37f.
65. Beasley-Murray, op. cit., pp.49ff.
66. Borsch, op. cit., pp.367ff.; Dibelius, *From Tradition to Gospel*, p.272; Dodd, op. cit., p.252; Voegelin, op. cit., pp.304f.
67. Cranfield, *The Baptism of Our Lord*, p.60. See further pp.227ff.
68. Schlier, op. cit., p.240; Dibelius, *From Tradition to Gospel*, p.272.
69. Dodd, op. cit., pp.252f.
70. E. O. James, *Sacrifice and Sacrament*, p. 255.

7 The Nativity Stories

THE MYTHOLOGICAL CHARACTER OF THE NATIVITY STORIES

The nativity stories contained in the gospels of Matthew and Luke stand apart from the rest of the New Testament in many ways. There is no parallel to them in Mark or John. The events which they describe are almost certainly not referred to anywhere else in the canonical New Testament. On the other hand, they attracted a great deal of attention in the apocryphal literature and have become central to the Christian liturgical year. Finally, they embody features of a kind which suggest that they may be of a mythological character.

A number of reasons have been advanced for describing these stories as myths, not all of which are valid but which merit consideration.

In accordance with his usual method, Strauss dubbed them mythological because they were unacceptable as historical narratives and this on two grounds. They could not be regarded as descriptions of historical facts because they offended the canons of empirical science. A virgin could not conceive. He also pointed to the inconsistencies found in the stories and claimed, therefore, that they failed to manifest that internal coherence on which the historian must insist. Even assuming the validity of his arguments, however, it must be said that Strauss did not thereby show that they were myths, but only that there was doubt as to their historical value.[1]

Far more pertinent was Strauss's recognition that certain elements were the result of theological motifs. They show a concern to convey certain ideas and beliefs. This is most evident in the fact that the events spoken of are provided with a kind of running commentary spoken by the angels. The reader is not left to guess at the significance of these events, but is given their meaning by the voices of angels speaking to those concerned in them. In view of this it may also be the case that the way in which the events themselves are told is also intended to convey certain Christian 'truths'. If this is the case, then we certainly have something which is at least akin to myth, i.e. a story the elements of which put forth certain truths about man and his relationship with the divine, in particular about one who is designated the Son of God.

A specifically mythological character may be attributed to them on the grounds of the place which they occupy in the development of Christian literature. On the one hand, they are not part of the earliest corpus of Christian material. On the other, they contain elements which are developed with great enthusiasm later. Particularly significant is the fact that these stories are taken up and embroidered in a clearly mythological way in the apocryphal literature. The uncanonical gospels rejoice in the mythological expression of their faith. That their authors should have found such agreeable material in the nativity stories suggests that they recognized that myth was already present in them. An equally important pointer in the same direction is the fact that these stories became the basis for an important part of the Christian liturgical year. Myth finds its natural expression in liturgical act and especially in annual celebration.

The really telling point is that these stories have a clear relationship with material which is acknowledged to be of a mythological character. Stories grew up round the birth of the Buddha which have an unmistakably mythological character, and there are certain formal similarities to the developing Christian tradition. This does not provide a warrant for any theory of dependence by the canonical gospels on Buddhism, for the only significant parallels are found in later material, but it does suggest that we are dealing with traditions of a comparable kind.[2] Dibelius explained this comparability as due to the 'law of biographical analogy',[3] but in this case it would be more aptly termed the law of mythological analogy. That is, in both cases the historical basis was provided with a similar mythological envelope. Parallels have also been noted with other mythical traditions, some of which were not anchored in any kind of biographical history, and again, while dependence cannot be shown, these resemblances suggest the propriety of an examination of the nativity stories in terms of the category of myth. As Jung perceived, our stories contain features common to a large number of child-myths,[4] and the significance of this fact cannot be ignored.

There does, therefore, appear to be a *prima facie* case for considering the nativity stories to be of a mythological character, at least in part. On the other hand, it has to be admitted, along with those scholars who oppose this conclusion, that there are fundamental differences between the evangelists' narratives and the pagan myths.

Pagan myths were always polytheistic, while this feature is clearly absent from our stories.[5] For Matthew and Luke there is but one God, and even he does not appear as a character in the drama but remains hidden in the backstage of transcendence. Here is the undoubted influence of the development in Judaism of a radical monotheism.

In the myths there is commonly a degree of sensualism, sometimes of a particularly gross kind. The story of Jesus, on the other hand, maintains the highest moral tone throughout.[6] The ideals of behaviour reflect those of Judaism rather than those prevalent in the Graeco-Roman world.

The maintenance of such a moral tone, moreover, is the result of the most important difference of all. The Jew could not indulge in thoughts of divine metamorphosis, which was such a stock ingredient of the pagan stories. In consequence he could not think of God bringing about a birth in many of the ways commonly found in the myths.

In pagan stories the deity might come to a maid in a variety of ways. Sometimes it would be in a dream. Often the deity was said to have taken one of three forms.

(*a*) The deity might turn himself into some natural element or endow it with the capacity for bringing conception about. So Perseus was the result of Zeus coming to the virgin Danae as a shower of gold, Alexander was said to have been born of a thunderbolt and his mother, Olympias, while Apis was conceived by a ray of the moon's light.

(*b*) Theriomorphism frequently played a part. Zeus came to Leda as a swan, giving birth to Helen, Castor and Pollux, while

Apollo came to the mother of Augustus as a serpent while she was asleep in his temple.[7] In one version of the story of the birth of Alexander, Zeus comes to Olympias also as a serpent. The birth of the Buddha took place after Maya had been impregnated by an elephant.

(c) In cultures where the gods were commonly thought of anthropomorphically, the myths then spoke of a personal god who acted in all respects like a man.[8]

All three forms suggested some kind of physical contact; theriomorphism tended to indicate that this was of a very crude kind, while a robust anthropomorphism gave rise inevitably to stories of a sensual character. So C. K. Barrett remarks that in pagan narratives 'it is never implied that conception was due to anything other than the ordinary sexual act with accompanying loss of virginity'.[9] As against this, Christian scholars have been at pains to point out that the nativity story does not even contain an allusion to any kind of physical contact between God and Mary. 'Nothing is said regarding a mechanical operation on the body of Mary.'[10] In no sense is it suggested that a supernatural seed replaced the natural seed. Physical contact with the deity is lacking.[11]

Some scholars would go so far as to argue that the Christian story is not mythological at all because it does not speak of a union of the divine Spirit with the mother of Jesus.[12] This judgment appears, however, to be based on the assumption that the myths were intended to be understood in a literal manner, while the biblical language is to be taken as metaphorical.[13] But such a line of argument does justice neither to the symbolic character of the pagan myths nor to the ontology intended by the gospel stories. While there can be little doubt that the myths were often understood in a crudely literal manner, as indeed the Christian story has been at times, it must also be seen that myth is by its nature symbolic, as J. G. Machen half recognized in this context.[14] The distinction between the two sets of narratives, therefore, is not that one is mythological and the other not, but rather that the Jewish-Christian stories of Jesus' birth are heirs to the steady eradication of divine anthropomorphism which had taken place in Jewish thought. In consequence their symbolism is drastically restrained, avoiding the dangers inherent in the morphology of paganism. On the other hand, while the targumists probably explained away as a substantive the title Son of God, as a result of 'the reaction of abstract Jewish monotheism against a manner of speech which savoured of mythology',[15] the Christians readily embraced the concept and the inevitable mythological character of their narrative portrayal of it which this entailed.

Nevertheless, we can appreciate the antagonism which the early church felt towards the pagan myths, while admitting with Justin Martyr[16] that there are formal similarities. This was due to the fact that they share a common narrative mode, i.e. a mythological one. What the differences do suggest quite unmistakably is that the mythological background in which we should search for an explication of the Christian symbolism here is Jewish rather than pagan.

At first this seems to present an insuperable obstacle, for where is there to be found any Jewish myth in which a child is born to a virgin mother? There was at least, however, a Judaic basis for the development of this idea.

To the Hebrew, as to many others, the process of birth was a divine mystery.[17] It was not to be understood in biological terms alone, but as an act of God, a divine gift. So the rabbis said that God was present and active in every birth. 'There are three partners in man, the Holy One, blessed be He, the father and the mother.'[18] As the woman is dependent on the man and the man on the woman, so both are dependent on the divine Spirit in the process of conception.[19] The idea that God participated in the production of a baby was not foreign, therefore, to the Jewish mind.

Further, the Jew believed that in certain cases God was involved in a much more direct manner. The Old Testament describes the births of Isaac, Samson and Samuel in some detail,[20] and this suggests that there was a pattern of Hebraic thought about the origin of outstanding men. The human circumstances, the age of the woman and the barrenness of the couple to date are against it, and yet a birth takes place, prophesied by God or his angel and apparently as an act of special divine grace. Moreover, the name and character of the child are determined beforehand, suggesting that while the human parents remained responsible biologically, God himself determined that the child should be endowed with certain qualities.[21] The nativity stories are undoubtedly related to this pattern of thinking, the parallelism between the narratives of the births of Jesus and Isaac being particularly noteworthy. J. Weiss even went so far as to argue that the story of the virgin birth 'was conceived according to the analogy, e.g., of the birth of Isaac'.[22]

Another class of Old Testament narrative with which Luke 1.26–38 appears to have much in common is that used when speaking of divine vocation. The calls of Moses and Gideon may be compared with the Lukan story.[23] In all three an angel appears, a mission is suggested, and the recipient pleads an excuse which is overruled by a promise of help leading to final acceptance of the role God had commanded. In consequence J. Daniélou concludes that 'there is a recognized literary form for describing annunciations'[24] of which Luke has made use. In Luke's gospel the birth of Jesus is seen as one which takes place in the special grace and providence of God, and its vocational aspect is brought into prominence.

As yet, however, there is no suggestion that the birth was anything other than a normal one in the biological sense. Despite attempts to play down the notion of a virginal conception and to regard Luke 1.34, the only explicit verse, as an interpolation, it remains stubbornly as an ingredient of the nativity story. While the text may not explicitly state that there was no intercourse between Joseph and Mary before the birth of Jesus, there is no doubt that this was intended. The idea appears to be so thoroughly un-Jewish that Conzelmann declares that it must derive from polytheism.[25]

This judgment has a good deal of weight. On the other hand, there is some basis for it in the Hebraic tradition. In Gen. 21.1 Yahweh is said to have 'visited' Sarah, with the result that she conceived and bore Isaac. It would be in accordance with Jewish usage to take 'visit' here in a sexual sense.[26] Another such ambiguous expression is used at Exod. 2.25 (RSV), when it is said that Yahweh 'knew' the children of Israel. This could also be taken as a euphemism for sexual intercourse. While there is no hint of this in the text of Exodus, it may have been so understood in certain rabbinic circles.[27] On the basis of these two texts, therefore, it could well have been held that both Isaac and Moses had Yahweh for their father, not in an ordinary physical sense but as men whose conception was due to the immediate and miraculous action of the divine Spirit.[28]

The evidence may be somewhat slender, but there is sufficient to show that the idea of God's direct involvement in certain births in the Old Testament already noted could be extended in the direction required by our narratives. There is no doubt that the early Christians did develop ideas found in their canonical scriptures in order to produce a theology which was distinctively new and one text, at least, favoured the production of an idea of virgin conception.

The importance of Isa. 7.14 in this connection has been recognized by a number of scholars,[29] and in view of the fact that it is quoted by Matthew at 1.23, its relevance must be acknowledged. It is the Greek version of the text which could be germinative of the idea. The young maiden could easily become the virgin who would conceive. If we add to this the fact that Hellenistic Judaism had embraced the idea of a pneumatic conception and the elimination of an earthly father and note also that Gen. 18.14 is alluded to in Luke 1.37, we must come to the conclusion that the idea of Christ's virginal conception probably arose in Hellenistic Jewish Christianity as an extension of certain ideas latent in the scriptures,[30] and was developed to represent a distinctive theological concept which had pressed itself upon them. Here use was made of certain motifs which set forth the significance of Jesus' birth in terms of the ancient Hebrew creation mythology.

THE EVANGELISTIC SYMBOLS AND THEIR MEANING

The only indications given by the evangelists as to the manner in which Christ's conception came about are to be found in Luke 1.35. It was the result of the Holy Spirit coming upon Mary and of the Most High overshadowing her. This is restraint indeed, but there is nevertheless a wealth of imagery in these phrases.

The word 'spirit' had a rich multivalence in the Hebrew and the Greek languages. In all its uses, however, it pointed back, for the Jew, to the creation story of Gen. 1. It could refer to the wind which in Genesis stirs up the waters of the *tehōm* and brings the world into being. It could also stand for the breath which made Adam a living being. Finally, it was that self-giving whereby God endowed men with the qualities required to carry out his purposes. Thus the word referred to the impersonal imagery of the wind and the very personal and anthropomorphic idea of breath, and to the transcending of both in the familiar symbol of God's presence and activity. In consequence it is a mistake to rejoice in the impersonal nature of the word in order to draw a contrast with pagan anthropomorphism.[31] The fact that conception by the breath appears in such stories as that of the birth of Quetzalcoatl from the Father-God and Chilmalman must not make us forget that it was a symbol considered appropriate to use both in Genesis and John 20.22 in a symbolically analogous context. It was a 'concrete and material representation of a highly religious idea'.[32] It asserts the direct activity of God in the conception of Jesus under symbols derived from the creation story.

The reference to Mary being overshadowed by the power of God takes us back to the same source. The word was used in connection with the cloud of the tabernacle in the LXX of Exod. 40.35, and this is echoed in its use in the story of the transfiguration.[33] It may be explained, therefore, simply as an indication of the presence of God against this background.[34] In view of the idiom found in Jotham's parable in which to be under the shadow refers to protection, it may also be considered to be an image intended to suggest God's protective presence.[35] This idea could have derived from the use of the royal parasol, under whose shadow there was kingly protection,[36] but in a Hebraic context it is more likely to stem from the image of 'the sheltering of a trustful little bird under the wings of parental love'.[37] The same word is used of a bird in the LXX of Ps. 91.4, and in Exod. 25.20 and 37.9 the cherubim overshadow the mercy seat with their wings. The word was therefore connected with the imagery in which God is likened to a great bird who flies protectingly over his people, and under whose wings the Elect One may dwell.[38]

Yet there may be more to the use of 'overshadow' than a reference to God's protective presence. We may probably see another reference to the imagery of the bird in Gen. 1.2.[39] The creative wind is connected with the action of the divine bird in

Egyptian mythology and elsewhere.[40] It may well lie in the
background of the imagery which Luke is using here. At this
time it was not difficult to pick up the threads leading back to
ancient myth, because they were still alive and important in
contemporary culture. So it was easy for the author of the
Christian Sibyllines, VIII, 462, to make use of the old creation
myth in connection with Christ's nativity and to speak of
Mary's conception taking place by the action of the divine
breath – which was both the wind of creation and that which
vivified the first Adam.

An interpretation of these images in terms of the Hebraic
creation myth is made all the more likely by the evident concern
of the evangelists to set their stories in this context. Matthew
begins his gospel by calling it the book of the *genesis* of Jesus
Christ.[41] Now this word was undoubtedly chosen for the variety
of meaning which it could carry. It could mean genealogy,
birth or biography and so was at once a title for the genealogy
contained in ch. 1, for the story of Jesus' nativity and for the
book as a whole.[42] Further, the word points back to the opening
of the Old Testament and to the creation story, in which the
word is twice used. In Gen. 2.4 it refers to the creation of the
heavens and the earth, and in Gen. 5.1 to the creation and
genealogy of Adam. In view of Matthew's use of the same word
again at 1.18 of the birth of Jesus, the conclusion of Daniélou is
inevitably that 'Matthew is establishing a parallel between the
creation of Adam and the Incarnation of the Word'.[43]

Luke's gospel makes the same point by carrying the genealogy
of Jesus back all the way to Adam, who is pointedly called the
son of God. This leaves little room for doubt that Luke intended
his readers to see in Jesus a second Adam[44] and with him the
coming of a new creation. In this lay the real meaning of the
virginal conception. A new world had begun and a new Adam
was born, not of the will of man but of God. He could therefore
have no father but God.

THE COSMOS REJOICES

Accompanying the nativity of Jesus are certain episodes of a
peculiar nature. In Luke angels appear to shepherds in the field
and hail his birth, while in Matthew a star guides the magi to

Bethlehem. These are not peripheral elements but essential ingredients of the stories, intended in their own special manner to point up the significance of the event.

The meaning of Luke's narrative is to be found in the presence of a choir of the heavenly host praising God and in the message of the angel,[45] and the clue to the interpretation of both is provided by Job 38.7 which speaks of the time:

> When the morning stars sang together,
> And all the sons of God shouted for joy.

The heavenly host is probably to be taken here, as elsewhere, as referring to the stars.[46] In Job the stars are those of the morning, for they are singing over the creation which God is bringing into being. So also in Luke's nativity story the heavenly host sings the praises of the God who initiates the new creation by the birth of Jesus at Bethlehem. Moreover, while only angels could shout for joy at the original creation, the angel in Luke's story can call upon the shepherds to join with them in the cosmic jubilation.

Matthew's story of the star and the magi[47] includes some further elements, but is probably to be seen as containing the same fundamental motif. In the literature of the ancient world the birth of a great one and his accession to the throne are often said to have been accompanied by the appearance of unusual heavenly phenomena.[48] Such stories were told, for example, of Augustus and Mithridates. Nor were they confined to pagan material. A star heralds the birth of Abraham in rabbinic sources. An unusually large and bright star appeared in the east and swallowed up the four stars standing at the corners of the heavens.[49] Matthew's story contains the idea of a heavenly witness to the birth of Jesus in a form similar to that found elsewhere and to be embroidered upon in typically mythological fashion by the apocryphal gospels. To this basic motif Matthew has added a number of subsidiary elements probably being influenced in particular by Isa. 60.

Matt. 4.16 shows that the appearance of the Christ was for our author the coming of God's light into the world of darkness.[50] In the nativity story this light is represented by the star. It is a regular feature of mythological narrative that two apparently distinct entities, in this case the child and the star, should be complementary symbols, so that the one can stand for the other. Here the star is both the herald of the child's birth and also, in symbolic fashion, the child himself.[51] The magi see the star 'at its rising', and so they know that 'the glory of the Lord is risen',[52] which is none other than Jesus' birth at Bethlehem. It is for this reason that as early as Irenaeus the star was identified with that in the prophecy of Balaam, in which it was a metaphor for the ruler to come.[53] Num. 24.17 is unlikely to have been Matthew's source,[54] although it is frequently referred to in the Qumran literature, for Matthew does not quote it, although he is concerned throughout to set forth the Old Testament prophecies. He is rather thinking in terms of his primary source, Isa. 60.

Matthew probably derived both the wise men and their gifts from this source. The kings of Persia had also to be magi, and Isa. 60.6 mentions two of the gifts brought by them.[55]

In view of the appearance of magi in the story, it would have seemed inevitable that it should have taken on the character of a witness by astrological science. This, however, appears to have been resisted. Although the time of the star's rising is carefully noted, this is solely for the purpose of determining the time of the birth and not in order to construct a horoscope.[56] Jesus is not so much born under this star as represented by it. Hence the story would seem rather to set forth the subordination of false prophecy to Jesus and to suggest that the Christian had nothing to fear from it.[57] There is little here, therefore, which conflicts with the early church's opposition to astrology. Matthew, as well as Ignatius, probably saw in the birth of Jesus the end of the sorcerer's power.[58]

Finally, we must note that the function of the star is primarily to bring these men from a distant country and to designate the place of the Messiah's birth.[59] This is a first fulfilment of the prophecy in Isa. 60.3f., which says that nations will come to this light and sons from afar off. The people of the darkness come to the source of light. That source, moreover, is to be found in the ancient city of David, in the heart of ancient Jewish territory, and indicated by a star which so often in mythology designates the place of revelation, of spiritual feeding and of new creation. But these are ideas which must be taken up in more detail later.

THE PERSECUTION OF THE CHILD

Built into Matthew's story of the star and the magi is another. Seeing in the prophecy of a new king of Israel a threat to his own power, Herod the Great determines to kill the child. Frustrated by the failure of the magi to return with precise information, he attempts to fulfil his object by ordering the deaths of all the children born since the appearance of the star. Even so the plan fails, for the holy family has taken refuge in Egypt and stays there until there is a new ruler in Jerusalem.

Now while there can be little doubt that Matthew was here influenced in large part again by Old Testament motifs such as the descent into Egypt, the Exodus and Hos. 11.1, it is also pertinent to note that similar stories were told about the childhood of Cyrus of Persia, Augustus of Rome and many others.[60] Matthew has written a Jewish variant of a story with wide currency. The significance of this for our purpose lies in the fact that the development of legends of this type on such a scale almost certainly indicates that a mythological root exists for the recurring motif.[61] This theme appears in a number of myths. Such stories were also told, for example, of Horus, Heracles and Krishna.[62] It appears in classic form in the myth of Leto and Apollo. In this story the goddess Leto, with child by Zeus, is pursued by the dragon Python because a prophecy has been made that the child would destroy him. Leto is saved, however, by Boreas, the god of the north. He takes Leto to Poseidon, who provides her with refuge on an island where she is able to give birth in safety to the god Apollo. Later the prophecy is fulfilled and Python is slain by Apollo on Mount Parnassus.

We have, therefore, a motif which appears in mythology proper and derivatively in legends about historical personages. The relationship between the two forms is made plain by the archetypal character of mythology. When the story appears in a legendary form, it is reasonable to suppose that the mythological archetype has been applied to history. This is precisely what appears to have been the case in Matthew, for the archetypal myth lying behind this story is to be found within the New Testament itself. In Rev. 12.1–4 the familiar mythological characterizations appear. A woman about to give birth to a ruler of the nations is pursued by a seven-headed dragon whose will it is to devour the child at birth. In subsequent verses the woman has probably become a symbol for the church,[63] but lying behind this we can recognize a continuation of the common myth: a place of safety is made for the mother in the wilderness while the child is exalted to the throne of God. The mythological character of this episode is indisputable. In the description of the mother, one like unto Isis the queen of heaven can be recognized, and the dragon is a classic example of the theriomorphic form of the chaotic *tehōm*. The location of the action is in the heavens and its time probably primordial. Rev. 12 may then be said to provide 'the archetype of the earthly history of the Christ',[64] and in particular of the story in Matthew 2.

Once a connection of this sort is established, the full meaning of the story in Matthew readily appears. Just as the Pharaoh of Egypt could incarnate the primeval dragon for the Old Testament prophet, so here the part is played by Herod.[65] As a result of his enmity, the child has to take precarious refuge in Egypt, a country which had become for the Jews a symbol of exile and even of the demonic.[66] The children are slaughtered as they once were in Egypt at the time of Moses' birth, but this does not prevent the child's survival to become the one who finally annihilates the dragon's power.

NOTES

1. For a recent summary of reasons for doubt as to historical accuracy see Fenton, op. cit., pp.33ff.

2. See A. M. Hocart, *Kingship*, Oxford University Press 1927, p.125; Zaehner, op. cit., pp.357ff.

3. Dibelius, *From Tradition to Gospel*, p.127; cf. p.107.

4. See Jones, op. cit., p.263.

5. Machen, op. cit., p.338.

6. J. Orr, *The Virgin Birth of Christ*, Hodder and Stoughton 1907, p.168.

7. Suetonius, *Augustus* 94.

8. Cf. Orr, op. cit., p.168; see the story of Paulina and Mundus in Josephus, *Antt.* XVIII, 3.4.

9. Barrett, *The Holy Spirit and the Gospel Tradition*, p.7.

10. G. Delling, *'Parthenos'*, *Theological Dictionary of the New Testament*, ed. Kittel and Friedrich, Vol. V, p.835.

11. Conzelmann, op. cit., p.78; Hahn, op. cit., pp.295f.

12. Delling, loc. cit.; Hahn, op. cit., p.296; Karl Barth, *Church Dogmatics* IV 1, T. and T. Clark 1956, pp.206ff.

13. Orr, op. cit., pp.151–81; Dodd, op. cit., pp.251f.

14. Machen, op. cit., p.337.

15. Manson, *Jesus the Messiah*, pp.105f.

16. Cf. Justin, *Apol.* I, 22; *Dial. Tryph.*, 67; Machen, op. cit., pp.319ff.

17. Macquarrie, op. cit., pp.258f.

18. *Niddah* 31a.

19. *Gen. R.* 8.9; cf. 71.1; *Sotah* 17a.

20. Gen. 18.9–15; 21.1f.; Judg. 13.2f.; I Sam. 1.1–20.

21. See Gordon, op. cit., pp.244f.

22. Weiss, op. cit., p.147.

23. Exod. 3; Judg. 6.11–16.

24. Daniélou, *The Infancy Narratives*, p.25.

25. Conzelmann, op. cit., p.78.

26. Widengren, op. cit., p.184.

27. See D. Daube, *The New Testament and Rabbinic Judaism*, Athlone Press 1956, pp.5–8; cf. p.34.

28. On Philo's allegorical treatment of God's fatherhood in such cases see Barrett, *The Holy Spirit and the Gospel Tradition*, pp.9f. See also Plutarch, *Numa* 4: 'And yet the Aegyptians make a distinction here which is thought plausible, namely, that while a woman can be approached by a divine spirit and made pregnant, there is no such thing as carnal intercourse and communion between a man and a divinity.'

29. E.g. Lobstein, op. cit., p.75.

30. Fuller, op. cit., pp.195f.

31. See Barrett, *The Holy Spirit and the Gospel Tradition*, pp. 7,10.

32. Lobstein, op. cit., pp.66f.

33. Matt. 17.5 par.

34. Cf. G. H. Box, *The Virgin Birth of Jesus*, Pitman 1916, pp.37f.

35. Judg. 9.15.

36. T. H. Gaster, *Myth, Legend and Custom in the Old Testament*, Duckworth 1969, p.427.

37. W. K. Lowther Clarke, *New Testament Problems*, SPCK1 929, p.75.

38. I Enoch 39.6f.

39. Cf. W. D. Davies, op. cit., p.40.

40. See G. E. Smith, op. cit., p.43; Gaster, *Myth, Legend and Custom in the Old Testament*, pp.4f.

41. Matt. 1.1.

42. Fenton, op. cit., pp.35f.

43. Daniélou, *The Infancy Narratives*, p.12.

44. Beare, op. cit., p.30, cf. p.42; H. Flender, *St Luke, Theologian of Redemptive History*, SPCK 1967, pp.50ff. Note also the dawning of the new day at Luke 1.78f.

45. Luke 2.9f., 13f.

46. Cf. Acts 7.42.

47. Matt. 2.1–12.

48. Cf. Origen, *Contra Celsum*, I, 59.

49. Rappoport, op. cit., Vol. I, p.226; Strauss, op. cit., Vol. II, p.71; cf. Gen. 37.9.

50. Cf. Isa. 9.1ff.

51. See Rev. 2.28; 22.16.

52. Isa. 60.1; cf. Matt. 2.2.

53. Num. 24.17; Irenaeus, *Adv. Haer.* III, 9.2.

54. Strauss, op. cit., Vol. II, p. 77.

55. See E. C. Selwyn, *First Christian Ideas*, Murray 1919, pp.54ff., 56f.,61f.

56. Cf. Daniélou, *The Infancy Narratives*, pp.76ff.

57. See C. S. Mann, 'The Historicity of the Birth Narratives', *Historicity and Chronology in the New Testament*, by D. E. Nineham and others, SPCK 1965, pp. 50f.

58. Ignatius, *Eph.* 19.

59. Matt. 2.1,9.

60. Herodotus I, 108ff.; Suetonius, *Augustus* 94; cf. Dibelius, *From Tradition to Gospel*, pp.129ff.; M. Noth, *Exodus*, SCM Press 1962, pp.26f.

61. Cf. Pfleiderer, op. cit., pp.6of.

62. C. G. Jung and C. Kerényi, *Introduction to a Science of Mythology*, Routledge and Kegan Paul 1951, pp.38ff.; Bultmann, *The History of the Synoptic Tradition*, p.293; Strauss, op. cit., Vol. II, pp.69f.; Clemen, op. cit., p.302.

63. Cf. II (4) Esd. 9.38–10.59; Gal. 4.26; Hermas, *Vis.* II, 4.1; IV, 2.1f.

64. M. Rist, 'The Revelation of St John the Divine', *The Interpreter's Bible*, ed. Buttrick, Vol. XII, p.455.

65. Isa. 30.7; 51.9f.; Ezek. 29.3,5; see Cheyne, op. cit., pp.79–91; Clemen, op. cit., p.305; Pfleiderer, op. cit., pp.59f.; Selwyn, *First Christian Ideas*, p.72.

66. See Daniélou, *The Infancy Narratives*, pp.84f. on the symbolism of 'Damascus' in the Qumran literature.

8   Descended from Heaven

THE INTRODUCTION OF NEW SYMBOLIC FORMS
IN JOHN'S GOSPEL

In John's gospel the Son of God is repeatedly said to have come
from heaven and to have been pre-existent. With the introduction of these ideas, John moves into an entirely new mode of
authenticating Jesus and there is a radical departure from the
thinking of the synoptists.

In the first three gospels there is no suggestion that Jesus,
even as the Son of Man, is either a heavenly figure or a pre-
existent one. They speak of the descent of angels, of the Spirit
and of fire,[1] but the origin of Jesus is never described in this
way. At most it could be argued that they speak of an eschatological descent, but even this is unlikely. The coming on the
clouds of heaven in Mark 14.62 par., almost certainly denotes
exaltation and not descent.[2] For the synoptists Jesus is the man
who is raised to heaven, not the one who descends from it. Of
any concept of Christ's pre-existence there is no trace at all.[3]

The Fourth Gospel continues to use the common Judaic
imagery found in the synoptists. The Word is said to tabernacle
among men and the manna to descend,[4] but this type of
terminology is extended and used in a dramatically new way.
It is the man from Nazareth who is said to have come from
above, to have descended from heaven into the world of men.[5]
Spatial imagery is used to express the relationship of Jesus to
God the Father. That this is the intention is clear from the
parallel expressions in which he is said to have come from the
Father or to have proceeded and come forth from God.[6] In
John, therefore, Jesus' exaltation to the Father is seen as an
ascension to where he was before.[7] That this language is to be
understood figuratively is clear from the fact that Jesus is
equated with the bread which descended and that John the

Baptist is said to have come from God.[8] What we have to do
with here is the use of a symbolic device whereby a spiritual
event is portrayed in spatial terms. Just as death may be
described as a descent into Sheol, so birth is here spoken of as a
descent from heaven. It expresses John's conviction that Jesus
came from the Father. He is the one who came from heaven in
order that others might also be born from above.[9]

The equally dramatic language in which Jesus is declared to
have been with God before the foundation of the world and to
have possessed the glory and love of God before creation must
also be interpreted figuratively.[10] Temporal symbolism here
complements the spatial in order to express the transcendence
and pre-eminence of Jesus as the Christ.

But this incursion into the wider realms of symbolic discourse
raises issues of considerable depth and perplexity. In particular
it must be considered whether it is to be understood as mythological in character and whether its imagery derives from a
Hebraic or non-Hebraic background.

THE PROPER LANGUAGE AND CULTURAL CONTEXT

The primary problem is to determine the proper context of
language and thought forms in which to place the statements
made in the Fourth Gospel. Only by locating these in the correct
framework can we hope to see their full meaning. Any attempt
to place them within an alien structure must distort their
message.

A mind developed in the traditions of Western philosophy
naturally tends to understand John's statements in terms of
metaphysics. The prologue to the gospel encourages this procedure, for ideas are to be found there which have a recognizable affinity with philosophic modes of thought. In particular,
the first five verses make use of the concept of the *logos* which
played such a prominent part in Hellenistic speculation. But
despite the undoubted relevance of these connections, it is
probably inappropriate to think of John as making statements
of a primarily philosophic type.

John's opening words immediately dissolve into narrative.
The apparently discursive propositions of philosophy are seen

to be part of a story to be told, and the *logos* is quickly identified as a person who plays a part first in pre-cosmic time as creator of the world and subsequently as the saviour of it from within his incarnation in the flesh. If this is philosophic at all, it is philosophy overtly showing its parentage in the language of mythology. Myth lived on for a considerable time within the structures of philosophic thought until a gradual process of demythologization attempted to cut it free from its roots in the more ancient modes in which man sought to state the meaning of the cosmos for himself. In John the connections with myth have not yet been severed.

This does not mean that John does not assert a relationship between Jesus and God which may be properly spoken of as metaphysical, but his language must nevertheless be interpreted primarily from within the context of mythological forms. John does not preach his gospel in a series of discursive statements, but speaks of personal relationships set within a narrative embracing both pre-cosmic and historical time. John's doctrine of the *logos* is to be understood best, therefore, when it is seen as a distinctive development of that mythological hypostatization of the divine which we find in the ancient Near East. Examples of this are to be found in the theological mythology of Egypt, where Maat and Thoth were deities who represented two aspects of the sacred. In Hellenistic Judaism the concept of wisdom had appeared, which sometimes bears a remarkable resemblance to the Egyptian Isis and certainly has the character of a hypostatization of elements in Yahweh's character and rule. In all probability there was no conscious dependence of Judaism on foreign religious thought, but the latter probably assisted the process whereby mythological hypostatizations were re-admitted into Judaic thought so that the abstract concept of the divine wisdom could come to be spoken of as a character in a cosmic myth.[11] In view of this development it is likely that John's presentation of Jesus as the *logos* owes something to Hellenistic Judaic modes of thought, and so makes use of ancient mythological forms being revived in contemporary Judaism.

It is equally important to determine to which cultural stream the mythology of the Fourth Gospel belongs. Some scholars have been prepared to argue that non-Jewish thought influenced the Fourth Evangelist directly, and not merely through the mediation of the wisdom literature.

It has been argued that the Son of Man figure, in the synoptists as well as in John, was derived from Iranian mythology. The Persian primeval Man, Gayomart, is the heavenly son of Ahura and his daughter Spendarmad or the earth. He falls victim to the powers of evil. From his seed a plant grows from which come the first human pair. From his dead body come the metals of the earth and from the slain ox associated with him come all the other living things of earth. With the arrival of the Saoshyant or Messiah, Gayomart will be raised from the dead, and following this will arise the first human pair and the rest of mankind. Yet whatever truth there may be in the contention that the Gayomart myth contributed to later gnostic speculations about the *anthropos*, there are good reasons for doubting that it had any effect on early Christian thought.[12] Gayomart is not mentioned in the Gathas, the earliest Zoroastrian material. He appears occasionally in the *Avesta*, but this, as we have it, is a very late recension, possibly well after the time of Christ. Only in the later literature does the myth outlined above emerge with any clarity.

Another line of thought relies heavily on the existence of parallels between the Fourth Gospel and the Mandaean literature. Having been content at first to derive John's language from Jewish Wisdom speculation, Bultmann later proposed that both were derived from an ancient oriental gnostic myth which also manifested itself in the Adamic mythology of Jewish Christianity. The basic features of this myth are similar in many respects to those of Gayomart. The *anthropos* here is also a heavenly man who pre-exists the world in the *aeons* of the *pleroma*, but he descends from this world of light to the world of darkness to redeem men trapped in it who are none other than lost sparks of his own being. He does battle with the evil forces, but after an initial defeat in which he is dragged down into the abyss, he rescues himself and with the aid of his heavenly knowledge enables others to share in his redemption and return to the world of light. This is, of course, a hypothetical reconstruction bringing together elements found scattered in gnostic literature. It is in fact a co-ordinating myth the features of which can easily be enlarged, as indeed they are in the descriptions given by Mowinckel and Borsch.[13] It is, as Borsch says, 'a pervasive conception', but as a whole it appears in no one place. Each specific example is but a fusion of certain elements from the total pattern. All that such a co-ordinating myth proves is that these gnostic systems have taken over elements which were common to a number of mythological schemes and which can also be found in cultures far from the Judaeo-Christian stream of development. The idea of a descending Man-redeemer who becomes incarnate is distinctive, but no one has been able to show that it was pre-Christian.[14] It could even be argued, therefore, that this post-Christian material owes something to the Johannine presentation of Jesus as the Son of God.

Of even more importance than the discrepancy in the required dating of these traditions in order to establish early Christian dependence on them is the outstanding difference in underlying ideas behind the two mythologies. The Iranian and gnostic literatures are dominated by a thoroughgoing dualism which is absent from the gospels. In the evangelists the world is at enmity with God in its disobedience, but not of its necessary nature. There may be no room for the holy family in the inn, the people of Nazareth may reject their Lord and the Son of Man may have nowhere to lay his head, but this is attributed to the morally degenerated will of men and not to their being flesh and blood. John is so clear as to this distinction that he confidently speaks of Jesus not belonging to the world, but he makes it clear that he uses 'world' ambivalently. It is alien to God in its sin and not by nature. The 'world' is not the earth but the realm of alienated man.[15] Further, the heavenly Man was in gnosticism a mythological representation of the soul of mankind. The Christ of John, on the other hand, was a man of flesh and blood who would make men one with him by establishing a corporate body made up of united but individual persons. And this is a typically Jewish concept.

It must be concluded, therefore, that the mythology to which we should look is to be found in the culture of Judaism rather than in paganism, and that if the *anthropos* speculation has played any part in the gospels, it is most likely to derive from Judaic developments of the concept of Adam.[16] And between the Jewish Adam and the gnostic *anthropos* there are vital differences.[17] The peculiar character of this Judaic Adam mythology will shortly be seen as we note its possible relevance when looking for the sources of John's terminology of descent and pre-existence.

THE MAN FROM HEAVEN

While pre-Christian Judaism does not appear to have had any one myth which would account for the Johannine concept of Jesus' descent from heaven, there had been certain developments which paved the way for it.

There had been an increasing emphasis on the transcendence of God in late Judaism, and this had often been expressed in the symbolism of space. God was said to be in heaven. Later Judaism began to speak of three heavens and designated the highest of these as the abode of God. By early Christian times the number of heavens had sometimes been increased to seven, and God's dwelling was even further removed from the realm of men.[18] Judaism had thus laid the foundation for John's talk of Christ's descent from heaven. It had provided the symbolism appropriately used to speak of one who was believed to have overcome the gulf of alienation between God and man.

A second development of some importance was also connected with the concept of God's transcendence. In the most primitive strata of Hebraic thought, God himself was thought of as being able to move amongst men and talk with them. As the doctrine of the otherness of God came to the fore, language of this kind became increasingly embarrassing. It was asserted, therefore, that it was not God himself who appeared among men but his angel. This was at first no more than a means of designating the presence of God without transgressing the divine transcendence. Very little distinction was made between the angel of the Lord and God himself. Later, however, this distinction was pressed. An angel became a distinct intermediary being between God and man. While God remained in his other-worldly height, his angels descended to do his will among men. This notion is clearly reflected in all our gospels, as we have already noted. In John it may have been put to christological use. There are some indications that Jesus has replaced angelic mediation for the Fourth Evangelist.[19] In

Christ God was present in the flesh and blood of a man. It is possible, therefore, that John was led to speak of Christ as descending from heaven, in order to assert that the angelic mediation of God to man had been replaced by the mission of Jesus.

Another possible contributory factor was the growing belief that a number of specially chosen people had been exalted to heaven and that one or more of these would return at the eschaton.[20] The idea that certain prophetic figures from the past would return in the end-time certainly appears to have played a part in early Christian thinking. Underlying parts of the synoptic narratives can be recognized traditions in which Jesus is thought of as Moses or Elijah *redivivus*.[21] John, of course, clearly represents a stage in christological development which has passed beyond these notions. For the Fourth Evangelist, Jesus is superior to all the Old Testament figures. Nevertheless, the idea may have had a negative influence on John's thinking. John 3.13 is a very difficult text to interpret, but it may constitute a denial of the exaltation of the apocalyptic saints and a re-affirmation of the view that heavenly wisdom is denied to men.[22] If this is correct, then no earthly saint, no matter how exalted, could return to earth with divine knowledge. Jesus, on the other hand, is asserted to have a knowledge superior even to that credited to Abraham in late Judaism.[23] He has possessed such wisdom from the beginning and as of right. He was not raised to heaven that he might receive it, but he came from heaven that he might spread it among men. It may well be, therefore, that John thought of Jesus not only as having replaced the mediation of the angels, but also as having made unnecessary any hope for the return of one of the translated saints.

Of rather special importance in this connection is the speculation taking place in Judaism around the figure of Adam. A number of themes were being developed which may have influenced Johannine concepts. No one of these would account for the distinctive character of this christology, but they may well have provided a background of ideas against which the Fourth Evangelist could set out his new and unique claim for Jesus.

It must be seen first of all that Judaism had developed the

idea of an eschatological Adam. This appears in Dan. 7, which
is 'shaped by the primitive myth of creation'.[24] The primeval
battle is fought anew in the eschaton. Yahweh again defeats the
beast who emerges from the sea. Having accomplished his
victory, Yahweh hands over dominion to the Son of Man, in
whom we can recognize the figure of the new Adam. As the old
Adam had been ruler of the primordial world, so the new Adam
would be sovereign over the eschatological age.[25] The concept
of the eschaton as a new creation had inevitably suggested the
appearance of a new Adam as it did in Persia, where it was held
that Yima would re-emerge at the end of time.[26] When the
author of Daniel makes use of this mythological concept, of
course, he does so in order to assert that his nation is the rightful
heir to Adam's rule. It is Israel who is identified with the son
and heir to Adam's sovereignty. In Daniel the Adamic figure is
merely representative of the chosen people. In later literature
the figure of the Son of Man was further developed so that he
came to be thought of as distinct from Israel.[27] He then became a particularized mythological figure, the heavenly Adam
of the new age who would get dominion over all things.

Closely connected with this development was another in
which the Adamic figure became the Messiah of the last times.
Early Messianic thought had merely envisaged one who would
restore the righteous rule of God's people on earth. With the
development of apocalyptic thought and its use of mythological
motifs, the Messiah became a transcendental figure and began
to take on certain Adamic characteristics. He would regain
what had been lost by the first Adam. Like his primordial
archetype he would become world ruler. According to later
Jewish tradition, Adam should have lived for a thousand years
but forfeited this longevity by his sin. The Messiah restores the
millennial life. He gives to men that for which the Jew so often
prayed, a long life on earth.[28] Indeed, all the blessings of the
paradisal age are restored by the work of the Messiah.

It would seem, therefore, that the figurative pattern associated with Adam had found echoes in the work assigned to both
the Son of Man and the Messiah. This being the case, it is
possible to say that Judaism, too, developed the concept of an
eschatological Adam, and that this has most probably influenced
the thought of the evangelists. By speaking of Jesus as Son of

Man and Messiah, they have identified him with the Adamic
figure in his eschatological coming.

We must now consider another group of traditions which
made it possible for this eschatological figure to be thought of
as coming from heaven.

The first Adam appears in Paul as the archetypal sinner, but
he was not always seen in this way. Already in pre-Christian
Judaism 'the perfection of Adam is a fairly common theme'.[29]
Adam was said to have repented and done penance for his sin,
and there was emerging the idea that he was the first of the
righteous patriarchs.[30] In consequence there was developed in
some circles a new form of the Adam myth appropriate to the
character now being assigned to the father of the human race.
In particular he was placed among the translated ones. He is
said to have been buried by angels, and taken up into paradise,
and so could be seen by Isaiah in the seventh heaven.[31] Adam
had therefore become a heavenly figure, and this implied that he
awaited the eschaton along with Elijah, Enoch and others.

In Philo another concept is developed which can also speak
of Adam as a heavenly being.[32] The Alexandrian Jew argued
that the first two chapters of Genesis spoke of not one but two
Adams. The Adam of Gen. 2 was held to be the earthly copy of
the heavenly Adam described in the first chapter. In Philo's
thought, therefore, it is not the terrestial but the heavenly Adam
who is the archetypal man. As a super-terrestial and purely
spiritual being, this Adam alone may be properly thought of as
made in the image of God and described not only as righteous
but as incorruptible and immortal. Judaism did not normally
distinguish in this way between the two Adams, but Philo's
concept was consonant with Hebraic thought.[33] The doctrine
of heavenly counterparts was common among the rabbis, and
this was probably no more than a more precise formulation of
older Hebraic ideas.[34] Under the influence of Platonism, Philo
has applied this concept to Adam and in so doing has reconciled
the contradictory elements in the developing Adamic tradition.
There was both a righteous and an unrighteous Adam. The
latter was of the earth, while the former was a heavenly being.
One had lived in the terrestial Eden, while the other belonged
to its celestial counterpart.

The Jewish notion of heavenly counterparts has a further

relevance here. It was commonly held that the celestial realities would descend at the end-time. There is no reference to the idea of Adam descending with the eschaton in this context, but, as we have seen, the Adamic figure had come to be subsumed under that of the Son of Man or Messiah. With his coming it may be said that there was envisaged the coming of the Man from heaven. There was an adequate basis, therefore, in contemporary Jewish thought for the notion of an eschatological age in which the true Adam would descend from heaven to rule over the new creation. Rabbinic thought saw no need to develop the eschatological Adam myth, whereas early Christianity seems to have had some interest in doing so. It had to speak of a man who was believed to be the archetypal pattern of a new humanity. What more appropriate way of stating this than to assert that he was the heavenly Adam sent by God to establish a new and heavenly race?

So while John's description of Jesus as the man from heaven may have been a novel one in his day, it had its roots in various developments taking place in Jewish thought. His heavenly origin designated the totality of his revelation of God's will for man. His descent meant that this was no longer mediated by angels, by vision or by Torah. It was shown to men in the flesh.[35]

THE PRE-EXISTENT WORD

The Johannine idea of Jesus' pre-existence as the Word also seems to have had its source in various ideas prevalent in contemporary Judaism. In John these have converged and, as with his doctrine of the descent of the Son of Man, become centred on Jesus as the Lord.

Allied to the notion of heavenly counterparts which would be revealed in the eschaton was the idea that these things were pre-existent, ready to become earthly realities from before the time of creation. The *Babylonian Talmud* regularly maintains that there were seven such pre-existent entities: the Torah, repentance, paradise, Gehenna, the throne of glory, the temple and the name of the Messiah.[36] The concept of pre-existence was therefore not in the least strange to rabbinic Judaism. This was, however, but a development of earlier speculation.

The notion of heavenly pre-existence had already been developed in connection with the Wisdom of God. In Prov. 8.22–31 Wisdom is personified. She is said to have been the first creative act of God and so to have been brought into being before the beginning of the world. This heavenly and pre-existent being is then described as being 'like a master-workman', a helper in the work of creation. Scattered in the Wisdom literature are other elements belonging to this myth. She is said to have sought her dwelling among men but to have been rejected by them. She therefore retired to her heavenly abode and came to be hidden from all but a few receptive saints.[37] This Wisdom was, of course, no more than a personification of an attribute of God himself. The myth was only intended to portray God's desire that men should share in his own moral perfection and to show how his will had been rejected by all but the saints of Israel. It was entirely consonant with the intentions of the original myth, therefore, when Ben Sira and the rabbis identified this Wisdom figure with the Torah. In the divinely revealed law was to be found the Wisdom which God offered to men. The mythological form given to this thought, however, spoke of a pre-existent heavenly being.

Another book belonging to this school shows the roots of this idea of Wisdom in Adamic mythology. In Job 15.7ff. reference is made to 'the first man that was born', who was 'brought forth before the hills' and who 'listened in the council of God'. The figure spoken of here is clearly parallel to that of Wisdom in Proverbs, but here the echoes of the Adamic myth are plain.[38] This Adam, however, is declared to have preceded the creation. He is no longer the first man on earth but a pre-existent heavenly being. As such he participates in a knowledge superior to that of the sages and has that unique understanding which is elsewhere attributed to Wisdom.

In apocalyptic literature these characteristics were taken over by the Son of Man. In II (4) Esd. there is an unmistakable allusion to his pre-existence,[39] while his heavenly character is frequently assumed. In this figure also it is possible to see a development of Adamic mythology which was probably the Judaic basis from which most notions of heavenly pre-existence are to be derived.

This is not so strange as might at first appear. In the book of
Genesis, Adam is a purely terrestrial figure who lived at the
beginning of history. In mythology proper, however, the first
man is not located in historical time or in empirical space. He is
placed in a time and space which are not of this world. In any
re-assertion of mythological thinking such as we find in late
Jewish thought, therefore, this time and space would be
recognized for what they originally were, something other than
that in which man's history takes place. Adam would be
restored to his proper mythological status and spoken of as one
who lived in the primordial otherness of God's time and space.

The concept of pre-existence was therefore by no means
unknown to late Jewish thought, and there is little need to
search for the source of John's symbolism outside it. The fact
that Jewish literature does not provide a close parallel to the
Johannine scheme does not invalidate this claim. Judaism had
no need of it, but was moving in a different direction. The
emphasis of late Judaism was placed on the divine wisdom
mediated to man in the Torah. The mythological imagery
which John applies to Jesus was therefore generally connected
by the rabbis with the law. It was to the Torah that they were
primarily concerned to ascribe heavenly pre-existence in order
to assert its truth and finality. This may already have been the
case in John's day, and if so, then it would appear that he has
deliberately used such imagery of Jesus in order to assert that in
him a man may find what the rabbi sought in the law.[40] By his
use of the accepted imagery of transcendental primordiality,
John has declared that in Jesus men may have a knowledge of
God and his will far superior to that contained in the prescriptions of the Torah. In him they may see the archetypal ideal of
manhood in the flesh. By declaring that Jesus had come from
the space-time of myth, John is able to say that in the incarnate
Word, the previously inaccessible things of God have been
brought into the very midst of human life. In Jesus the heavenly
has become flesh and the pre-temporal brought within time.
This is the strange fact presented throughout John's gospel, and
that which Jesus' hearers are shown as finding so difficult to
understand. The Jews have to grapple with a new concept –
the presence of mythological primordiality and otherness in the
person of a man like themselves. Earlier christological formula-

tions whereby Jesus had been presented as the inspired prophet of the eschatological age, the chosen Son of God or the child brought into being by God to save his people Israel, had now been superseded. They are replaced by a description of Christ's origin which left no doubt as to the supremacy claimed for him by faith. By the use of language derived largely from the Adamic mythology of Judaism, Jesus is set forth as the one who reveals the archetypal ideal of manhood and so alone may be 'the source and pattern'[41] of the new race which God had willed to be from before the beginning of time.

NOTES

1. Matt. 3.16; 28.2; Mark 1.10; Luke 9.54.
2. See pp.234f.
3. Cf. H. E. Tödt, *The Son of Man in the Synoptic Tradition*, SCM Press 1965, pp.284f.
4. John 1.14; 6.33f.
5. John 3.31; 6.38,41f.; 8.23; 11.27; 18.37.
6. John 8.42; 16.28.
7. John 6.62.
8. John 1.6; 6.41.
9. John 3.7.
10. John 17.5,24; cf. 8.56,58.
11. Cf. J. T. Sanders, *The New Testament Christological Hymns*, Cambridge University Press 1971; p.56; W. L. Knox, 'The Divine Wisdom', *Journal of Theological Studies* XXXVIII, 1937, pp.230–7.
12. See Albright, *From the Stone Age to Christianity*, pp.378ff.; Manson, *Jesus the Messiah*, p.184; Stauffer, op. cit., p.104.
13. Mowinckel, *He That Cometh*, pp.427ff.; Borsch, op. cit., pp.70f.,87.
14. Borsch, op. cit., p.259; Fuller, op. cit., p.97.
15. John 17.11,16,18.
16. C. H. Dodd, *The Bible and the Greeks*, Hodder and Stoughton 1935, p.146 n. 1; W. D. Davies, op. cit., pp.44f.; cf. R. N. Longenecker, *The Christology of Early Jewish Christianity*, SCM Press 1970, pp.58–62, who points out that the descent-ascent motif was an accepted element in the language of early Palestinian Christianity.
17. See H. Jonas, *The Gnostic Religion*, Beacon Press ²1963, p.155.
18. II (4) Esd. 7.81–87; II Enoch 8.1ff.; II Cor. 12.2; *Hagigah* 12b.
19. See John 1.51; 5.1–9. See p.290.
20. Deut. 18.15 and Mal. 4.5 lay the foundation for the idea that Moses or Elijah would return; see Ecclus. 48.10; Matt. 16.14; 17.10ff. par. It came to be believed that Enoch, Ezra, Baruch and Jeremiah had also been

translated and would return with the Messiah; see II (4) Esd. 6.26; cf. 7.28; 13.52; 14.9; Ecclus. 44.16; Wisd. 4.10f.; Jub. 4.23; I Enoch 39.3f.; 60.1f.; 70.1–3; 89.52; II Enoch 36.2; II Macc. 2.1f.; 15.13; II Bar. 13.3; 46.7; 48.30; 76.2.

21. See pp.114f.

22. See Prov. 30.3f.; II (4) Esd. 4.2; Wisd. 9.16–18; I Bar. 3.29; Sukkah 5a; *Sanhedrin* 39a.

23. John 3.32; 5.19f.,37; 7.15f.; 8.23,26,38; 12.60; *Gen. R.* 44.22; *Mid. Tel.* Pss. 1.13; 16.7.

24. Hooker, op. cit., p.17; cf. Farrer, *A Study in St Mark*, pp.258–62.

25. Cf. Wisd. 10.2; II Enoch 30.12.

26. See Borsch, op. cit., p.79.

27. Hooker, op. cit., pp.29f.; Stauffer, op cit., pp.108f.

28. Jub. 4.30; II Bar. 17.3; Rev. 20.4,6.

29. Fuller, op. cit., p.77; cf. Ps. 8.5.

30. *Cant. R.* 1.4.1.

31. Life of Adam and Eve 48.4–6; Apoc. Moses 37; Asc. Isa. 9.7,28.

32. Philo, *De Opificio Mundi* 134; *Legum Allegoria* I, 31f.

33. See the discussion of this problem in W. D. Davies, op. cit., pp.44–9; cf. I Cor. 15.47–49.

34. See p.211.

35. Contrast the Pauline treatment of the notion of the first and second Adams in I Cor. 15.45–49.

36. *Pesahim* 54a; *Nedarim* 39b.

37. See Bultmann, *The Gospel of John*, pp.22f.

38. Cf. II Enoch 30.12; *Gen. R.* 24.2; *Num. R.* 19.3; *Eccles. R.* 7.23; E.M. Sidebottom, *The Christ of the Fourth Gospel*, SPCK 1961, pp.110f.

39. II (4) Esd. 13.3,26,52; cf. I Enoch 48.2f.,6; 62.7; Mowinckel, *He That Cometh*, p.370 n. 2.

40. Compare the attribution of pre-existence to Moses in Ass. Moses 1.14.

41. Barrett, *The Gospel according to St John*, pp.61f.; see John 19.5, but compare Borsch, op. cit., p.269.

PART THREE

Jesus at the Centre

9　Jerusalem and its Rivals

THE IMPORTANCE OF JERUSALEM

Although Jesus is a man from Galilee and although much of
the synoptic narrative is located in the north, it is Jerusalem
which dominates the whole story. To Jerusalem Jesus must
eventually go and there meet with his death at the hands of his
enemies. There is never any suggestion of an alternative. No
other end is thinkable. In John, Jesus visits Jerusalem many
times and is often in its locality, and the final visit has a sense of
inevitability about it. So in all the gospels there is a deep-rooted
theological necessity for the passion to take place in Jerusalem.
It is not the result of a fortuitous combination of circumstances.
Rather, it is done according to the will of God to which Jesus
willingly and deliberately conforms.

We are faced, therefore, with an important question. What
significance attached to Jerusalem for the evangelists that it
should be so central to the plot of this drama? For subsequent
Christians, Jerusalem became a place of pilgrimage and the
centre of devotion as a result of its connection with Jesus. For
Muslims, too, Jerusalem became of fundamental religious significance. But before all this Jerusalem was the holy city of the
Jews, the one place to which a Jew had to go and towards which
he was constantly turned in spirit. It is an understanding of this
which we must seek in order to answer our question. Only if we
can discover what Jerusalem really meant to the Jew, can we
hope to ascertain its significance in the gospel story. The evangelists themselves do not explain, because the knowledge we
require was common to the people of their day. What was left
unsaid must for us be explicitly set out.

Numerous scholars have undertaken to give us carefully

documented pictures of the political, religious and social life of Jerusalem so that we may better understand the events which took place there. Archaeologists have attempted to show us where the walls stood and to reconstruct the route of the *via dolorosa*. Yet for our purpose, all such studies must be deemed inadequate. While the machinations of politicians, soldiers and priests are to be allotted an important part in the story, and while the physical structure of the city is most relevant to historical reconstruction, these things cannot solve our problem. It is beyond the realm of empirical study, as the fate of Christ was beyond the will of men. Such study tells us nothing about the mystique which attached to the rocks and dust of this minor capital of an occupied people. To gain this we must go back not only to the growth of the Jew's feelings about Jerusalem but also into the depths of ancient myth.

THE CENTRAL MOUNTAIN AND THE HOLY CITY

The Jews were not alone in having a city which was of mystical significance to the people.[1] We need only remind ourselves of Babylon, Delphi, Angkor Wat, Rome and Byzantium. Each one claimed for itself an exclusive position such as we find accorded to the city of Jerusalem. They were all of more importance to the people than can be explained by their geography or history. Many of the claims made about them seem strangely baffling, until we look beyond the location and time of the cities themselves and trace back the claims made to a concept rooted in a mythology of space more ancient than any example of it in the first pages of our history books.

Central to mythological cosmography is the idea of the earth as a great mountain rising out of the sea. This meant that the highest place on earth was of primary importance. This would be the first part of creation to emerge from the primeval ocean.[2] Here life first flourished, and hence it was the location of the garden in which the first man and woman lived. From it the life of the world spread out in all directions. The highest point was also, therefore, equated with the centre of the earth.

Parallel to the earth was the heaven above and the astral bodies within it. As the earth had its centre, so too did the heavens denoted by the north or pole star, around which the rest appeared to revolve. As earth and heaven were related in this way, the pole star stood directly above the topmost tip of the mountain at the centre of the earth. For this reason earth's centre was frequently understood to be in the north. Here was the axis of the world and the point at which heaven and earth met.[3]

As the bond between heaven and earth, the centre was inevitably understood to be the place of revelation, the point at which God and men might meet. Here the abode of God was located. The conjunction of heaven and earth at this point made it at once a temple in the heavens and a dwelling on the heights of earth.

Such was this mythological picture of the world. By itself, however, it would have been merely a tale without relevance. To be of practical use for religion and society it had to be brought into relationship with the physical space in which a people actually lived.

This was achieved by identifying a particular site within the domain of a race with the sacred mountain. In this way a national capital could be invested with all the mythological significance of the centre. The rule of its kings could be identified with the lordship of God whom the king represented. The temple in the heart of the capital was none other than the very dwelling of God himself.

It will be seen that this was an illogical claim to make for any city other than one located at the north pole. Fortunately for those whose religion and political economy depended on such an identification, mythological cosmography was not geographical cartography but symbolic portrayal. It was possible, therefore, for a city to be invested with all the attributes of the centre, even though it was not located in the north, because it functioned as though it were so placed. Here we come across an important aspect of mythological symbolism. The status of a place, an object or a person was determined not by conformity in physical terms, but by the possession of the ability to exercise the appropriate functions. It was even possible both to identify one's city with the centre, and even to build an artificial hill to be the cosmic mountain, and yet at the same time to continue to speak of that other centre which was far away in the north. In this way both the nearness and the remoteness of God could be expressed and experienced. Both the mythological original and its physical derivative persisted because both exercised an important function in the religious lives of the people.

With this outline before us, we can now consider whether such a complex of ideas can throw any light upon the role of Jerusalem in Judaic culture, remembering that the considerations of empirical geography will be largely irrelevant.

THE IDENTIFICATION OF JERUSALEM WITH THE CENTRE

The idea that Jerusalem was located at the centre of the earth is only explicitly asserted in the post-exilic literature.[4] By the time of Jesus, however, it had probably become a commonplace, as we can see from its presence in Jewish apocryphal literature[5] and in Josephus.[6] Later it appears in rabbinic and patristic writings.[7]

This evidence may be misleading, however, in that it suggests that the notion was a late one in Judaism. This may not in fact have been the case. We know that it existed long before the exilic period among Israel's neighbours, and this leads us to suspect that its comparatively late appearance in Old Testament literature may have something to do with the peculiarities of Hebrew development. In particular we are reminded that Jerusalem did not have an exclusive claim to loyalty among the Hebrews, even after the Deuteronomic reform. It would therefore be late before Jerusalem could be thought of as destined to be 'a blessing in the midst of the earth', as it is in Isaiah.[8] The notion may have been earlier attached to other sites such as Bethel and Tabor, as the names may suggest. When the 'high places' other than Jerusalem were finally overcome, their claims would tend to be suppressed, especially if they were linked with concepts of deity suspicious to prophetic puritanism. It would take time for the old traditions of a central high place to attach themselves without harm again to Mount Zion. Whatever decision be taken about the antiquity of the concept in Israel, however, we do know that it was firmly established by the time of Christ. Moreover, we can see that it was not merely a meaningless convention, but part of Israel's living mythology. This is clear from the way in which the hill of Jerusalem was invested with the vital characteristics of the central mountain. Of these, three may be taken as showing that the concept was of primary importance to the religion of the Jew.

(*a*) *Mount Zion and the land of Israel.* In rabbinic writings there is an evident concern with the height of Jerusalem,[9] which is only explicable in terms of the kind of thought we are considering. It derives from the notion of the psalmist that the mountains of God were as great as the ocean was deep.[10] If Jerusalem was to be equated with the earthly dwelling of God, then it must be seen atop a great mountain. But this it certainly was not. Zion was only a little hill, and the fact was a source of embarrassment. There were two ways in which such an objection could be overcome.

One way out of the difficulty was to assert that the whole land of Israel was higher than the rest of the world. However small in themselves, the mountains of Israel would then be the highest on earth. This idea lay behind the rabbinic statement that the land of Israel had not been submerged by the flood.[11] This was indeed a common notion. That part of the earth which was able to remain dry as the waters rose over the rest of the earth was clearly the highest.

Alternatively, it could be admitted that Jerusalem did not conform in stature in the manner required at the present time. Its religious significance then had to be safeguarded by the assertion that it was the place chosen to become the great mountain in the new age. This is found first in Isa. 2.2f., and becomes common later.[12] In some passages this is not understood as a raising of Jerusalem, but rather as an abasement of all other highlands.[13] In this way all other pretenders to the role of the centre are said to be doomed, and Zion alone is left to fulfil the myth of the mountain of the gods.[14]

(*b*) *Jerusalem in the north.* If Jerusalem was to function as the spiritual centre of the earth, it would also have to be related to the idea that the central mountain stood under the pole star, on the unmoving axis of the universe. If this feature was absent, grave doubts would have to be voiced as to the existence of the complex of ideas we are studying having been part of Hebrew culture at all. Yet despite the apparent unlikelihood of such a claim, it does in fact appear.

A number of Old Testament passages refer to the mountain of God located in the far north, from which it may be concluded that the Hebrews shared with their neighbours the myth of the polar mountain.

Isaiah makes use of the myth when describing the pretensions of the king of Babylon.[15] The self-glorification of the Babylonian monarch is portrayed as an attempt to ascend into heaven, to exalt his throne above the stars of God, to sit upon the mount of congregation in the furthest parts of the north, to ascend above the clouds. These claims are not the result of Isaiah's poetic fancy, but are such as a sacral king would have made, and the basis of the allegiance he demanded from his subjects. Divine kingship involved for the Babylonians and for Isaiah an assertion that the monarch's throne was mythologically, and therefore in spiritual reality, located on top of the mountain of the north.

As the dwelling place of Yahweh, the north was also that direction from which came the elemental manifestations of his activity. From it came the cold north wind which was the very breath of God.[16] From that direction came the golden splendour and the terrible majesty of God.[17] Out of the north Yahweh appears to Ezekiel in his vision.[18] The significance of the northern quarter in these passages is only explicable because we know that there the central mountain of the earth 'reached to heaven like the throne of God'.[19]

The same complex of ideas also makes sense of an otherwise puzzling reference in the book of Job to God stretching out the north over empty space when he hung the earth over nothingness.[20] The author might appropriately have used a hanging umbrella as an analogy for the concept in mind, its point reaching up to the pole star and the whole earth suspended from it.

From these allusions it is clear that the Hebrews did associate the mountain of God with the north and probably with the pole star.[21] It may have been taken over from one of the neighbouring cultures,[22] or it may have been a mythological image which appeared among the Hebrews as among other peoples by means of a simple logic based on the observation of the fixed point of the pole star.

Of even more importance than the presence of the general notion in Israel, is the evidence for its application to the hill of Jerusalem. From this it can be seen that the concept was of real importance within the mythologically-based cultus of Judaism. To the polar mountain man could never go, and in that lay part of its religious value, but it was also necessary that man should be able cultically to overcome the barrier between himself and God conceived in terms of space. For this reason, an accessible mountain had to be identified with the place of God.

There is no direct statement of this in the Old Testament. On the other hand, there are passages which necessitate recognition that allusions to it are present for the purposes of a meaningful interpretation. In Ps. 48.2, Mount Zion is said to be beautiful in elevation, the joy of the whole earth and to be 'on the sides of the north'. The psalmist has applied the myth of the northern mountain to Zion,[23] so that the centre of the Israelite cultus should be authenticated as being within the acknowledged complex of the northern and sacred mountain. There may also be an implied polemic, the claim of Zion to be the true slope of Zaphon being made against the same claim made for Ugarit.[24] An even stranger assertion from the geographical point of view appears in Ps. 133.3, where the dew of Hermon is said to come down upon the mountains of Zion, because it is on the latter that the Lord has commanded the blessing of life. This appeared to represent such an anachronism to Oesterley that he wished, following A. Jirku and Gunkel, to amend the text, reading '*Iyyon*, i.e. the hilly country on the south-west foot of Hermon, for Zion.[25] This is unnecessary, and would not in any case explain why the text was eventually made to refer to Zion. The answer must surely be that Hermon was at one time a synonym for the northern mountain whose blessing descends upon Zion, because the latter is for practical religious purposes identified with Hermon's slopes.[26] A similar usage appears in later Jewish texts when the temple is referred to as Lebanon.[27]

(c) *The exclusive mountain.* By claiming that Jerusalem was the high mountain of the north which constituted the centre of the universe, the Hebrews were forced to assert further that Jerusalem was alone the mountain of God's choice. This, however, entailed difficulties which were felt most acutely with regard to other mountains of fundamental importance within the Judaic tradition.

The Israelites had recognized a number of vitally important mountains as religiously significant during the course of their cultural development. During the period of tribal independence, various mountains could be used and have an exclusive status within the tribe in whose territory it lay. With the unification of the tribes, this would no longer be possible. A political unity could only survive if local cultic centres could be forced to surrender their importance. Something of the processes involved is reflected in the vicissitudes of Israel's history. David's centralization of his kingdom on the newly-captured Jerusalem, which was probably already an important cultic centre, would pose a problem for many of the tribes, and the assertion of the rights of Dan and Beersheba by Jeroboam was a rejection of any exclusive claim made for David's capital. The later centralization of worship in the Deuteronomic reform on Jerusalem at the expense of the local high places was another vital phase in the process of making Jerusalem the exclusive mountain.

Sinai posed a special problem because, although it was of key importance to their religious history, it lay outside the land which they came to inhabit.[28] In Old Testament times, Sinai could probably be neglected as a mythological problem because there was never any question of its being in practice a continuing political or cultic centre, though certain prophetic movements may have harked back to it (e.g. the Rechabites). The problem was keenly felt by some rabbis, however, who were offended by the fact that it lay outside what had become firmly, for them, the holy land. One rabbi therefore explained that Sinai had been chosen by God for the giving of the law in preference to Tabor and Carmel because, although they had the requisite height, they had been places of idolatry.[29] Ancient and mountainous cultic centres in the land had forfeited their rights. For another rabbinical writer, this does not go far enough in solving the problem. He preserves the pre-eminence of Mount Moriah, on which the temple was built, according to II Chron. 3.1, by explaining that Sinai had plucked itself out of

Moriah.[30] In this way the extra-territorial mountain is derived mythologically from that which had become the centre of the Israelite cultus.

Thus although Jub. 8.19 had perhaps attempted to give an adequate place to Sinai by calling it 'the centre of the desert', the solution was eventually seen to lie in a process of assimilation. This is already taking place in the work of the Chronicler, who identifies the temple site with Ornan's threshing floor and Jerusalem with Mount Moriah.[31] It was carried further in the course of the polemic against Mount Gerizim, as we shall see, and became a fixed idea in the Judaic mind. What could not be so assimilated now in view of the evident and confessed facts of geography, could be assimilated eschatologically. So the midrash on Ps. 87 says that God will bring Sinai, Tabor and Carmel together and put Jerusalem on top of them.

To say that two or more quite distinct mountains, located at some distance from one another, are now or will become one, seems extremely strange to us. To the mythological mind, however, this was not so because, as B. S. Childs remarks, 'spaces possessing the same content transcend distance'.[32] Spatial similarity may become identity when the symbolic or mythological function is one. This was easiest when the cultic centres to be assimilated lay within the bounds of one culture. When this was not the case, men were forced to proceed by way of denial and counter assertion. This is how the Jews had to meet Samaritan claims about Mount Gerizim.

Mount Gerizim, along with Mount Ebal, had been a sacred mountain from ancient times.[33] The Samaritans maintained a vigorous claim that this was the place chosen by Yahweh as his holy mountain down to and beyond New Testament times. According to Memar Markah III, 2, this was 'the place which the True One has chosen, the place of blessing, the dwelling place of the angels, the house of the great Divine One, the place of his glory, the place of forgiveness by the True One'.[34] The Samaritans had assimilated all places of religious importance to this region in the centre of their land, just as the Jews had done with regard to Jerusalem. It was identified with the place of the original creation of man, with the burial sites of Joseph, Joshua and other patriarchal figures, There the first altar had been set up on earth by Adam, and it was there that Seth,

Noah, Abraham, Isaac and Jacob had built their altars. This
indeed, then, must be the place designated in Deut. 12.11, 14
and 27.12 to be the one sanctuary, and not Jerusalem as the
Jews supposed.[35] So Gerizim was identified with the great
mountain which had not been covered by the flood.

In their polemic against the claims of Samaria, the Jews
could only assert their own contrary process of assimilation.
They could agree that the descendants of Shem had been
accorded the privilege of dwelling at the centre of the earth,[36]
but must disagree as to the location of the holy place within
Shem's portion. For the Jew it was Jerusalem and it was there,
and not in Samaria, that all the great religious centres of the
past were to be found. Salem, the city of Melchizedek, was
Jerusalem and not Shechem, as the Samaritans held. The
Samaritans might point with some confidence to Judg. 9.37,
which seems to locate the centre of the land hard by Shechem,
and to Gen. 28.19, which designates Bethel as the place at which
Jacob set up his pillar. With a fine disregard for historical
geography, however, the Jew held that Jacob's dream had taken
place in Jerusalem and his stone was none other than the sacred
rock of the Jewish temple.[37] In this way no acknowledged
incident in Hebrew history was allowed to detract from the
glory of Jerusalem's hill, and the identification of the site so
vaguely referred to in Deuteronomy with Jerusalem was preserved.[38]

THE HORIZONTAL AND THE VERTICAL BOND

From the short review we have made, it is clear that the Jew
was prepared to make what to us appear to be quite extravagant
claims on behalf of his holy city. Taken as examples of national
pride alone, they are not merely extravagant but frivolous. It
is only when the ultimate aim of all this casuistry is seen that
they can be justified. Assertions concerning the height of Jerusalem, its relationship to the northern mountain and its identification with all the sites of past theophany were designed to
safeguard the functional value of Jerusalem for the Jew as the
place where he could meet with Yahweh, and as the unifying
centre of the Jewish people. In symbolic and mythological
terms, Jerusalem had to be maintained as the bond uniting

heaven and earth, and as the bond uniting the people. Only then could it be the valid centre of both cultic and political life.[39]

It was into a society held together by such a veneration and love for Jerusalem that Jesus was born. It was to Jerusalem that his family were always turned in spirit, and it was to that city that they took their newborn child as did every other Jewish family.[40] They attended the statutory feasts in Jerusalem, and it was there that Luke's tradition says that Jesus knew that he must be about his Father's business.[41] Consequently we may assume that Jesus was familiar with and at least initially accepted the role which the Jews attributed to Jerusalem in the spiritual life of man.

As an adult Jesus continued to attend the feasts in the holy city. It remained for him the city of God.[42] When he speaks of it there is a sigh of great tenderness and a terrible anguish for the city whose humiliation and destruction he foresaw. As it was the great mountain of God, he naturally spoke like other Jews of going up to Jerusalem,[43] for the ideology of Jerusalem was built into the very language which he used. It probably suggested some of his metaphors such as that of 'the city built on a hill which cannot be hid', which would have had an impact upon his audience largely lost on us, who have at best a second-hand knowledge of what Jerusalem meant to the Jew, and very little of that tremendous feeling for the city which found it impossible to conceive of its destruction.[44]

It would be reasonable, therefore, to assume that Jerusalem constituted both the vertical and the horizontal bond also for Jesus. When we turn to the gospels, however, we have to allow for the fact that they were written after a revolution had taken place in the minds of his followers. There would seem, moreover, to be evidence of an important development lying between the writing of the synoptic gospels and the formulation of the concepts embodied in John.

To some extent the synoptic gospels seem to retain the Judaic concept of Jerusalem. This is perhaps most evident in the case of Luke's gospel, as we shall see. On the other hand, there is also a kind of negation of the concept which is centred upon the idea of the kingdom of God. This takes up the symbolism of the central bond, but divorces it from its connection with the land and capital of Israel. In view of the fact that the preaching of the kingdom belongs to the most primitive tradition and was dropped very early within the New Testament period, it is likely that the synoptic viewpoint originated with Jesus himself. The synoptic tradition goes a stage further. Especially in Matthew, there is a tendency to identify the symbolism of the centre with Jesus himself. This finds specific expression in John's gospel, where the change is completed and Jesus in his person is shown to replace Jerusalem as both the vertical and the horizontal bond.

Later, full consideration will be given to the idea of Jerusalem and of Jesus as the vertical bond between heaven and earth. At this point we can illustrate the development outlined by noting the way that the Jewish concept of the horizontal bond is appropriated and transformed in the gospels.

THE BOND OF THE PEOPLES

In ancient and modern times it is common to find nations arrogating to themselves positions of world rule combined with and dependent on a sense of world mission. There is usually, at least ostensibly, a claim that they can radiate from their national centre the benefits of enlightenment of which the rest of the world stands in need. So military and economic expansionism is defended on the grounds of spiritual, moral, cultural or political superiority. In the ancient world these ideas were generally expressed in the language of mythological cosmography. The concept of the world centre was appropriated for this purpose. So Herodotus, for example, tells us how the Persians organized their government in a hierarchy of space. Those at the centre had the place of most honour, and governed both themselves and those nearest to them. The latter in turn were responsible for governing those further from the mystic centre.[45] Similarly, in China those nearest the centre of political and spiritual power were held to have the most privileged position, while those who lived at the greatest distance from it had the least.

Lacking imperial status, the Jews were unable to translate this idea into political fact but were nevertheless dominated by the same concept. It is expressed most eloquently in one of the *Sibylline Oracles* which asserts that 'the godlike heavenly race of the blessed Jews. . . . dwell around the city of God at the centre of earth'.[46] This only makes explicit what was in the mind of Isaiah when he called upon the inhabitants of Zion to shout and sing for joy because the Holy One of Israel dwelt in their midst.[47] For Isaiah, people were naturally divided into those who were afar off and those who were near.[48] For Ezekiel, too, Jerusalem was set in the midst of the nations and so occupied the most privileged position, although it had been abused by her people.[49]

To the psalmist, therefore, the Gentiles were the spiritually underprivileged by virtue of the fact that they dwelt 'at earth's farthest bounds'.[50] The Psalms in fact 'bear many echoes of a piety for which remoteness from the holy place meant separation from the source of life'.[51] The sense of misfortune attaching to such a habitation even led to terminology which suggested that 'the place of punishment is the uttermost darkness at the edge of the world'.[52]

The people who lived anywhere other than at the centre were commonly said to inhabit one of the four quarters of the world. Such a division of the compass was common in Israel and in Babylonia, where Sargon of Akkad called himself the ruler of the four quarters.[53] This probably derived in many cases from the idea that the earth was a quadrangle and that the world mountain was like a four-sided pyramid. There are numerous indications that the division of the world into four was connected with mythological portrayals of the centre. From paradise at the centre four rivers flowed. The same division was also to be found in the heavens, of which there were four winds.[54] The heavenly rule was therefore appropriately delegated to four archangels by the author of I Enoch 40. 2,9f.[55] Heaven and earth, as so often, parallel one another. And for both, the centre was the place of supremacy and rule. For the Jew, Jerusalem stood on this central spot beneath the heavenly throne, and so performed the function of being the bond of the peoples located in the quarters.[56]

It followed within this complex of ideas that the hope of those living afar off at the ends of the earth must rest on their relationship with the centre. This was felt particularly with regard to the Hebrew dispersion. The Jew saw the scattering of Israel among the nations of the world as one of the greatest

punishments which God had inflicted upon his people.[57] To
be among the Gentiles was to be taken 'from the midst of the
land'.[58] They found comfort, however, in the belief that it was
God's merciful and saving purpose to bring his scattered people
home again.[59] In the eschatological age, the lost sheep of Israel
would be gathered in from among the Gentiles to partake in the
blessings which God would provide for his people in the new
Jerusalem. In some writings this ultimate convergence on Jerusalem will include the Gentiles. Isaiah 26.6–9 spoke of all peoples
coming to the mountain of Jerusalem for the feast which God
would provide at the end-time.[60] The *Testaments of the Twelve
Patriarchs* are informed by a spirit of universalism. Through
Israel the Gentiles will be saved, and the righteous among them
will be gathered in along with the Jews.[61] In the two centuries
preceding Christ, however, Jewish thought often became bitter.
The Gentiles would come to Jerusalem, but not to share in
God's salvation. They would come to see the glory of Israel, to
be judged and to suffer the Lord's vengeance.[62]

When we turn to the New Testament, it is possible to see how
these ideas have played a part in the language and thought of the
first Christians, although they are immediately modified in such
a way as to make room for new conceptions.

Jesus restricted his ministry to the Jews. When he goes outside the land of Israel, he is not undertaking an evangelistic
mission, but is in fact surprised when Gentiles press upon him
and show greater spiritual acumen than the Jews.[63] Matthew
seems to do no more than make this attitude explicit when he
has Jesus restrict the mission of the twelve to 'the cities of
Israel'.[64]

It is probable, however, that Jesus shared the liberal Jewish
expectation that the Gentiles would be gathered in at the end
of history. The evangelists certainly portray him in this way.
While his earthly ministry is restricted to the Israelite land and
people, the Gentiles are destined nevertheless to take part in the
final convergence of mankind round 'the mountain of God'.[65]
Thus although Matthew's gospel most emphasizes the spatial
restrictions imposed on Jesus' earthly ministry, it looks forward
to a time when the elect are gathered from one end of heaven to
the other before the throne, and in preparation for this the
disciples are sent out after the resurrection into the whole

world.[66] Similarly, in Mark there is to be a gathering which is universal in scope, men coming from the four winds, from the ends of the earth and from the ends of heaven.[67] Luke also reflects this apocalyptic expectation when people will come from the four quarters to the kingdom of God, but now it is asserted that many who believe that they have a reserved place will find themselves outside.[68] The confidence derived from a belief in the efficacy of having been born in the holy land of patriarchal lineage is undermined in favour of a righteousness which is purely spiritual in character, and not the prerogative of a holy race.

The gospel writers have continued to make use of the current mythological symbolism of space, but do so in order to put forward a new perspective. The gathering in to which the pious Jew looked forward is seen in a new light. Its results will be other than many expect. This is portrayed with the utmost simplicity and yet with great subtlety in the parable of the prodigal son.[69] It makes use of the symbolism of space in a manner which every Jew would recognize, but like every good story has an unexpected twist. By going away into a far country, the son makes himself one with those who are alienated from God. This is further emphasized by his having at last to eat the food of swine. The spiritually renegade Jew is thus finally identified with the unfortunate Gentiles of the outer lands. The prodigal then proceeds to act in a manner expected of such people by the Jews. He will be grateful even to be accepted as a servant if he may return. The story reaches a climax, however, when the father does not wait to receive his son's submission, but goes out to meet him while he is still afar off. By this action the father crosses over the spiritual barrier represented by spatial distance, and so the story-teller lays the foundation of the doctrine that God wills to overcome the division which has been set up between the Jews of the centre and other men, whether they be prodigal Jews or Gentiles. If Pharisaic piety could not accept the reality of such divine grace, then they themselves, like the elder brother, would find themselves outside on the day of the feast.

In the story of the Pharisee and the publican, the symbolism of the near and the far is used to another, but related end.[70] Now the Pharisaic claim to spiritual superiority is radically

called in question. The two men act in a manner which was
thought entirely proper. The publican stands afar off, while
the Pharisee expresses his sense of privilege by approaching close
within the temple precincts. Yet the very point of the parable
is that the Pharisee's confidence in his own superior righteousness is misplaced. The publican is in fact closer to God, despite
his inferior placing in the hierarchy of space. The symbolism
is now beginning to be used in a way quite different from that
which obtained in mythological cosmography. Spatial distance
is now simply an image for expressing a man's relationship to
the salvation and righteousness of God of an interior kind.

The city of Jerusalem and the righteousness which it represents ceases to be the goal of man's spiritual pilgrimage. All
traces of nationalism are removed, and in place of a hope for a
kingdom of David there emerges the idea of the kingdom of God
which is not a spatial concept at all, although the imagery of
space continues to be employed in connection with it. This
kingdom is within the heart of a man.[71] A man's closeness to
that kingdom, therefore, is determined by his spiritual relationship to the will of God.[72]

A further change takes place which was of the utmost importance for the development of Christian thought. In what is
probably the older stratum of gospel material, Jesus is the gatherer into the kingdom of the Spirit which he proclaims, antici-
pating the work of the apocalyptic Son of Man. He was the
one sent to bring in the lost sheep of the house of Israel.[73] He
wills with great emotion to gather the people of Jerusalem as a
hen does her chicks.[74] Indeed, his ministry can be summed up
as a gathering in, and the discipleship of a man may be determined by knowing whether he participates in this. If not, he is
a scatterer of men, and so drives them into the spiritual wilderness.[75] But Jesus as the gatherer gives way in other passages to
the idea that it is to Jesus himself that men are brought in.
He becomes the centre which all men seek and in which lies their
salvation. The symbolism of the near and the far is now used in
the gospels to show how the outcasts from God's land find their
hope in him. The demoniac, denied the privileges of the holy
society, comes to Jesus from afar to be healed.[76] The Gentiles
also come to him from far away.[77] The preacher has become that
of which he spoke. Jesus and the kingdom are one and so he

begins to function as the bond of men, the centre of the human race.

An even more dramatic development inevitably followed from the identification of Jesus with the centre. For the evangelists, his status as the bond of men was totally exclusive of all others. There was no other to whom men could go.[78] This meant that all other centres were negated, and in particular that the role of Jerusalem as the bond of earth had ultimately to be rejected, however difficult this might be for a disciple of Jesus brought up from childhood to regard the holy city as that on which his hope of salvation must be fixed. The old concept appears to be retained in the story of the cleansing of the temple. It is cleared in order that it may be a house of prayer for all the people.[79] This older tradition, in which Jesus remains strictly within Jewish ideas as to the function of Jerusalem and its temple, is, however, completely rejected in another tradition found in John. Here the Gentiles come not to Jerusalem but to Jesus, and it is to the crucified one that all men are to be drawn.[80] A similar thought is probably to be found in Matthew's nativity story. The magi come to the baby Jesus with gold, frankincense and myrrh. The converted pagans of Isaiah come to Jerusalem with their gifts, but in Matthew they bring them to Jesus.[81] The same idea seems to lie behind Matt. 12.42. The Jews are compared unfavourably with the queen of the south who came from the ends of the earth to listen to the wisdom of Solomon. But this implies that the centre to which those afar off come is Jesus, rather than Jerusalem.

The evangelists also make the point that by rejecting the Son of Man who comes to the old centre, its people have forfeited their territorial privileges. Jesus comes to the centre, both proleptically to his *patris* and to Jerusalem, but in both cases he is rejected. He is cast out from Nazareth and does his mighty works elsewhere.[82] He is condemned in Jerusalem, but his death opens the doors to the Gentiles.[83] The same idea is found in Matt. 12.6. Jesus' sabbath work is defended on the grounds that he is greater than the temple. Here there is already the seed of the idea that Jerusalem is rejected as the centre in favour of Jesus, which is given fully explicit formulation in John's account of Jesus' meeting with the woman of Samaria.[84] The woman gives typical expression to the rival claims of Jerusalem and Gerizim, saying, 'Our fathers worshipped on this mountain; and you say that in Jerusalem is the place where men ought to worship.' Jesus replies to this by saying that 'the hour is coming when neither on this mountain nor in Jerusalem will you worship with the Father'.[85] Worship 'in spirit and truth' is about to become a reality.

There is something more to this than an exaltation of the spirituality of true worship, as Bultmann notes.[86] In order to discover what this is, we may compare the description of a very similar situation and dialogue found in a midrash.[87] In this, a Jew on the way to Jerusalem is invited by a Samaritan to worship on 'this holy mountain and not to pray in that vile ruin', referring to Gerizim and the fallen Jerusalem respectively. The Samaritan supports the claims of Gerizim by repeating the familiar story that it was the mountain not covered by the flood. This is countered, however, by the ass-driver of the Jew who proves from the text that all mountains were flooded. From this remarkably close parallel it can be seen that a discussion of the sort referred to in John's gospel was a common one, and concerned the claim of Gerizim to be the divinely chosen place of worship and the high mountain of mythology. As John Marsh rightly observes, therefore, John shows here that Samaria's worship is now transcended, just as he has previously shown that this is the case with the religion of Judaism.[88] Further, however, it is to be noted that the two stories are quite different in their result. Jesus does not engage in any attempt to rebut the Samaritan claim along the accepted lines of the debate. The whole basis of this is swept away and a quite new factor is introduced. 'The place' gives way to 'the person' of the Messiah. This is reinforced by the earlier part of the conversation, in which Jesus is identified with the source of living water.[89] This asserts that Jesus as the Christ has taken on the function of the central mountain. As Messiah in and by whom the spiritual worship comes, Jesus is also the fulfilment of those hopes for the eschatological exaltation of the sacred hill.

The gospel writers have not been concerned with issues about the height and centrality of Jerusalem found in Jewish literature. They never become involved with the idea that the city is located in the north. This is undoubtedly due to the fact that they have a new perspective on these ancient mythological ideas. These ideas can be allowed to remain in the background because the whole structure is seen in an entirely new light. The purely spatial elements of the picture have now become irrelevant, for they pin their hope not on a holy place but on a divine person. They still attach great importance to the idea of the exclusive centre, but the total claim once made for Jerusalem or Gerizim is now made for Jesus as the Christ. This dramatic development could not take place all in a moment, however. It was a gradual process, and the new outlook had to be thought out slowly and with care. In consequence, there are to be found in the gospel material elements which are not entirely consonant with one another. Fortunately for the historian of early Christian ideas, the evangelists do not eradicate the old when the new appears. Indeed, to have done so would have meant discarding much of the basis of the gospel story, with its roots in the history of Jesus of Nazareth himself. In this chapter, therefore, we have been able to see how the idea of the horizontal bond is first attached to the land of Israel, but is eventually found to have its fulfilment in Christ. As we turn to other aspects of the role of the Jerusalem myth, we shall find comparable developments taking place.

NOTES

1. A. Jeremias, op. cit., Vol. I, pp.54f. remarked that 'every country has a mountain which is the throne of the Divinity and place of Paradise, a centre of gravity (navel) . . . a sacred river . . . an entrance to the Underworld and so on'.

2. Note the order of creation in Prov. 8; cf. *Erubin* 22b.

3. See S. A. Cook, *The Religion of Ancient Palestine in the Light of Archaeology*, Oxford University Press 1930, p.120; S. B. Frost, *Old Testament Apocalyptic*, Epworth Press 1952, p.107; Gaster, *Thespis*, pp.181ff.; A. Jeremias, op. cit., Vol. I, pp.33, 103; H.G. Q. Wales, *The Mountain of God*, B. Quaritch 1953, p.10; A. J. Wensinck, *The Ideas of the Western Semites concerning the Navel of the Earth*, Müller 1916, p.15; cf. Astley, op. cit., p.89.

4. Ezek. 5.5; 38.12; cf. 5.12; 34.26; Ps. 74.12; Zech. 14.8.

5. Jub. 8.19; I Enoch 26.1; 90.26; Sib. Or. V, 249–50. Cf. Wensinck, op. cit., p.22.

6. Josephus, *War* III, 3.5.

7. *Sanhedrin* 37a; *Gen. R.* 33.6; *Lev. R.* 31.10; Clem. Alex., *Strom.* V, 6.

8. Isa. 19.24f.

9. *Kiddushin* 69a: 'The Temple is higher than the rest of Eretz Ysrael, and Eretz Ysrael is higher than all [other] countries'; cf. *Gen. R.* 69.7; *Cant. R.* 4.4,9.

10. Ps. 36.6.

11. *Gen. R.* 33.6; *Lev. R.* 31.10; *Cant. R.* 1,15.4; 4,1.2.

12. Ezek. 17.22–24; 20.40; 40.2; Micah 4.1f.; *Baba Bathra* 75b; see G. von Rad, *The Problem of the Hexateuch and other Esasys*, Oliver and Boyd 1966, pp.233f.

13. Zech 14.10; Psalms of Solomon 11.2–5.

14. Frost, op. cit., p.138.

15. Isa. 14.13f.

16. Job 37.9; cf. Wales, op. cit., p.12.

17. Job 37.22.

18. Ezek. 1.4ff.

19. I Enoch 18.8; cf. 24.2; 25.3; 77.3; Frost, op. cit., pp.106f.

20. Job 26.7.

21. See also Goodenough, op. cit., Vol. III, illus. no. 1042, which shows an *omphalos*-type mound with a star.

22. See Childs, op. cit., p.89. In this connection note that the Hebrew word for north may be related to the name of the sacred mountain, Zaphon, in the Ras Shamra texts: Clements, op. cit., p.5.

23. W. O. E. Oesterley, *The Psalms*, SPCK 1953, pp.262.; Jacob, op. cit., p.198.

24. Clements, op. cit., p.49 n. 1; cf. pp.8f.

25. Oesterley, *The Psalms*, p.536.

26. See Deut. 4.48; cf. Selwyn, *The Oracles of the New Testament*, p.271.

27. *Gen. R.* 15.1; 16.2; *Ex. R.* 23.5; 35.1; *Num. R.* 8.1; 11.3; cf. *Lev. R.* 1.2; B. Gärtner, *The Temple and the Community in Qumran and the New Testament*, Cambridge University Press 1965, pp.43f.; G. Vermes, 'The Symbolical Interpretation of Lebanon in the Targums', *Journal of Theological Studies* IX, 1958, pp.1–12.

28. Wensinck, op. cit., p.46, pointed out that Sinai is situated beneath the navel of heaven in Deut. 4.11.

29. *Gen. R.* 99.1; cf. *Num. R.* 13.3.

30. *Mid. Tel.* Ps. 68.9.

31. I Chron. 22.1; II Chron. 3.1; cf. Gen. 22.2.

32. Childs, op. cit., p.85.

33. Stadelmann, op. cit., pp.152f. In this tradition the city of Shechem is between two sacred mountains, see Wensinck, op. cit., p.13.

34. Quoted J. Macdonald, *The Theology of the Samaritans*, SCM Press 1964, p.327; cf. Josephus, *Antt.* XVIII, 4.1; *War* III, 7.32.

35. Cf. Deut. 11.29; 27.12; see Marsh, op. cit., p.216.

36. Jub. 8.12.

37. *Mid. Tel.* Ps. 91.7; cf. *Gen. R.* 69.7.

38. *Sanhedrin* 11.2; cf. Josephus, *Antt.* XIII, 3.4.

39. See E. Burrows, 'Some Cosmological Patterns in Babylonian Religion', *The Labyrinth*, ed. S. H. Hooke, SPCK 1935, pp.52f.
40. Luke 2.22.
41. Luke 2.49.
42. Matt. 5.35.
43. Matt. 20.17f.; Luke 2.42; 18.31; 19.28; cf. Luke 10.30.
44. Matt. 5.14. See p.259.
45. Herodotus I, 134.
46. Sib. Or. V, 249f.
47. Isa. 12.6.
48. Isa. 33.13.
49. Ezek. 5.5f. Cf Voegelin, op. cit., p.28.
50. Ps. 65.8.
51. Jacob, op. cit., p.178.
52. Conzelmann, *An Outline of the Theology of the New Testament*, p.17; cf. Farrer, *The Revelation of St John the Divine*, p.207, who suggests that the text may mean that 'the unreconciled are tucked away in lands remote from the centre'.
53. E.g. Isa. 11.12; Ezek. 7.2; Stadelmann, op. cit., pp.131–4; Voegelin, op. cit., p.25. For further examples see Lord Raglan, *The Temple and the House*, Routledge and Kegan Paul 1964, pp.159–68.
54. Ezek. 37.9; Dan. 7.2.
55. Cf. I Enoch 9.1; Qumran, *War Rule*, IX, 15f.
56. See Wensinck, op. cit., pp.17,40; cf. Rev. 21.12ff., where the new Jerusalem is a square with four walls and twelve gates facing to the four quarters.
57. Deut. 28.64.
58. Jub. 1.13.
59. Jub. 1.15; cf. Deut. 30.1–5.
60. Cf. Isa. 2.2f.; 66. 19–21; Micah 4.1f.; Zech. 2.10f.; 14.16ff.
61. Test. Napht. 8.3; Benj. 9.2; cf. Levi 2.11; 4.4; 8.14; 18.9; Judah 22.2; 24.6; Zebulun 9.8; Dan 6.7; Asher 7.3; Benj. 10.5.
62. See Psalms of Solomon 14.6–10; 17.21–32; II (4) Esd. 13.37f.; 49; Charles, op. cit., pp.294, 518 note on II Bar. 72.4–6.
63. Matt. 8.5–10; Mark 7.28f.
64. Matt. 10.5,23.
65. See Jeremias, *New Testament Theology*, Vol. I, pp.245–7.
66. Matt. 24.31; 28.19; cf. 25.32.
67. Mark 13.27.
68. Luke 13.28f.
69. Luke 15.11–32.
70. Luke 18.10–14.
71. Luke 17.21.
72. Mark 12.34.
73. Matt. 10.6.
74. Matt. 23.37; Luke 13.34f.
75. Matt. 12.30; Luke 11.23.
76. Mark 5.6.

77. See p.304.
78. John 6.68.
79. Mark 11.17.
80. John 12.20ff., 32.
81. Isa. 60.6; see Daniélou, *The Infancy Narratives*, p.93.
82. Mark 6.1–6.
83. Matt. 28.19.
84. John 4.1–42.
85. John 4.20f.
86. Bultmann, *The Gospel of John*, p.190 and n. 4.
87. *Cant. R.* 4.4,5; cf. *Gen. R.* 32.10.
88. Marsh, op cit., pp.214–21.
89. John 4.14; cf. John 1.51.

10 *Christ Entombed and Risen*

At the very centre of the earliest and the continuing gospel of
the Christian church has been that sequence of events in which
Jesus is said to have suffered, died, been buried and to have
risen from the dead. These are also the events which to some
have seemed to have most in common with the myths of the
ancient world. In these also there are stories of gods who died
and rose again. On the other hand, the gospel story is distinctive in many ways, and it has been impossible to find an origin
for it in any one myth and ritual pattern which is earlier than
the gospel itself. The special character of the gospel story may
with some confidence be attributed to its being based on a
historical foundation. The documentary evidence for the crucifixion is compelling, and the resurrection is most certainly
based on the experience by the disciples of the risen Christ. This
does not mean, however, that mythological elements are completely absent. On the contrary, it would appear natural enough
to the evangelists to make use of symbolism derived from myth
in order to portray the significance of these events as they saw
them. In particular, they appear to have made use of the
Hebrew myth of the holy mountain in order to portray in narrative form the doctrine of Christ's descent into hell, his raising
of the dead and his rebirth in resurrection.

DESCENT INTO HELL

Although absent from the primitive kerygma of the early
church, the doctrine of Christ's descent into hell quickly found
a place in the teaching of the church and was incorporated in
the Apostles' Creed. Perhaps the inherent strangeness of the
idea to modern man has been largely responsible for the fact
that it has frequently been derived from pagan mythology.

Three apparently convincing reasons may be advanced in support of this contention.

Pre-Christian Judaism appeared to offer very little basis upon which the doctrine could have been built. The Jewish tradition was full of stories of men who had ascended into heaven but 'few, if any, persons in Jewish myth are supposed to have had a peep into Hell'.[1] Lack of a Hebraic source implied an intrusion from paganism.

The idea seemed to have appeared relatively late in Christian thought. Few have seen any indication of it in the gospel accounts, while its presence in the rest of the New Testament has been disputed.[2] In view of the fact that a good deal of pagan influence is generally admitted to have found a place in post-canonical Christianity, there seemed every reason to see in the doctrine the invasion of a heathen idea.

Most convincing of all has been the known presence of such stories in pagan mythology. Osiris, Attis, Ishtar, Baal, Heracles, Orpheus and Hibil-Ziva, for example, were all said to have descended into the realm of the dead. Such a source seemed all the more plausible because Christ was known to have been assimilated to deities like these during the spread of Christianity through the Graeco-Roman world. In particular he was represented in the catacombs as Orpheus, and this led Conybeare to conclude that 'we may safely attribute to the influence of the old Orphic hymns and mysteries this class of Christian myth'.[3] However, as we shall see, there are 'more contrasts than similarities' between the pagan and the Christian traditions.[4] The only common factor is that of a descent into and rise from the place of the dead.

If a pagan origin for the idea of Christ's descent into hell is to be denied, therefore, it is necessary to show that there was a basis for it in Judaism from which the doctrine could have grown, that it was present in some at least embryonic form in the early documents of Christianity, and that the differences when compared with pagan myth are such as to make such a source most improbable.

THE JEWISH BASIS FOR THE DOCTRINE

The Hebrews probably inherited the idea of the place of death as a gloomy underworld from the Assyro-Babylonian religion. By the time of Christ the concept of Sheol was fully established within Jewish thought. Although the place of death and evil could be thought of as lying in the wastes at the edge of the earth, it was most commonly seen in terms of the mythological model which divided the cosmos into three or more levels. The dead were interred in the ground and so placed in the netherworld. Described in accordance with this mythological cosmography, the dead had gone to a world below the earth, or even beneath the ocean on which it lay.[5] The Hebraic concept of death, therefore, provided a basis for the idea of funereal descent. Judaism thought of all men as undertaking a journey into the netherworld. To be laid in the grave was to enter Sheol, to descend into the pit.[6]

Moreover, there was also a basis in Judaism for the idea of a heroic descent into hell and of salvation from it. The book of Jonah makes it abundantly clear that the prophet's sojourn in the belly of the fish was to be understood as a descent into the underworld. A number of complementary expressions are used to convey this. Jonah is thrown into the ocean, goes down into the deep and to 'the heart of the seas'. He went down to 'the roots of the mountains', to the prison and to the pit.[7] The fish which swallows Jonah turns out, moreover, to be none other than the zoomorphic form of the primordial ocean so that he cries out from 'the belly of Sheol'.[8] The author has left the reader in no doubt that he is making use of the common mythological motif in which swallowing by a fish-monster can represent the fate of the dead.[9]

There was, then, a complex of thought in the Old Testament itself from which the idea could be developed, and it is on this basis that the evangelists appear to have built.

THE IDEA IN THE GOSPELS

Three passages refer to 'the sign of Jonah'.[10] In view of the probability that Jonah was already symbolic of death and resurrection,[11] it is likely that Matthew and Luke could assume that the sign would be understood. In Matt. 12.39f., however, its meaning is made explicit. The sign is said to consist in the parallelism which will exist between the descent of Jonah into the belly of the fish and that of the Son of Man into the heart of the earth. The Son of Man, like Jonah, would descend into hell and rise again.[12]

The Jonah myth also suggests a partial solution to the oft-debated question of the origin of the idea that the resurrection of Jesus would take place after three days,[13] for, as the gospels record it, the resurrection happened on the third day. Although this period of time also appears in some pagan myths and rituals, it is evident from the explicit connection made between the two by Matthew that the immediate source from which the three days and nights tradition came was the book of Jonah.[14]

The idea of a descent into Hades also seems to lie behind the story of Christ's death and burial. The mere fact that Jesus is said to have died and been buried would have been understood to constitute a descent into Sheol.[15] This by itself accounts for the one element which is all that F. Loofs found the Christian story to have in common with the supposed pagan parallels.[16] If we take note of the fact that the dying gods of paganism were also said to rise again from the dead, a pagan origin still remains unnecessary. What Jesus is said to have done was no more than to anticipate what Pharisaic piety hoped for all the righteous at the time of the new creation. It is, however, possible to go further than this. The evangelists all record that, contrary to normal practice, the body of the crucified Jesus did not share the common grave of convicted felons. As a result of special pleading on the part of Joseph of Arimathea he was buried in a rock-hewn tomb which had not previously been used.[17] This was clearly of some importance to the evangelists, for they describe the burial in considerable detail. It is certain that they did not do this in order to provide a mythological basis for a subsequent cultic veneration of the site. Christians of the earliest period showed no interest in the tomb. They followed the advice of the angels to the disciples on the resurrection morning and so did not look for the living among the dead.[18] Nor could the story have been for the purpose of validating the resurrection. Neither in the gospels nor elsewhere in the New Testament, with the possible exception of Acts 2.29ff., is the empty tomb an argument for the resurrection. The evangelists in fact make it clear that the empty tomb merely puzzled the disciples or drove them deeper into despair.[19] The resurrection

was made known by the appearances of the risen Christ, and
not deduced from the disappearance of the body from the
sepulchre. Another reason must lie behind their interest in the
details of Jesus' burial.

A preliminary clue is found by remembering the evangelistic
insistence that Jesus had to die in Jerusalem and nowhere else.[20]
This meant in turn that his body would be interred in the
vicinity of the holy mountain of Jerusalem, to all intents and
purposes within it. An understanding of the significance which
the burial had for the gospel writers, therefore, would seem to lie
in an appreciation of the role played by the myth of the sacred
mountain.

There was a widespread connection made between the
mountain and death. It was common practice among a great
many peoples to bury their dead either on a mountain or in a
tumulus which was its miniature representation.[21] The archetypal basis for this is found in the myths in which a god was said
to have been buried on the heights of the mountain like Baal or
in its rock like Mithras.[22] The reasons appear to have been
manifold, but fundamental to most of them was the idea that the
mountain was the connecting link both with heaven and hell.
The Jews undoubtedly shared this concept, with the result that
the site of Christ's burial may be suspected of possessing similar
symbolic value. He was interred at the very place where the
entry point of the great abyss was located in Jewish myth.

The Hebrew spoke of the flood waters of death lying immediately below the mountain of Jerusalem.[23] The city of
Yahweh stood directly above, and so victorious over, the realm
of death and destruction. Consequently the psalmist contrasted
the rock of Zion with the pit of death,[24] and the author of I
Enoch located the abyss at the centre of the earth.[25] Rabbinic
literature developed the idea and made it most explicit. The
rock of Jerusalem was said to stand exactly over the *tehōm*,
the temple mountain closing its mouth and holding down the
subterranean waters of the flood.[26]

Judaic tradition also posed another relationship between
the rock of Zion and the place of death, but this too kept the
close connection between them. This was suggested by the historical geography of Jerusalem. Over against the city lay the
valley of Hinnom which had been a place of heathen sacrifice.

This was seen as a type of death in its most horrible aspect, and gave its name to the Hebrew hell, which was known as Gehinnom or Gehenna. As it had been a place of cultic holocaust, so it was an appropriate image for the place in which the wicked were to be punished. So again the house of Zion could be seen to be set over against the house of Satan.[27] The abyss could be spoken of as lying 'to the right of the house' as in I Enoch 90.26. Gehinnom and paradise were adjacent to one another in the midrash so that one was visible from the other as in Luke 16.23ff.[28] This clearly derived from the typological character accorded to the valley of Hinnom and the mountain of Zion respectively. As the one was the image of death, the other was the symbol of life.

Both these imageries throw light on the passion narrative. For one who was buried outside the city walls, the thought of Hinnom may well have suggested exclusion from life in the place of the dead. As one who was buried within the rock of Jerusalem, Jesus had passed through the portal leading to the great abyss. Here more than anywhere else, then, for the Jew was to be found the entrance into Hades.[29]

Not only the site of the tomb was suggestive of this idea. The mausoleum itself represented the whole concept in microcosmic form. Burials are normally carried out in such a way as to suggest a people's belief about the world and about death. To this the Hebrews were no exception. Their tombs were normally hewn out of rock and had the entrance closed by a great stone. This usage portrayed first of all that the dead were imprisoned in Sheol.[30] The stone was nothing less than the locked door of Hades. The idea of death as a prison was so deeply rooted that 'the gates of Hades' was a common term for death.[31] The rock laid at the entrance of a tomb was a miniature of the great rock lying in the mouth of the abyss which the Jew identified with Zion.[32] When the evangelists relate that Jesus was bound with burial-cloths and placed in a rock-hewn tomb which was closed with a rock and sealed by the soldiers, it would seem certain that they intend the reader to see in this event Christ's descent into Sheol. Only then can their story have the impact they require when the burial cloths fail to bind him and neither rock nor seal can hold him. The gates of Hades cannot prevail against the church, because they could not remain fixed against her Lord.[33]

The stone is removed by an earthquake,[34] which cracks open the sealed mountain of Christ's tomb.

The concept of Christ's descent into hell, therefore, appears to have been given explicit mention in the gospels and also to have been embodied in the evangelists' story of the burial. In the doctrinal speculation of the later church, however, the idea was usually accompanied by some description of the work achieved by Christ in his descent. Two assertions were commonly made. One held that Christ descended into the realm of death in order to defeat and bind its lord. The devil is chained and thrust into Tartarus. The other spoke of Christ preaching to the dead, especially the message of deliverance to the saints of old.[35] In this way the descent became an integral part of his saving work. The question must arise as to whether these ideas have also found a place in the gospel story.

THE BINDING OF BELIAR

In the *Testament of Levi* the binding of Beliar is an essential element in the work of the Messiah.[36] The gospels do not connect this with the descent into the grave, but the reason is not difficult to find. In the schemes of the evangelists, Beliar has already been bound before Jesus ascends the cross, and the results of that act are shown to be in process long before the crucifixion.

Early in Mark's story, Jesus declares that Beelzebub has already been bound.[37] As evidence of this he cites the fact that the devil has allowed his house to be plundered, for Jesus has wrested from him the unfortunates who were held in his grip, preyed upon by his demons. The exorcisms of Jesus, therefore, were seen as proof that he had already overcome the one who held the power of disease and death over man. And it is because he has done this that Jesus faces no real opposition when he 'muzzles' the demon in the synagogue or on the sea.[38] His miraculous ministry is a procession in which his triumph over death is repeatedly proclaimed.

If we ask at what point that triumph had taken place, we are forced back to the very beginning of the ministry. This was recognized by many early Christian writers, who saw it as having taken place at the time of his baptism.[39] In order to portray this, the *Odes of Solomon* describe the baptism as a descent into hell. The abysses open and Jesus descends to triumph over Satan.[40] In the Markan tradition the victory is also given as a prelude to the ministry, but is centred on the temptation incident. Although Jesus has to confront the forces of the devil throughout his ministry, he is merely mopping up the remnants of an army whose leader has already been decisively defeated in the desert.

It was not long, however, before this victory was transferred to the time of Christ's death. Mark could not have assented to the words of Origen who said that Christ 'began by binding the Devil on the Cross, and, entering into his house, that is, into Hell . . . took with him the captives',[41] but the idea is already beginning to develop in John and Matthew.

THE RAISING OF THE DEAD

Mark records that Jesus raised the daughter of Jairus from the dead and Luke that he brought back to life the son of the widow of Nain.[42] But while these stories are clearly intended as demonstrations of Jesus' power over death, neither suggests any connection with the idea of descent into hell. In both cases the raising takes place immediately after death. Thought of a descent into Hades would only arise in connection with the raising of those who had already been laid in their tombs. In John and Matthew this is exactly what takes place.

The Gospel of John contains both a discourse on the resurrection of the dead and an exemplification of it. In John 5, death and life are spoken of in two senses. On the one hand they are spiritual facts. In the present, Jesus, as the Son, gives life to those who are dead. The hearer of his word and the believer in him are said to have already passed from death to life.[43] John is speaking of spiritual death and of that eternal life which becomes the present possession of the believer's soul. But John does not intend that the gift of life in Jesus should be understood solely in a spiritual or existential sense. His voice is to be heard not only by the living dead but also by those lying in their tombs.[44] When the hour comes, a clear reference in John to the time of the passion, these will obey the voice of the one who has life in himself and come forth from their graves.

In John 11 the raising of Lazarus is described. A period of time is deliberately allowed to lapse before Jesus goes to Bethany after having heard of Lazarus' death. The reason for this is given. It is that his friends may believe that he is not only capable of giving the power of life to the living, which Martha and Mary readily accept, but is able also to overcome the death and putrefaction of the body. Further, the point is made that the resurrection which they expect to take place in the eschaton may become a present reality in him. In words which forcibly recall those of ch. 5, Jesus calls into the tomb with a loud voice and Lazarus comes forth, released from the grip of death. The raising of Lazarus may be seen, therefore, as a typological demonstration of the event which is to take place at the hour of the crucifixion when the dead will hear the voice of the Son of God and live.

In Matthew the connection between the death of Christ and the raising of the dead is given explicit expression in dramatic form. In 27. 51–53 the evangelist tells of tombs being opened and the dead coming forth at the time of Christ's death to be seen of many after his resurrection. Matthew appears to wish to connect the event with both the death and the resurrection of Christ. That he should have timed the opening of the tombs to coincide with the death of Christ only appears to be explicable on the assumption that he saw in Christ's death a descent into Hades in order to free its captives. It is, as Loofs remarked, 'an incomplete and coarse reminiscence of the descent story'.[45] This was certainly understood by the author of the *Acts of Pilate*, who saw in it the rising of men with Christ out of hell.[46] Matthew has surely made clear what was also probably implicit in John, that the dead are raised from their tombs only by virtue of the fact that Jesus himself enters the domain of death in order to free its prisoners.

Matthew's story also has a feature which reinforces what has been said about the significance of the earthquake which removes the containing rock of Christ's tomb.

There is an echo in Matt. 27.51 of the idea of the earth as a mountain being rent apart and so being forced to surrender its dead. Some basis for the concept may be found in Zech. 14.4, which tells how the Mount of Olives will be cleaved at the eschaton. In the *Testament of Levi* the imagery is more fully developed and used in connection with the raising of the dead.

> . . . The rocks are being rent,
> And the sun quenched,
> And the waters dried up . . .
> And Hades is despoiled through the passion of the Most
>   High. [47]

In the context of a description of the end-event by means of all the primary mythological symbols, mention is made of precisely the sort of event to which Christians referred when they spoke of Christ's plundering of hell, and it comes about by the cleavage of the earth. Perhaps reflecting this imagery, a scene is portrayed in the synagogue of Dura Europos in which a mountain is shown split by an earthquake, with a building falling to the ground. There are ten men in white who are probably the risen saints, and a figure in pink stands at the side of the mountain who may be intended to represent Ezekiel. [48] It would appear, therefore, that Matthew has not only made use of the descent motif, but also spoken of it in terms derived from part of the mountain myth.

In conclusion, therefore, it may be said that all the elements which were gathered together to form the later doctrine of Christ's descent into hell are to be found in the gospels. The evangelists, however, saw the saving work which it represented as something which was accomplished through the total ministry of Christ. From their perspective, therefore, it would have appeared misleading to have elaborated on the period between the crucifixion and the resurrection. For them the victory had been achieved long before, so that the very appearance of the Christ on the threshold of death was sufficient to destroy its gates and release its prisoners. This manner of dealing with common mythological material is in itself some indication that the evangelists are not dependent on the myths current in paganism. They manifest a freedom of treatment which militates most strongly against any theory of borrowing from an alien culture. This becomes even clearer as note is taken of the differences in theological intent and of narrative form.

THE PAGAN MYTHS OF DESCENT AND THE GOSPELS

Pagan myths invariably tell of a deity who displays heroic strength like Heracles or strikes a bargain with Hades as did Demeter. He may even fail in his task and be cheated as Orpheus was in his bid to rescue Eurydice. In contrast the gospels never hint at anything of this sort. Christ's conflicts are with men. Death is merely powerless before him.

Many scholars have failed to see any reference to Christ's descent into hell in the gospels because there is no adventurous tale of his travel into the netherworld, as is usually the case in such myths. What this does suggest is that a developed mythological form for Christ's descent has not yet come into being. The ingredients are present, but they have not yet been worked up. In this, too, the gospels show their independence.

Most important of all is the absence from the gospel story of a deity trapped in Hades and from the pagan myths of any suggestion that the descent takes place in order that the dead as such should be raised. Pagan stories of descent usually involve an attempt by one deity to rescue another. Dionysos descends to rescue his mother Semele, and Ishtar goes in search of Tammuz. At no point in the Christian tradition is there any suggestion of this. Yahweh does not descend to raise Christ from the dead. There is a reference to the earth being made 'to rumble and the ghosts to come forth from their tombs' in Ovid's story of Medea, to which Conybeare drew attention.[49] But the apparent similarity with Matt. 27.51–53 is superficial. Medea is boasting of the many feats she can accomplish when aided by the powers of the gods. She can cause unnatural things to happen. The opening of the tombs by Medea is not connected with her death, and there is no suggestion that this is a work of saving grace. In the Akkadian version based on the myth of Inanna or Innini, Ishtar threatens to break down the gates of the underworld, releasing the dead so that they would outnumber the living. This is not the purpose of the descent. It is a threat to overturn the proper order of nature in order to gain another objective.[50]

In view of these basic differences, it would seem that the gospels only share with the pagan myths the common notion of a descent into the realm of the dead. But both its form and its meaning are quite different. The myths are often speaking of personifications of cosmic forces, whereas the gospels speak of a man in whom death is overcome.[51] If any influence has come from the ancient myths, it has been through the medium of Judaism, and the idea has been used for quite new purposes.

EMERGENCE FROM THE ROCK

Burial within the sacred mountain was also a ritual act which pointed towards the hope for future life. The entombment of Christ, therefore, can never be considered without reference also to the function of the cave in the rock as a symbol of new birth.

The sacred mountain was usually said to be at the navel or *omphalos* of the earth. It was here that the birth of creation had taken place and the point at which the divine nourishment flowed into it.[52] A grave-mound was a replica of the mountain and so by its very nature an *omphalos*.[53] When a grave was made into an *omphalos*, its inhabitant was understood to have been interred in the cosmogonic womb. This symbolism is even more apparent when the dead are placed in a cave cut out of the mountain.[54] Myths present this idea in archetypal form by speaking of the mountain cave as both the burial tomb and the birthplace of the gods.[55] This is well illustrated by the Mithras myth. The story of his birth takes place before creation, for it is archetypal in character. The scene is a mountain on the banks of a river and beneath a sacred tree. In this creation and paradisal situation Mithras comes forth from a rock.[56] His death is finally a return to the same rock, as he is interred in its cave. Hence the prominence given to the use of caves in the rites of Mithras, Attis and others. Against this background the burial of Everyman in the navel-tomb took on vital significance.

This was so deeply rooted in the human understanding of death that it retained a place in Jewish thought despite the obvious dangers of its being associated with numerous pagan cults. 'The underworld and the chambers of souls are like the womb' declared the author of II(4) Esdras.[57] It is hardly surprising, therefore, that the idea should appear in connection with the birth and death of the patriarchs. To the canonical tradition which spoke of Abraham's interment in the cave of

Machpelah[58] was added the idea that he was also born in a cave.[59] The birth of Moses was also located in a cave,[60] while the cryptic references to his death in Deut. 34 were developed to include the motif at this point also, the Palestinian targum on Deut. 33.21 describing the cave in which he was buried to await his emergence for his future task.[61] Judaism, therefore, not only knew but was prepared to make use of the idea that the funereal cave was also a womb of rebirth.

In early Christian literature the cave motif is found most prominently in the post-canonical nativity literature.[62] Neither Matthew nor Luke make use of it in telling the story of Jesus' birth, but it appears already in the earliest Armenian manuscript of Matt. 2.9, which says that '*the star stood over the cave where the child was*',[63] while in the third century Origen wrote that 'the cave at Bethlehem is shown where he was born and the manger in the cave where he was wrapped in swaddling-clothes'.[64]

Some writers have been so unaware of the mythological significance of the birth-cave motif that they have seen in it nothing more than a desire to give the birth of Christ a humble setting.[65] But as Dibelius remarked, the cave 'is an old mythological motif' commonly used in connection with the birth of a divine child.[66] Before turning to what may well be the channel whereby this mythological motif became a part of Christian nativity hagiography, note should be taken of the idea which appears in one of the sayings attributed to the Baptist by Matthew and Luke.[67] Speaking to the Pharisees and Sadducees who have come to him for baptism, John warns them against claiming privileges by virtue of their patriarchal ancestry, and tells them that 'God is able from these stones to raise up children to Abraham'. The stones are referred to because they are apparently lifeless but, if 'raise up' is a Semitism, the Baptist asserts that God can cause them to give birth to true Israelites. In order to appreciate the full significance of John's words we must remind ourselves of two Old Testament passages. There is a reference first of all to Isa. 51.1–2, which speaks of Abraham as the rock from which the righteous are hewn and from whom they are born.[68] But the Baptist reminds his hearers that God is the ultimate source of their life. In accordance with Deut. 32.18 he tells them that Yahweh is the rock which gave them birth.

The imagery of the child-bearing rock or mountain is therefore carried over into the New Testament and finds a place in the gospel story. For the Christian, however, the symbol of the life-bearing rock had been given a new content by the resurrection of Christ.

The rock from which Jesus rose was understood symbolically as a womb of new birth. The small opening which caused the disciples to bend in order to enter the tomb is in itself suggestive of womb symbolism,[69] but the idea finds far more explicit formulation. Not only do the gospels record Jesus as having been buried in the place which was, to the Jews, the navel of the earth, but the New Testament writers assert that by being raised from the dead, Christ was 'declared *to be* the Son of God with power' and 'the firstborn from the dead'.[70] So while it has been the fashion to attempt a clear distinction between resurrection and rebirth, this is not one which is maintained in the New Testament itself. On Easter morning there were fulfilled in Christ the words of the psalmist who addressed the king as one who 'was begotten on the holy mountain from the womb of dawn'.[71] The evangelists, whether consciously or not, describe the resurrection as taking place in the age-old mythological setting of the cosmogonic mountain. The writers of the apocryphal nativity understood this symbolism well and found it impossible to think that Christ's other birth, of Mary, could have taken place anywhere else than in a cave. That compulsion was no doubt indebted to the continued presence of the common mythical symbol, but their more immediate justification lay in the story of Christ's entombment and of his birth to new life from the rock.

NOTES

1. Rappoport, op. cit., Vol. I, p.111.

2. See Eph. 4.9; Heb. 11.39f.; 12.22ff.; I Peter 3.18f.; 4.6; Rev. 1.18; E. C. Selwyn, *The First Epistle of Peter*, Macmillan 1946, pp.314–62; Throckmorton, *The New Testament and Mythology*, p.119.

3. Conybeare, op. cit., p.286.

4. F. Loofs, 'Christ's Descent into Hell', *Transactions of the Third International Congress for the History of Religions*, ed. P. S. Allen, Clarendon Press 1908, Vol. II, p.300.

5. Job 26.5; cf. Gen. 37.35; 44.29,31.

6. Pss. 28.1; 30.3; 88.4–11; 143.7; Isa. 14.19.

7. Jonah 2.1–6.

8. Cf. Prov. 27.20; 30.16; Isa. 5.14; Hab. 2.5.

9. See M. Eliade, *Rites and Symbols of Initiation*, pp.35f., 48f., 62ff.

10. Matt. 12.39f.; 16.4; Luke 11.29.

11. Gärtner, op. cit., pp.112f.; Goodenough, op. cit., Vol. II, pp.225–7.

12. Palmer, op. cit., p.52.

13. Mark 8.31; 9.31; 10.34.

14. Goodenough, op. cit., Vol. II, p.225; cf. Albright, *From the Stone Age to Christianity*, p.397 n. 81.

15. Acts 2.31; Rom. 10.7; Eph. 4.9.

16. Loofs, op. cit., pp.300f.

17. Matt. 27.57–60 par.

18. Luke 24.5.

19. Mark 16.8; Luke 24.22–24.

20. Matt. 16.21; 20.18; Mark 10.33; Luke 9.31,51; 13.33; cf. Grant, op. cit., pp.131ff.

21. Gaster, *Myth, Legend and Custom in the Old Testament*, pp.234f.; cf. R. de Vaux, *Ancient Israel*, Darton, Longman and Todd 1961, p.287.

22. Gordon, op. cit., p.201.

23. Ps. 29.10; 93.

24. Ps. 28.1; cf. 9.14.

25. I Enoch 90.26.

26. B. Chudoba, *Early History and Christ*, Alba House, 1969, pp.96f. See *Parah* 3.3; *Erubin* 19a; *Sukkah* 53a; *Lev. R.* 27.1; O. Cullmann, *'Petra'*, *Theological Dictionary of the New Testament*, ed. Kittel and Friedrich, Vol. VI, p.96; Wensinck, op. cit., pp.26f.

27. E. Lohmeyer, *Lord of the Temple*, Oliver and Boyd 1961, p.67.

28. *Eccles. R.* 7.14.3.

29. *Erubin* 19a.

30. Job 17.16; Jonah 2.6; cf. Rev. 1.18; 9.1; 20.1; Qumran, *Hymns* V.

31. Job 38.17; Pss. 9.14; 107.18; Isa. 38.10.

32. Cf. Hebert, 'The Resurrection Narrative in St Mark's Gospel', pp. 66ff.

33. Matt. 16.18.

34. Matt. 28.2.

35. I Peter 4.6; Gospel of Peter 10.41f.; Irenaeus, *Adv. Haer.* III, 20.4; IV, 22.1; IV, 27.2; etc.

36. Test. Levi 18.12.

37. Mark 3.27.

38. Mark 1.25; 4.39. Simpson, op. cit., p.11, sees in the stilling of the storm an echo of the descent into hell motif.

39. See pp.125f. above.

40. Odes of Solomon 22.5; 24.1–3.

41. Origen, *Comm. Rom.* 5.10, quoted Daniélou, *A History of Early Christian Doctrine*. pp.241f.

42. Mark 5.21–24,35–43; Luke 7.11–15.

43. John 5.21,24.

44. John 5.25,28f.

45. Loofs, op. cit., p.299.

46. Acts of Pilate I(XVII) Latin B.

47. Test. Levi 4.1. The text given follows the notes in Charles, op. cit., Vol. II, p. 307, understanding the passage as a Christian interpolation.

48. Goodenough, op. cit., Vol. X, pp.183f.; Vol. XI, illus. XXI; cf. *Ketuboth* 111b: 'R. Ḥiyya b. Joseph said: A time will come when the just will break through [the soil] and rise up in Jerusalem.'

49. Ovid, *Metamorphoses* 7.205f.; Conybeare, op. cit., p.286.

50. Cf. Pfleiderer, op. cit., pp.105f.

51. Cf. Künneth, op. cit., pp.56ff.

52. See pp.238ff. below.

53. Wensinck, op. cit., p. xi, wrote that 'the Omphalos was often represented as a grave', but rather a grave is represented as an *omphalos*; see Butterworth, op. cit., p.31.

54. Eliade, *Rites and Symbols of Initiation*, p.58, cf. pp.69,97; Gaster, *Myth, Legend and Custom in the Old Testament*, pp.608f.

55. See A. B. Cook, *Zeus*, Cambridge University Press 1925, Vol. I, pp. 149f., 157–63.

56. See Justin, *Dial. Tryph.* 70; Boslooper, op. cit., p.158.

57. II (4) Esd. 4.41; cf. Prov. 30.16; Jer. 2.27.

58. Gen. 25.9.

59. Ginzberg, op. cit., p.88; Rappoport, op. cit., Vol. I, p.229.

60. *Sotah* 12a.

61. See W. A. Meeks, *The Prophet-King*, Brill 1967, p.212 and n. 3.

62. The Protoevangelium of James 18.1; 19.3; 21.3; Pseudo-Matt. 14; Justin, *Dial.* 78; Jerome, *Ep.* 58.3; 147.4.

63. Quoted Clemen, op. cit., p.300.

64. Origen, *Contra Celsum* 1.51, trans. Chadwick, op. cit.

65. E.g. Doane, op. cit., pp.155f.

66. M. Dibelius, *A Fresh Approach to the New Testament and Early Christian Literature*, Ivor Nicholson and Watson 1936, p.88. See also Arnobius, *Adv. Gentes* 5.5, where Acdestis, son of Jupiter, is said to have been rock-born.

67. Matt. 3.9; Luke 3.8.

68. See J. Jeremias, *'Lithos'*, *Theological Dictionary of the New Testament*, ed. Kittel and Friedrich, Vol. IV, pp.270f.

69. G. Vann, OP, *The Eagle's Word*, Collins 1961, pp.53ff.

70. Acts 13.33; Rom 1.4; Col. 1.18; Rev. 1.5.

71. Jacob, op. cit., p.328; Ps. 110.

The temple in Jerusalem was the centre of Jewish life in almost
all of its aspects. Most of all, it was the avenue of the Jew's approach to God and to the world of the spirit. It was the focus of
his worship and the representation of his view upon life. In
order to function in this way, the temple was furnished with an
abundance of symbolism, much of which was rooted in Hebrew
mythology. It is this which must now be explored, for the
Hebrew concept of the temple on the holy hill not only played
a vital part in the thinking of Christ himself, but also gave to the
evangelists the means whereby they could present their understanding of his meaning for them. As so often, it is necessary to
consider this subject at two levels. On one level the gospel story
moves within the complex of thought obtaining in contemporary Judaism. On the other, note has to be taken of new usages
which arose out of the developing christology of the early church.

ASCENT TO THE TEMPLE OF GOD IN JUDAISM

Coupled with the notion of Christ's descent into Hades in the
Apostle's Creed is that of his ascension. The supposition of a
pagan origin for the idea is not so often made in this case. Although numerous parallels can be cited in pagan mythology,[1]
the concept is known to have been present in Judaism long before the time of Christ and to have been prominent in apocalyptic literature.[2] Moreover, it is already asserted of Christ within
the New Testament in a quite explicit manner. The most
which can be claimed in this case is that the Jewish-Christian
tradition shares with pagan mythology a motif which was in
some instances developed along similar lines. If a real understanding of the Christian assertion is to be attained, therefore,

an effort must be made to appreciate the nature of its roots in
Jewish thought.

Mention of Christ's ascension immediately recalls for most
readers the story which Luke included in the first chapter of
Acts. The notion of ascent was, however, a complex one and the
Lukan story is probably the most misleading place at which to
begin a study of the idea, When a Jew spoke of ascending, he
might well have a quite different concept in mind. In Judaism
there were two basic usages. One spoke of ascension as an event
entirely within this life. The other used it to refer to the leaving
of this life to be with God.

Talk of ascension in contemporary Judaism most commonly
referred to the journeys undertaken to Jerusalem to keep the
obligatory festivals there. At such times the character of the
temple as God's house built upon the sacred mountain was
paramount. A pilgrimage to Jerusalem constituted an ascension
of the hill of the Lord. The idiom of speech reflected the idea of
the sacred hill up which the pilgrim must go to 'see God' in the
place which he had designated.[3] The notion of attaining the
mount was in fact of more importance fundamentally than arrival at the temple, for it was Zion which gave the temple its
sanctity. Mountains had always been places of revelation and
worship, and when Jerusalem's hill was exalted above all others
by the command of Yahweh, it attracted to itself all the features
of the mountain cultus. When the Jewish pilgrim journeyed to
Jerusalem, therefore, it was so that he might go up the sacred
hill and in so doing enact ritualistically what he willed that his
spirit should accomplish.

The use of ascension imagery in which to speak of the mode
whereby a man might leave this life can be less summarily
itemized. Just as a man might be said to have descended into
Sheol through death, so it was also possible to speak of his
ascending via the grave into the place of the blessed. At one
time, Sheol had been regarded as the lot of almost all men, but
the doctrine had steadily developed in certain Jewish circles
that the righteous attained a place of beatitude through death.
Of such it was therefore appropriate to say that they had ascended. Ascension was also used to speak of the end met with by
certain favoured saints. These were held to have been permitted
to attain the heavenly court without passing through the sleep

of death. They were said to have been translated directly into the presence of God.[4] This may have been no more than a graphic way of describing a saint's immediate arrival into the state of blessedness through death, but it is usually done with the aid of symbolism which strongly suggests a bodily assumption.

The imagery used for these ascents, however, also shows a lack of complete homogeneity. In some cases the old mythological cosmography comes into play. In others it is replaced by the more recent vertical cosmography. On occasion, the two are allowed to run into one another.

In the more ancient cosmographical scheme, the place of the blessed was generally located in the inaccessible parts of the earth. In order to reach it, therefore, the dead had to undertake a long and hazardous journey, whether their destination was the Elysian Fields, the Isles of the Blessed or Mount Olympus. Privileged persons might be wrapt away like Tithonus to live by the streams of ocean at the ends of the earth,[5] or be carried off to serve the gods in the house of Zeus like Ganymede,[6] but for ordinary mortals the only path to such glory lay through burial in the cavernous tomb of the holy mountain. In this way the humblest peasant interred in his tumulus might hope to emulate the ascent of Baal[7] to the polar mountain. Death or translation might therefore be described as a going up to the heights of the sacred mountain.

The later idea probably developed out of the earlier.[8] The notion of attaining a place beyond the clouds in the heavens was easily derived from that of reaching the unseen summit of the great mountain. An ascension mythology of this type, moreover, was able to make use of solar symbolism, which may even have been instrumental in promoting it. So both Elijah and Mithras were said to have ascended by means of the chariot symbol of the sun.[9] At all events, by New Testament times the idea of an ascent to heaven was well established. Nor was it something which only happened to extraordinary people. Every righteous Jew could hope that his soul might one day be safely hidden beneath the throne of glory,[10] for the reward of the righteous was in heaven.[11]

These two mythological schemes were not always mutually exclusive. In the growth of ideas about the death of Moses it is possible to see how various elements have been brought together. Although the Hebrew had a strong sense of the unity of body and soul, it became possible for him to make a distinction between them.[12] In death, body and soul could be envisaged as separating, the life which God gave being taken back to be with himself. Use is made of the possibilities inherent in this by the author of the *Assumption of Moses* in order to combine the idea of the prophet's death with the privilege of translation, and also to make use of both mythological cosmographies. Moses is said to have been buried among the ravines of the mountain. In this way the text of Deuteronomy is adhered to, while it is indicated that the body of Moses finds its final resting place within the holy mountain. The author is no longer content with this symbolism, however, and also tells how the soul of Moses ascends to the realm above.[13]

Corresponding to the two notions of ascent was the idea that there were two temples, one on earth and the other in heaven. The first was to be found in David's ancient capital, while the second was normally hidden from mortal eyes in the heavenly Jerusalem. The extraordinary importance which the Jew attached to his temple was dependent on the idea that it was the means whereby he might enter the fuller world which it represented.

Like the mountain on which it stood, the temple represented the whole cosmos. It was a cosmic replica.[14] There is some doubt as to whether the temple of Solomon was symbolic in this way, but that described by Ezekiel certainly was.[15] To rabbinic Judaism there was no incongruity in drawing a comparison between the creation narrative of Genesis and the building, destruction and rebuilding of the temple.[16] In the temple the Jew was in God's world. He saw there in ritual terms his ideal for the whole of life on earth.

The temple also stood for the heavenly realm whose beatitude it mirrored in a disjointed world.[17] The earthly temple was held to be placed immediately below the heavenly reality of which it was a counterpart.[18] In it, the ritual copied that which took place in the temple above. As the priest brought an offering to the altar on earth, the angel Michael presented it in heaven.[19] In the temple, therefore, a worshipper might see a ritual reflection of the reality for which he yearned or even be transported in spirit into the purity of God's holiness itself.[20]

All this had been made possible because the temple of Jerusalem had not been built at the whim of an earthly architect. It had been built as a copy of the heavenly reality shown to the patriarchs. According to II Bar. 4.2–6, God had given both Abraham and Moses a glimpse of the heavenly Jerusalem.[21] They had seen a temple which was created before the world, whose foundation pits were more ancient even than the great abyss.[22]

The idea of heavenly counterparts, of there being ideal realities of which earthly things were but imperfect copies, also appears in Platonism, but it is clear that while late Judaism may have been influenced by this, there were sources for the concept deep within its own culture. It was in fact an ancient Sumerian idea,[23] and has already found a place in Hebrew thought by the time of the Priestly Code.[24] Apocalyptic and rabbinic writers took up the notion, so that by the first century it must be assumed to have been common in Pharisaic circles. Both Jesus and his disciples, therefore, are likely to have been familiar with this complex of thought and traces of it to appear in the gospel story.

THE PILGRIMAGE AND ASCENSION OF THE CHRIST

While argument rages concerning Jesus' attitude towards the sabbath and other elements in the scribal code of behaviour, there is never any suggestion that he did not keep the obligatory feasts in Jerusalem. Indeed, Jesus' pilgrimage to keep the Passover there constitutes an important element in the evangelistic narrative. Stress is laid upon his desire to celebrate the feast in Jerusalem even at the cost of his life.[25] Much is made of his triumphal entry into Jerusalem, when he is greeted with the singing of one of the Hallel psalms normally sung as a welcome to weary pilgrims.[26] Although no significant action is performed on this occasion, the point is made that Jesus completes his journey by entering the temple like a true pilgrim. Matthew and Luke go further than this. For them, the whole of his ministry constituted a pilgrimage. In Luke this last journey is made to embrace a large part of his earthly activity. In Matthew the mission of the twelve disciples in turned into a pilgrimage by

slight but significant changes in the Markan wording.[27] They
are now given the same instructions as were laid down in the
Mishnah for those undertaking a journey to the temple mount.[28]
In this way, Matthew indicates that the life-work of the apostles
is to be seen as one with that of their Lord.

Jesus is no ordinary pilgrim, however, in the eyes of the
evangelists. He comes as the lowly one to be vindicated as the
righteous one before the tribunal, not of men, but of God. He
is none other than the king of Zech. 9.9. As such, his actions in
the spiritual capital of Judaism take on peculiar authority.
As its Lord he can receive the blind and the lame who had
contravened the law by entering the temple, for he is in reality
the source of healing which the temple could only represent.[29]
He ensures the cleanliness of the temple by making the unclean
clean and by throwing out the merchants. The temple is now
to fulfil its ordained function and become through him the
place of salvation for all people. The new age is being inaugurated.[30]

The pilgrimage of the Christ, however, appears to end in
rejection and disgrace. Instead of a triumphal installation in
Jerusalem, he is handed over to the executioners and identified
with felons. And yet, for the first Christians this was not the real
end of the story. His rights in the earthly temple may have been
denied, but by his death he had been welcomed into the heavenly temple by the Father.

The idea of the Jerusalem above appears in Paul's letter to
the Galatians and is a key concept in the book of Revelation.[31]
What this means for the interpretation of Christ's earthly end is
explained at some length by the author of the *Epistle to the
Hebrews*. He acknowledges that the earthly temple was built in
accordance with that shown to Moses on the mountain,[32] but
rejoices in the fact that while the people dare not come near
even to touch that mount, in Christ the heavenly reality itself
has been made accessible to them.[33] The pilgrimage of Jesus
did not end for him in Jerusalem on earth, but in heaven.
Through his death he entered into the holy place[34] and made
it available to all, for Christ is now the high priest of the heavenly temple and its worship.

F. V. Filson remarks that the author of Hebrews 'hurries on
past the earthly triumph over physical death . . . to the heavenly

ministry and triumph'.[35] The resurrection is pushed into the background because thought is concentrated on Christ's entry into the heavenly tabernacle achieved through the crucifixion. This perspective is one which the author probably shares with early Christian tradition.

The words to the thief on the cross in Luke[36] have been a constant source of embarrassment to those who attempt to see a sequence of chronological events in which the crucifixion, resurrection and ascension follow one another after certain temporal intervals. These words suggest an immediate translation on death into the place of the blessed. They presuppose that the resurrection and ascension are virtually one with the crucifixion. This turns out not to be an isolated case, but to reflect a pattern of ideas built on typically Jewish concepts of ascension.

The idea of Christ's journey to Mount Zion is always associated in the minds of the evangelists with death. They remind us constantly that in going up to Jerusalem, Jesus is travelling to the cross. This is very explicit in John, who makes use of the ambiguity inherent in the word *anabainein*. It was a word properly used for the 'going up' which constituted a festival pilgrimage, and it could also be employed to speak of the ascent of death.[37] Similarly, to be 'received up' in Acts 1.2 could mean simply to die.[38] Christ's ascension, therefore, could be understood both as his journey to Zion and his being lifted up in crucifixion.

In the Markan tradition this ascension in death to the temple of God appears to have been indicated by use of the idea that the earthly temple was a copy of the heavenly. Mark 15.38 records that at the moment of Christ's death, the veil of the temple was torn from top to bottom. Various explanations of this verse have been offered. It has been seen as an omen of the temple's destruction or symbolic of the temple mourning for what was to come in AD 70.[39] Daniélou saw in it an allusion to Pentecost on the basis of the *Testament of Benjamin*.[40] Frequently it is understood as a removal of the barrier between Jew and Gentile.[41] None of these explanations, however, do justice to the fact that it is said to happen at the precise moment of Christ's death, or take notice of the representational value of the earthly temple. Just as Matthew could indicate a descent into Hades by the cracking open of the earth at the time of the crucifixion, so Mark has probably suggested Christ's entry into the heavenly temple by another symbolic device.

Again, a comparison with the baptism narrative is illuminating, for just as it was early felt to contain the idea of descent into Hades, so there may be embodied in it a reference to ascension. H. Schlier, for example, sees a connection between the opening of the heavens in Mark 1.10 and the rending of the temple veil.[42] This idea, moreover, seems to lie behind the reading in some MSS of Matthew 3.16, which says that the heavens opened 'unto him'. It may well be, therefore, that when Mark speaks of Jesus 'going up' out of the water and the heavens being torn open, that he sees in the baptism the foretaste of an ascent from death to life which is completed on the cross.[43]

Note must also be taken of John 19.23, in which Jesus' tunic is said to have been 'without seam, woven from top to bottom' and to have been disposed of by lot so that it should not be torn. Two ideas may lie behind this. The coat is described as being like that of the high priest and that attributed to Adam probably because he was understood to have been the primordial priest-king.[44] John may therefore be suggesting that Jesus is the new and true high priest who has entered the heavenly sanctuary.[45] The contrast with the fate of the temple veil could hardly go unnoticed. The one is destroyed and the other preserved. The idea of Christ's entry into the heavenly temple soon made the earthly temple of Jerusalem obsolete for his followers.

In one strand of the gospel material, then, the ascension was understood to have been one with the death of Christ, a notion which was not unfamiliar to the Jew, and to have constituted an entry into the temple above as priest for ever. In John, this close association between death and ascension is partially weakened by the record of the appearance to Mary Magdalene in the garden.[46] Yet the text conveys the impression that the resurrection and ascension are really one event which is being interrupted by this meeting, Mary must not, therefore, cling to him, for ascension to prepare mansions in his father's house is the end and the work for which he was destined.[47]

In the developed Lukan tradition, the crucifixion and ascension are fully separated. Between them there is a gap of forty days.[48] Israel spent forty years in the wilderness before entering

the paradisal Canaan, and Adam was forty days after his creation before he was brought into the garden of Eden.[49] Luke's
chronology, therefore, may reinforce the notion that Jesus has
ascended to the heavenly paradise, through the cloud which
both denoted the presence of God and also constituted the veil
or curtain of the heavens which hid him.[50]

THE NEW TEMPLE

Seen from the perspective of this age, the true temple was hidden
from man and only gained through vision, death or translation.
In the eschaton, however, it was believed that the temple of
Hebrew desire would be built on earth. The temple of the
present would be destroyed to be replaced by a better. Sometimes this is seen as a purely historical event, a work of reconstruction being undertaken as it had been before. Of more importance for our purpose, however, are the writings which see
the new temple coming into being, not by the hand of men, but
by the direct action of God. Such speculations may be divided
into two categories. In the first, the dominant idea is that of a
reconstruction in a miraculous way of the glorious temple of
old. In II Macc. 2.4–8, for example, Jeremiah is said to have
hidden the tabernacle, the ark and the altar of incense in a cave
in the rock of the mountain of Moses' revelation. There it would
remain unknown until the day when God would gather his
people together again and reveal it. A similar tradition existed
among the Samaritans.[51] The roots of this symbolism in the
concept of the sacred mountain are clear. The temple to come
remains with God on the holy hill until it is revealed to the
men of the new age. In the second it is said that the new temple
will descend from heaven.[52] The archetypal temple of God above
will come to be among men when the time of shadows has
passed. Instead of a copy, men will possess the original. In
place of the symbolism of the old horizontal cosmography, the
second type of speculation relies on the newer vertical cosmography for its presentation of the coming of the eschatological
temple.

Both of these symbolic complexes were used in the New
Testament, but before we consider them we must note a further

factor of some importance. The temple was sometimes understood not as a building but as a community. This is particularly
well exemplified in the Qumran writers, who were probably led
into this kind of thought by their rejection of the Jerusalem
temple, just as rabbis later indulged in it when that temple no
longer stood. In Qumran, therefore, there was to be found 'a
house of holiness for Israel and a foundation of the holy of
holies for Aaron'.[53] When the evangelists speak of the new
temple as made of flesh and blood, it is not therefore a development unique to Christian thought. On the other hand, it must
be seen that the idea is expressed in a distinctive way. Jesus is
credited with a role never assigned to the Teacher of Righteousness in Qumran[54] or to the patriarchs in rabbinic Judaism.

Perhaps the oldest of the evangelistic presentations of Christ's
role in bringing the new temple into being is to be found in the
story of the transfiguration. This is at once most peculiar in
character and rich in meaning. Much of its strangeness is due
to the fact that it is the most clearly mythological narrative in
the gospels outside the accounts of Christ's resurrection appearances.[55] The story of Jesus here takes on an other-wordly
character. On the mount of transfiguration Jesus enters into a
space and time outside history. The place is a mythical one to
which the people cannot come.[56] Three disciples are allowed
to climb the mountain and to be spectators, but even they are
overcome by the strangeness of the world into which they have
entered. Here the gulf between earth and heaven is crossed, and
the barrier of time broken, as they see Jesus talking with saints
long dead.

No attempt is made in the gospels to give any geographical
location for the mountain. In consequence, there have been
many speculations as to possible sites on which the incident
might have taken place. The evangelists, however, have not
given the location of set purpose. This is not a geographical
but a mythical height. It is the mountain of God. The author of
II Peter 1.16–18, therefore, was fully justified in calling it
simply 'the holy mount'.

Comparisons have often been made (and rightly) with the
story of Moses' ascent of Sinai. Here are two outstanding
examples of the idea that the mountain is the appropriate place
of revelatory experience. There are, moreover, many points of

contact between the two narratives.[57] Both stories refer to the cloud, transfiguration and the hearing of God's voice. Both occasions are also connected with the idea of the exodus and the tabernacle. Behind the two narratives lies the symbolism of the sacred mountain of God, ascent of which leads into the heavenly world.

The ascent of Moses on Sinai was interpreted as an ascent into heaven.[58] There was an adequate basis for this interpretation in Exod. 24.10 and 25.9. In view of the parallelism between this and the transfiguration, it may well be that the latter event was also intended to be understood as an ascension into heaven. Numerous scholars have recognized the affinity of the story with those told of the resurrection, the ascension and the parousia, because it appears to describe Jesus in a heavenly state. This is how the author of the *Apocalypse of Peter* understood the event. He describes 'the holy mountain' in terms which make it clear that in going up the hill, Jesus has ascended to the garden of Eden and to heaven.[59] This is probably a correct reading of the evangelists' intentions from within an immediate knowledge of the mythological associations of the sacred hill. Not only is Jesus together with the translated ones of the past, but he is transfigured so that he is seen in the glorious light of his heavenly nature.[60] The ascension to come is thus clearly prefigured.[61] In this epiphany of Jesus in his destined heavenly status, his disciples are assured of divine vindication.[62]

Moses had ascended into the mountain of Sinai to be shown the pattern of the tabernacle to be built on earth. In the ascent of the transfiguration also the heavenly temple is shown to men. But now that which is presented to human vision is not a building but a man. The voice of God directs the attention of the disciples to Jesus. In him the revelation of God is now to be found. The incident therefore already points towards the obsolescence of the temple which is to be replaced by the person of Christ. Peter appears to have grasped the significance of the event to some extent in suggesting that they build tabernacles for Moses, Elijah and Jesus. He is aware that the Presence of God is on the mountain. What he has not fully realized is that Jesus in his person has been shown to him as the dwelling place of God. His thoughts are still rooted in the tradition of the past. The Presence is mediated to men by flesh, not tabernacle.

Peter has still to learn the full meaning of this epiphany, to know that heaven is to be found in the body and spirit of Christ.[63]

The vision of God's glory in the person of Jesus on the mount of transfiguration is probably seen as the basis in John 1.14 for the assertion that in him the Word has tabernacled amongst men. In John, however, the idea assumes much greater prominence and lies behind much of his narrative. Time and again the glory of the Christ is manifested so that men may know that the presence of God is to be found, not in architectural but in human form. At the outset of the ministry a promise is given to Nathanael that he will perceive this in imagery derived from the story of Jacob. This story was of very great significance to the Jew and the Samaritan because in it is related how the temple site was revealed to the father of Israel. Use is now made of it to show that the true temple is to be found elsewhere than in Jerusalem or Gerizim. Just as Jacob had been made aware of the fact that the presence of God was in Bethel by being shown angels ascending and descending on a ladder stretching up to heaven from that place, so by the same means Nathanael is to perceive that the Presence is with Jesus. The Christ is now to constitute the bond between heaven and earth, to be the tabernacle which mediates the glory of God. John may have been assisted in developing this thought by the fact that Gen. 28.12 was sometimes understood to make Jacob the bond between earth and heaven,[64] but the implications of John's exegesis are far more radical. John had probably derived his notion of the pre-existence and descent of Christ partly from Judaic ideas concerning the heavenly temple. In doing this he is led ultimately to see the heavenly temple coming to be a tabernacle on earth in the person of Jesus.

The idea which John has deliberately allowed to dominate the opening stages of Christ's life also finds expression at its end – and in this he probably follows older tradition.

In the synoptic gospels the coming of the new temple takes place with the resurrection. During his trial, certain witnesses declared that they had heard Jesus say that he would destroy the temple and build another not made by men.[65] In John 2.18ff. the request of the Jews for a sign is answered by the statement that if they destroy the temple, Jesus will rebuild it in three days. This is hardly playful repartee, but is seen correctly by John as a reference to the resurrection body.[66] The sign is almost identical with that of Jonah, but in this case appeal to the resurrection is probably combined with the idea of the ascended Christ descending as the new temple. The temple in Jerusalem will no longer be required when the heavenly temple made without hands by God himself has come.

All references to Christ's ascension contain the idea that his departure takes place in order that he might return. In Acts, the disciples looking up into heaven are told that they will see him come again in like manner. In John, the words of Jesus to Mary Magdalene imply that she may not possess him until he has ascended to the Father.[67] The purpose of the ascent is that a descent may follow. Some confusion arises here because of the ambiguous relationship in the New Testament between Christ and the Spirit. There can be little doubt, however, that the Spirit which could only be given after Christ's ascension was understood to be in some sense another giving of Christ himself. Certainly this is how the matter appears in John, where it is the Jesus who has already ascended who comes to breathe the Spirit into his disciples.[68] In this we may see the Judaic hope of the descent of the heavenly Jerusalem taking place according to the thinking of the evangelists. The new temple is constituted by Jesus' descent as the Spirit into his disciples. From henceforth he is with them wherever they go. As the ascended and descended one he is not confined in space and time, but is everywhere among his people. The records of the resurrection appearances show this being discovered by the disciples. If they take the road to Emmaus, he is with them. If they go to Galilee he is there. If they bolt their doors, he appears among them.[69] This is a communion which is to continue wherever they go into all the world.[70] No longer will they need to return constantly to the hill in Judaea, for the Lord will be amongst them. His going, therefore, is not a removal from their presence, but the means by which its permanence is established.[71] Indeed, the church has now become the temple and is made so by the presence of the Holy One within it. The house of David has become the house of God built by the Son out of the bodies of the faithful.[72] A temple has been built on another rock than that which lay in Zion.[73]

NOTES

1. See Pfleiderer, op. cit., pp.106–11; Weiss, op. cit., pp.26f.
2. J. G. Davies, *He Ascended into Heaven*, Lutterworth Press 1958, p.25, for example thinks that Luke saw Raphael in Tobit 12 as a type of Christ. For references to the idea of ascension in apocalyptic, see ch. 8 note 22.
3. See Ps. 24.3–6; cf. Matt. 5.8.
4. See ch. 8 note 20.
5. Hesiod, *Homeric Hymns* 5.217ff.
6. Hesiod, *Homeric Hymns* 5.202ff.
7. Widengren, op. cit., p.193.
8. G. Berguer, *Some Aspects of the Life of Jesus*, Williams and Norgate 1923, pp.57f.
9. II Kings 2.11f.; M. J. Vermaseren, *Mithras, The Secret God*, Chatto and Windus 1963, pp.104ff.
10. *Shabbath* 152b.
11. Matt. 5.12; 19.21; Mark 10.21; Luke 6.23; 18.22.
12. *Shabbath* 153a; Montefiore and Loewe, op. cit., p.313.
13. In Clem. Alex., *Strom.* VI, 15.
14. Clements, op. cit., pp.65ff.; cf. Ps. 78.69.
15. See Ezek. 43.13–17; cf. Ps. 78.69; W. Eichrodt, *Theology of the Old Testament*, SCM Press 1967, Vol. II, pp.193f.; Raglan, op. cit., pp.136f.; de Vaux, op. cit., pp.323,328f.
16. *Gen. R.* 2.5; cf. *Sukkah* 49a; A. Guilding, *The Fourth Gospel and Jewish Worship*, Clarendon Press 1960, p.175.
17. See I Kings 8.12f.; Ps. 11.4; II (4) Esd. 10.49; Childs, op. cit., p.86; G. B. Gray, *Sacrifice in the Old Testament*, Clarendon Press 1925, pp.149ff.; P. R. Ackroyd, *Exile and Restoration*, SCM Press 1968, pp.175,198.
18. *Cant. R.* 3. 10.4; 4.4.9; cf. *Gen. R.* 55.7; *Ex. R.* 33.4; *Mid. Tel.* Ps. 30.1.
19. *Mid. Tel.* Ps. 134.1; cf. Test. Levi 3.
20. Isa. 6.1–8.
21. Exod. 25.9; Wisd. 9.8; Asc. Isa. 7.10; cf. *Gen. R.* 69.7, which says that it was shown to Jacob.
22. *Pesahim* 54a; *Mid. Tel.* Ps. 11.2; cf. 90.12; 93.2–7.
23. See J. Moffatt, *Hebrews*, T. & T. Clark 1924, p.106, cf. pp.xxxii,xxxiv; Rappoport, op. cit., Vol. I, p.8.
24. Exod. 25.9,40.
25. See especially Luke 22.15.
26. Matt. 21.9 par.; cf. Ps. 118.25f.
27. Matt. 10.9f.; cf. Mark 6.8f.
28. *Berakoth* 9.5.
29. Matt. 21.14; cf. II Sam. 5.6; S. H. Hooke, *Alpha and Omega*, Nisbet 1961, p.193.
30. Cf. Gärtner, op. cit., pp.110f.
31. Gal. 4.26; Rev. 3.12; 21.1–22.5; cf. Phil. 3.20; Sib. Or. V, 420ff.; *Mid. Tel.* Ps. 122.4.
32. F. V. Filson, *Yesterday*, SCM Press 1967, p.45.
33. Heb. 12.18–27.

34. Heb. 9.12; cf. 4.14; 6.19f.; 9.24; 10.19f.

35. Filson, op. cit., p.38.

36. Luke 23.43.

37. John 3.13; 6.62; 20.17; see Barrett, *The Gospel according to St John*, p. 257.

38. P. A. Van Stempvoort, 'The Interpretation of the Ascension in Luke and Acts', *New Testament Studies* V, 1958/9, p.32. Cf. 'to be lifted up' in John 3.14; 8.28; 12.32–34, and see R. E. Brown, *The Gospel according to John*, Geoffrey Chapman 1971, pp.145f.

39. Strauss, op. cit., Vol. II, p.383; see *Yoma* 39b; *Clem. Recog.* I, 41; Suetonius, *Julius* 81; *Nero* 46; *Vespasian* 23; Tacitus, *Hist.* 5.13.

40. Daniélou, *A History of Early Christian Doctrine*, p.145.

41. Cf. Eph. 2.14f.

42. Schlier, op. cit., p.240.

43. See Borsch, op. cit., p.369; J. G. Davies, op. cit., pp.34ff.

44. See Exod. 28.31f.; Josephus, *Antt.* III, 7.4. There was much rabbinic speculation concerning Adam's garments. One tradition held that they were handed down from Adam through the firstborn to become the vestments of the High Priest (see Bowker, *The Targums and Rabbinic Literature*, pp.129f.).

45. Thorburn, op. cit., pp.260f.

46. John 20.11–18; cf. Apoc. Moses 31.3.

47. John 14.2f.

48. Acts 1.3ff.

49. Jub. 3.9; cf. Test. Benj. 9.4f.

50. Cf. Ps. 104.2; Isa. 40.22; Acts 1.9; Heb. 1.12; Rev. 6.14.

51. Macdonald, op. cit., pp.17f., 330.

52. II (4) Esd. 7.26; 13.36; I Enoch 90. 28; II Bar. 32.2; Rev. 21.2,10.

53. Qumran, *Community Rule*, VIII. 5ff. quoted Jeremias, *New Testament Theology*, Vol. I, p.173; cf. IX. 3ff.; Gärtner, op. cit., p.21.

54. Gärtner, op. cit., p.101.

55. Dibelius, *From Tradition to Gospel*, p.275; cf. J. M. Creed, *The Gospel according to St Luke*, Macmillan 1965, p.133.

56. H. Conzelmann, *The Theology of St Luke*, Faber 1960, pp.29,44.

57. J. A. Ziesler, 'The Transfiguration Story and the Markan Soteriology', *The Expository Times* LXXXI, 1970, pp.265ff.

58. *Mid. Tel.* Ps. 24.5; 106.2.

59. Apoc. Peter (Eth.) 15f.

60. So Mithras in the *Avesta* 'is described appearing in a golden glow on top of *Hara Běrězaiti*', Vermaseren, op. cit., p.76.

61. J. G. Davies, op. cit., pp.39ff.; id., 'The Prefigurement of the Ascension in the Third Gospel', *Journal of Theological Studies* VI, 1955, pp.229–33; cf. Grant, op. cit., p.155.

62. Creed, op. cit., pp.132f.

63. Cf. Caird, op. cit., p.133.

64. *Gen. R.* 69.3 on Gen. 28.13; cf. *Gen. R.* 68.12 on Gen. 28.12; see Barrett, *The Gospel according to St John*, p.156; Marsh, op. cit., p.136; Brown, op. cit., pp.88–91.

65. Mark 14.57f.

66. See F. P. Cheetham, 'Destroy this Temple, and in Three Days I will Raise it Up', *Journal of Theological Studies* XXIV, 1923, pp.315–7; cf. H. J. White, 'On the Saying attributed to Our Lord in John 11.19', *Expositor* XVII, 1919, pp.415–23.

67. John 20.17.

68. John 20.22.

69. Luke 24.15;John 20.19.

70. Matt. 28.20.

71. Cf. Aulen, op. cit., p.129.

72. Voegelin, op. cit., p.310.

73. Matt. 16.18.

12   *The King of Israel*

One of the commonest titles applied to Yahweh in the Old Testament is that of king.[1] It also appears in the New Testament, and probably had a key place in the teaching of Jesus, who announced the coming reign of God in his time.[2] In the gospels, however, it is Jesus himself who comes to be named as king of Israel and is regarded as having been enthroned as universal Lord by his ascension. Contributing to this imagery of kingship used in the Old and the New Testaments were a number of mythological ideas, the elucidation of which are of some value in appreciating the associations relied upon by the evangelists.

GOD AND KING

When speaking of the place of God's throne, both types of mythological cosmography were used. In I Enoch 25.3 the throne of God is the high mount on which he will sit 'to visit the earth with goodness'. Yahweh, like Zeus and Baal, is pictured as exalted above the earth on the dais of the central mountain.[3] In view of the tendency to identify this with Zion in the Hebrew tradition, it followed that Jerusalem would come to be thought of as the earthly capital of Yahweh's rule, and it seemed entirely natural for Jesus to speak of it as 'the city of the great King'.[4] By Jesus' time, however, it was also quite common to speak of God's throne raised above the earth in heaven.[5] With the development of a vertical cosmography, this usage had been long established. As part of the reaction against the dangers inherent in the use of the older model, Isa. 66.1f. even appears to have been intended to express a rejection of the idea that

Yahweh's palace was to be identified with the temple in Jerusalem.[6] While the temple as a place of worship might happily be seen as the earthly counterpart of the heavenly temple, prophetic Judaism had become increasingly distrustful of the notion that it was also a copy of the heavenly throne. Behind this suspicion lay the fear of sacral kingship against which there had been fought a long ideological battle.

A sacral king was one who not only governed in the name of God, but was also considered in some measure to represent him. Such a king could play the part of deity in the political and religious life of the people. His divine role was most clearly portrayed in the new year rites when he played the part of the creator in the re-enactment of the cosmogonic myth.[7] For such actions to be accounted valid, the king had to be recognized as one who had the closest possible relationship with God. He had to show that he had the necessary qualifications to act as vicegerent of deity. In order to do this he normally had to demonstrate that he was in fact a son of God. This was a status which he might acquire by a rite of adoption, a method particularly suitable when a new royal line was being established. Alternatively he could claim descent from the first king set on earth by God, the Adamic royal man. This was an easier course to pursue when he came to the throne as next in line of a long-established dynasty. The nature of the king's sonship attained in either of these ways was not always regarded, however, in the same light. In some cultures his sonship was regarded as being of an ontological kind. In this case the king was held to be himself a divine being. Other cultures were more cautious, and the king's sonship was regarded as no more than functional in character. In the latter case he was only the most exalted of the servants of God. Yet while this distinction is an important one, it must be noted that it cannot be pressed too closely. It was a distinction particularly difficult to maintain in a ritual setting, and not much less so in a social or political one. It was probably this difficulty which led to Judaism wishing to clear away any traces of sacral kingship in Israel in order to keep inviolate the concept of Yahweh as transcendent over all.

The eradication of sacral kingship ideas by prophetic Judaism was so successful that indications of its existence in ancient Israel are often ambiguous. Nevertheless, it is now generally

recognized that it did have a place at one time, and that Israel
was influenced in this by the practices of the Canaanites. Fuller
is probably correct, however, in stressing that the Hebrew
monarchy was a 'constitutional' one, emphasis being laid on the
idea that the king was adopted or elected, following the Assyrian
practice, as against the Egyptian concept of the king as son of
God in an ontological sense.[8] Even so, it must be admitted that
the idea was a mythological one. 'The prophetic persuasion
of Israel's election by the Most High, and of a divine purpose of
grace governing her institutions and history'[9] was a conviction
shared by other peoples, but in relation to their own place in the
scheme of things.

The prophetic revolt against the concept of sacral kingship,
however, does not mean that later Judaism ceased to be influenced by concepts derived from it. It led in the prophets
themselves to a stress upon the kingship of Yahweh and to the
idea of Israel as a theocracy. The imagery of earthly kingship
was applied to Yahweh in the strongest terms in order to counter
divine claims made for human kings in nearby cultures.
Further, when the prophets looked forward to the day when the
reign of God would be acknowledged by all peoples, they retained the old association between the kingship of God and the
seat of the ancient kings of Judah. In the eschatological age it is
to Jerusalem that the nations will be gathered to acknowledge
that the holy city of Israel is the throne of God. It is in the midst
of Israel that Yahweh will dwell, enthroned above all peoples.[10]
The influence of the ancient mythological concept of kingship
is even more pronounced in descriptions of the coming Messiah and of the Son of Man.[11] What had been considered danger-
ous to ascribe to kings in the present age, was confidently
predicted of the king to come. The eschatological hope of Israel
thus laid a foundation for the use of the mythology of sacral
kingship in the New Testament. While it may well be that the
Jesus of history was content to declare the approaching reign
of God, his disciples were certainly not slow to see in him the
Messianic king, and early Christian literature to set this forth
in imagery which had its origin in the sacral kingship of the
ancient Near East.

JESUS THE KING

If the symbolism of sacral kingship found a place in the gospel story as part of this process, there are certain features which might be expected to appear in it. Although ritual practices varied a good deal, a number of elements appear to have been fairly common and it is these which would be most likely to leave their mark. Before considering whether this is in fact the case, it will be of value to have these features broadly formulated.[12]

(i) The selection of a new king was always of considerable importance. He was expected to have certain qualities of a physical nature which showed him suitable for his sacred task.[13]

(ii) Having been chosen, the king-elect normally undertook some form of preparation which might include a period of fasting and a purificatory baptism.

(iii) He was acknowledged as son of God either by birth or adoption. In the latter case particularly he might be required to take part in a ritual of death and rebirth, and in either case he would generally be given a new name.

(iv) The blessing of immortality was usually bestowed upon him by means of his receiving the food and drink of life and by his being anointed with oil.

(v) The ritual would often include a form of combat in which the new king emerged victorious over the forces of destruction and evil. In this way he was identified ritualistically with the creator of the myth.[14]

(vi) Having been admonished to rule justly and invested with the royal garments, shoes, crown and other regalia, the new king would be installed on the raised and stepped throne 'which symbolized the mountain of the world'.[15] His reign would then be proclaimed and he would receive the homage of his subjects.

(vii) A number of other elements might also form part of the ceremonies. There was often an accompanying sacrifice, perhaps of a human victim in ancient times. Frequently there would be feasting and buffoonery. The queen naturally had a place, and the royal marriage might be held to consummate the union on earth of the gods above.

A hypothetical pattern of this kind is of considerable value in setting out the nature of a complex of thought, but it must be used with the utmost caution. While all of these elements may be found in the practices of the ancient world, they do not all appear together in any one cultus.[16] Certainly it is difficult to see anything like a complete pattern of such behaviour in the Old Testament, and in view of this it is unlikely that it should appear in the New. It is, of course, possible to see hints of virtually every element mentioned in the language of the gospels, but in many cases the sacral kingship scheme is unlikely to provide the correct background. The evangelistic use of wedding symbolism illustrates this very well. Marriage had become a common eschatological image among the Jews, but while it may be possible to trace a lineage for this in the sacral marriages of the past, this background is so remote from the apocalyptic sources on which the gospel writers were drawing that it should probably be regarded as irrelevant. Similarly, the description of Jesus as a shepherd is reminiscent of the common use of this title for kings in mythological times, but Bultmann had no hesitation in saying that there are in this 'no traces whatsoever of the kingly figure'.[17] While these and other symbols were used in sacral kingship ideology, they were also common enough in other contexts. If a particular idea found in the gospels is to be connected with the mythology of kingship, therefore, it is necessary to show that there is more evidence for this than a coincidence of a single symbolic device. In view of these strictures, therefore, attention is best confined to those elements in the gospels which appear to be difficult to explain against any other background.

THE ROYAL SON OF GOD

We may safely begin with the ascription of divine sonship to Jesus in the gospels. This was an idea which was basic to the thought of the evangelists. It is clearly associated with the concept of kingship, and it appears in narratives which are undoubtedly reminiscent of sacral kingship rituals.

This is most obvious in the story of Jesus' baptism. We have already noted that this makes use of mythological symbolism, and so we are further encouraged to consider whether it includes features which are most easily explicable in terms of sacral kingship. The story contains several elements which are in fact, familiar from ancient royal rites, and so Borsch is probably correct when he says that 'behind it we may catch sight of the dimensions of older stories concerning the adoption of one chosen to be a royal Son'.[18]

(*a*) The kingdom proclaimed by Jesus and later to be identified with him is announced by a precursor, John the Baptist.

(*b*) As the Pharaoh was purified by bathing in the sacred lake representing Nun, so Jesus is immersed in the waters of the Jordan.[19]

(*c*) By the opening of the heavens to him, Jesus is shown to be the person in whom heaven and earth meet. Like the kings of old, he has become the channel of divine communication.

(*d*) He is invested with the Spirit of God and so ordained to his kingly role. The symbolism of the Spirit as a dove is particularly noteworthy in that it may be compared to the way gods were said to appear in theriomorphic guise in Egyptian coronation mythology.[20]

(*e*) He is designated as the one chosen by God, and the royal epithets of 'Beloved' and 'Son of God' are applied to him. Ps. 2.7, which lies behind the words used at this point, may in fact be 'a Hebrew adaptation of the Babylonian formula of *adoption*',[21] or have its origin in a similar form of words found in the Egyptian pyramid texts. 'Thou art my beloved Son whom I begat' are the words used by Amon-Re to the archetypal king of Egypt, Horus,[22] and may be taken as typical of the language employed to indicate that a man had been raised to divine kingship. So here they suggest exaltation to kingly rule as the adopted Son of God. This was certainly how the words were understood by the *Gospel of the Hebrews*, in which God proclaims Jesus to be 'my first-begotten Son that reignest for ever', and it is probable that this does no more than draw out the original meaning.

(*f*) In the desert immediately afterwards, Jesus undergoes a period of seclusion and fasting such as royal rites often called for, and emerged victorious over the powers of evil, so showing that he was the one ordained to do the work of God on earth and able to defeat 'the primeval forces of darkness, evil and chaos', like the king-gods of the past.[23]

Seen against the background of sacral kingship, therefore, the story of Jesus' baptism takes on added dimension. All the

symbolism of the story previously noted is gathered up, and we
have a picture of one ordained to be king of God's world.

The gospels of Matthew and Luke are not content to have
Jesus' royal title dependent on a rite of adoption. Both evangelists provide genealogies which set out a claim to hereditary
kingship. Matthew traces Jesus' descent back to Abraham.
This was probably intended to assert not only his Jewish identity
but also his royal succession, for Abraham was held to have been
a king long before the election of Gideon or Saul to this office.[24]
Luke traces Jesus' ancestry back further still, to Adam, the son
of God. The reason for this is almost certainly in part to set forth
Jesus as a direct descendant of the first royal son of God. At
Ugarit and elsewhere the king was held to be son of God by
virtue of his being 'the representative of Primordial Man'.[25]
The same idea may have found a place in Hebraic thought.
Certainly Adam was regarded as the first king, especially in
Ezek. 28, where the guardian of God's garden is an anointed
one 'like a corresponding Mesopotamian figure, the Primordial
Man called Adapa'.[26] Moreover, Adam was seen as the arche-
type of any king who attempted to set himself up as equal with
God.[27] It may also be significant that David was described as
the 'firstborn'.[28] This would be a natural epithet to apply to
one regarded in some sense as a representative of the first man.
Finally, it may be noted that the concept of the Son of Man
probably owed something to this kind of thought in later
Judaism. Indeed, the very title could be taken as suggesting it.
When, therefore, Luke seeks to show that Jesus was a descendant of Adam and speaks of both as son of God, it is most likely
that he is making use of mythological symbolism derived from
the notion of sacral kingship founded on the archetypal royalty
of Adam.

The stories of Christ's baptism and birth have validated his
claim to the title of king in different ways, but both methods had
their roots in the concept of sacral kingship. For the evangelists,
however, this is the first occasion on which such a claim was
deemed to have been justified. Only with Jesus was the anointed one properly identified as the Son of God.

THE ENTHRONEMENT OF THE KING

The enthronement of the one designated as king in the baptismal and nativity stories of the evangelists could not take place until much later. Appropriately for one whose kingdom was not to be of this world, his enthronement was to be accomplished in a fashion quite different from anything encountered in the ancient rituals. It was to take place by means, not of a simulated death, but of a real one. His first throne was to be a cross near Jerusalem, and his lordship was to be exercised from a throne in heaven. Everything which the evangelists have to say about the kingship of Jesus is dominated by this. The procession of the king-designate is seen as the road to Calvary. Any suggestion of Jesus' exaltation to royal status which precedes the passion narrative is therefore only of an anticipatory kind.

Although monarchical symbolism is not explicit, the story of the transfiguration may well contain 'numerous echoes from royal liturgies and myths'.[29] It is made clear to the disciples, however, that this enthronement on the mount is not to be divulged until he has risen from the dead. It is a royal event only in the sense that it prepares the disciples so that they may understand that his passion is the means whereby he will attain to kingship bestowed upon him by God.[30] They are further prepared for the new concept of kingship when Jesus promises his disciples that he will have throne-mates like the kings of the past, and that the twelve will share his rule. Those who are to reign with him will do so by their identification of themselves with him in his death. Only so can they attain the glory which they seek.[31]

The first public declaration of Jesus' kingship is made at the triumphal entry. Ostensibly it is no more than the end of his pilgrimage to the festival, but the evangelists wish the reader to see a further significance in the event. John 12.16 points out that while they went unrecognized at the time, certain things took place then which were only understood after Jesus was glorified. According to Mark 11.10, the people declare that the kingdom of David is coming at this time, but do not refer to Jesus as king. Matthew, on the other hand, inserts quotations from Isa. 62.11 and Zech. 9.9 into his account, so that Jesus is now specifically identified with the king of Zion. Luke keeps closer to Mark's narrative, but makes a significant change in the Markan quotation from Ps. 118.25f., so that the title of king is introduced. In the later gospels, therefore, the entry is clearly intended to be understood as a coronation procession.[32] But equally clear is the fact that they could not have intended this in a political sense. The one who comes to the capital at this time is no earthly ruler but the king of heaven. The proper parallel to this event, therefore, is perhaps to be found in the cultic rites of Hebrew theocracy. As Yahweh ascended Mount Zion represented by his ark in the ancient new year festival,[33] so now his Son processes towards his divine enthronement.

Only from such a perspective does the concern of the evangelists for certain features of the narrative find adequate explanation. Particular attention is drawn to the procurement and use of the colt on which Jesus rides into Jerusalem. While a perfectly natural explanation can be offered for the fact that Jesus knew that an unbroken colt was tethered in the village, the story as the evangelists have it tends to suggest that Jesus exercised paranormal insight on this occasion.[34] Riding upon an ass appears to have been a princely status symbol in ancient Israel,[35] but there are indications that we are here concerned with something more than an outward symbol of prestige. The gospels link the incident with Zech. 9.9, and so assert its Messianic character. Further, they stress the fact that the animal had previously been unused. The act thus belongs to that class of events which is related to the making of all things new. On just such an animal would Adam have ridden at the beginning of history, and indeed there was a tradition to this effect.[36] Jesus was therefore no ordinary prince but the Son of Man, a new Adam, whose sovereignty was now acknowledged.

The decking of Christ's route may also be intended to point us in the same direction. In Mark the people lay down layers of leaves or straw, but Matthew says that they used branches for this purpose which John identifies as having come from palm trees. Palms were used on the arrival of a victor, but there was an older and more important association. Branches called 'hosannas' were carried at the feast of Tabernacles, when Ps. 118 was sung, as it is here.[37] Much of the symbolism of this feast was suggestive of the concept of paradise, and the trees of the garden were sometimes identified with palms. It would seem, therefore,

that this feature provides another reason for thinking that
the evangelists see in Jesus' entry into Jerusalem the new Adam
coming to the garden of God, represented by Jerusalem and its
temple on earth. But they undoubtedly looked beyond the cultic
representation and saw in this event a symbol of Jesus' entry
into the paradise which is above. The king to whom hosannas
are now given is not, like the kings of old, a merely temporary
representative of the primordial Man but is in reality to be the
father of a new mankind.

The triumphal procession becomes a *via dolorosa* as Jesus
makes his way to the cross. The hosannas are replaced by taunts.
The word king is used six times in Mark 15 and on each occasion
in contempt. He is ridiculed by the soldiers, given a reed for
a sceptre and crowned with a wreath of thorns. A pretence of
homage is accompanied by spitting and a game of blind man's
buff. This horse-play reaches a grim finale when his title as king
of the Jews is placarded above the cross, his supremacy being
acknowledged only in the formulation of his crime.[38]

There is nothing in all this which would have been unlikely
in the circumstances. It centres on the charge brought against
Jesus, and the behaviour of the soldiers is entirely credible as
expressive of their contempt for the Jews, and especially for any-
one who claimed to be their king. As part of a great military
machine, they could only have found the idea of this manacled
Jew as a king to be inexpressibly funny. Yet more has to be
said. While there are no adequate grounds for doubting the
historicity of these events, it is clear that the evangelists are
concerned to emphasize them. The mock kingship plays an
important part in their understanding of the passion. It is necessary, therefore, to consider what significance it had for them.

Writers of the Christ-myth school have usually seized upon
this sequence of events in order to support their denial of the
historicity of Jesus. Their argument is worth consideration here
not because the case for making the crucifixion fictitious is
proved, but because it points to a background of mythological
practice which may have played some part in the thinking of
the evangelists.

On the basis of suggestions put forward earlier by P. Wend-
land in 1898 and Frazer in 1900, Solomon Reinach elaborated
the theory that the passion narrative was myth dressed up as

history. An essential ingredient in his argument was the resemblance of the story to the Sacaea rites of Babylonia and Persia and to the Roman Saturnalia. In these a condemned man was led in triumphal procession, dressed up as a king and finally stripped, scourged and killed. It was not difficult for Pierre Batiffol to point out the weaknesses in Reinach's theory.[39] In particular, certain fundamental elements of the Sacaea were absent from the gospel narrative because it lacked the Bacchanalian character of the ritual orgy. The evangelists, however, may well have intended the reader to be aware of the similarity. Jesus' kingship was one which on this earth could be no more than an ironic testimony to his role as divine king of creation. There is clearly a contrast present in the minds of the gospel writers between the humiliation of the Christ at the hands of the political rulers of Jerusalem and the exaltation which is to follow. Luke ensures recognition of this at 23.42 where the thief looks forward to that elevation of Christ to kingly power at the very moment when all thought of earthly rule is excluded. The cross, therefore, is but the prelude to Jesus' enjoyment of the divine throne. The *Epistle of Barnabas* is not so far from the thought of the evangelists when it says that the reign of Jesus begins on the tree.[40]

The true enthronement of Christ, however, takes place beyond death, and is portrayed according to both the mythological models which are so frequently used. He is shown as king first on the mountain and then in heaven.

Matthew closes his gospel with a scene which takes place on 'the mountain' in Galilee. As Pfleiderer pointed out, 'the very scene of this event, "the mountain," gives us a hint that now again, at the close, we find ourselves upon the same *ideal* height' which has figured earlier in the gospel.[41] The significance of the hill here can be illustrated by a Heliopolitan coronation or mortuary text in which the king is asked to assume the role of the creator-god, standing on the primeval hill which has just emerged from the waters. The king, like the god, ascends the hill of cosmic order and so the reborn monarch joins his father Atum.[42] So Matthew no doubt intends the reader to understand that Jesus here assumes the role of the divine king who is enthroned over heaven and earth.[43] What is said of this event by Matthew assumes the form, moreover, of what J. Jeremias calls a 'triple-action coronation text',[44] which follows the ancient Egyptian coronation ritual. Jesus assumes total authority over heaven and earth. He commands his disciples to promulgate his law to all nations, utters the divine word of power and assures them of his continuing presence.

In Acts 1.8,12 the command to go out as witnesses into all the world is given by Luke as having taken place on Olivet. The choice of this mountain can hardly have been without significance. It was rich in associations for Israel, having been a noted place of prayer, vision and judgment.[45] It figures as the place where the resurrection of the righteous will take place,[46] and where the Messiah will come. In the Lukan scheme, however, the last mountain mentioned as part of the Christ-event takes on a new role. The time has not yet come for his kingdom to be established on earth and so it is not, as in Matthew, the place of his enthronement.[47] Jesus does indeed still give his disciples here his royal commission, but the scene is no more than the prelude to his true enthronement which takes place by means of the ascension to heaven. In this way Luke makes it clear that only those with eyes to see his heavenly exaltation will have understood the message of the road to the cross and see in it a procession through death to the only legitimate divine kingship in history.[48]

In Mark no enthronement ceremony is described, possibly because the end of the gospel has been lost. But at 14.62 the gospel may look forward to this event. Jesus here tells the high priest that he will see the Son of Man sitting at the right hand of power and coming on the clouds of heaven. The two elements in this prophecy have often been separated, the first being made to refer to Christ's exaltation and the latter to his eschatological return. But as the high priest is to see both of these events, it is more likely that they should be seen as two aspects of one event. In that case Jesus' coming on clouds was probably intended to denote the manifestation of the divine rule attained by his exaltation. This interpretation is suggested on the one hand by the use of the imagery of coming on clouds in Dan. 7.13 to describe the exaltation of the Son of Man in terms of royal enthronement, and on the other by its use in Exod. 19.9 and Ezek. 1.4 as part of the imagery of theophany.[49] In Mark also, therefore, the notion of Christ's heavenly enthronement and manifestation is to be found, and in a way which suggests a background in the Hebraic use for eschatological description of symbolism derived from sacral kingship.

Finally, R. Joshua ben Levi may help us to appreciate the contrast to which the evangelists have all along been pointing. The rabbi asserted that if Israel was unworthy, her Messiah would come '*lowly and riding upon an ass*',[50] but if she was worthy then he would come on clouds of heaven. This third-century contrast may well be one that had been made much earlier, and certainly it has something in common with the gospel presentation. For the evangelists Israel had indeed been found unworthy, promoting the crucifixion of her Messiah and mocking his right to rule. But while the kingship of Christ had been denied on earth, it had been recognized in heaven. Although the world might not be able to see the Lord of heaven and earth in the crucified Jew from Nazareth because he was so unlike the pretentious kings of worldy empire, the evangelists have attempted to show that the archetypal and mythological role to which such kings aspired had been granted to him. He in truth and spirit shared the throne of God.

NOTES

1. Pss. 5.2; 10.16; 24.10; 74.12; 84.3; Isa. 33.22; Jer. 10.10.

2. Matt. 18.23–35; 22.1–14; Mark 1.15; Luke 4.43.

3. A. B. Cook, op. cit., Vol. I, pp.124–48; cf. Gaster, *Thespis*, pp.218f.

4. Matt. 5.35; cf. I Chron. 29.23.

5. Matt. 23.22; Acts 7.49; Rev. 4.2.

6. Ps. 103.19; Ezek. 1.26; 10.1; cf. Ps. 11.4.

7. See A. Jeremias, op. cit., Vol. I, pp.58–60; J. R. Porter, 'The Interpretation of 2 Samuel vi and Psalm cxxxii', *Journal of Theological Studies* V, 1954, pp.161–73; N. H. Snaith, *The Jewish New Year Festival*, SPCK 1947; Widengren, op. cit., pp.199f.

8. Fuller, op. cit., pp.23f.,31; cf. Bentzen, op. cit., p.19; Wales, op. cit., pp.19f.

9. Manson, *Jesus the Messiah*, p.103.

10. Jer. 3.17; Jub. 1.28.

11. See H. Riesenfeld, *The Gospel Tradition*, Blackwell 1970, pp.33ff.

12. Cf. A. Corell, *Consummatum Est*, SPCK 1958, pp.17ff.

13. I Sam. 16.7; II Sam. 14.25; cf. Lev. 21.16: Gaster, *Thespis*, pp.218f. note.

14. Cf. Gaster, *Thespis*, p.170 note.

15. Mowinckel, *He That Cometh*, p.64; see Ps. 2.6.

16. Hocart, op. cit., pp.70f.

17. Bultmann, *The Gospel of John*, p.367; cf. Allegro, op. cit., p.4; Barrett, *The Gospel according to St John*, pp.310f.

18. Borsch, op. cit., p.370; cf. E. O. James, *Christian Myth and Ritual*, John Murray 1933, p.100.

19. Cf. James, *Christian Myth and Ritual*, p.59.

20. Ibid., p.101.

21. Dodd, *The Interpretation of the Fourth Gospel*, p.252; cf. Weiss, op. cit., p.40.

22. Voegelin, op. cit., pp.304f.; cf. Jones, op. cit., p.258.

23. Borsch, op. cit., p.93.

24. See LXX of Gen. 23.6; Gordon, op. cit., p.143 n. 2.

25. Widengren, op. cit., p.175: cf. Borsch, op. cit., pp.89f.

26. Widengren, op. cit., p.166; cf. Gen. 1.28; Ps. 8.6; Philo, *De Opificio Mundi*, 84; cf. Jacob, op. cit., p.327.

27. Isa. 14; Ezek. 28; Dan. 4.

28. Ps. 89.27; see Widengren, op. cit., pp.174f. Cf. Bentzen, op. cit., p.17 on the terms applied to the Messiah in Micah 5.1 and Isa. 9.5.

29. Borsch, op. cit., p.382. See Ps. 2.6; Zech. 3.7; Josephus, *Antt.* XIX, 8.2.

30. Mark 8.29–34; 9.9.

31. Mark 10.37ff.

32. Caird, op. cit., p.216.

33. Mowinckel, *He That Cometh*, p.26.

34. Vincent Taylor, *The Gospel according to St Mark*, Macmillan 1959, p.454.

35. Gen. 49.11; Judg. 5.10; 10.4; 12.14; II Sam. 19.26.

36. O. Michel, '*Hippos*', *Theological Dictionary of the New Testament*, ed. Kittel and Friedrich, Vol. III, p.337 n. 4.

37. Taylor, op. cit., p.456.

38. Mark 15.16–20,26,32 par.

39. S. Reinach, *Orpheus*, Heinemann 1909; P. Batiffol, *The Credibility of the Gospel*, Longmans, Green 1912; see Taylor, op. cit., pp.646–8.

40. Barnabas 8.5.

41. O. Pfleiderer, *Primitive Christianity*, Williams and Norgate 1909, Vol. II, p.375.

42. See Voegelin, op. cit., p.77.

43. Cf. Dodd, *The Interpretation of the Fourth Gospel*, p.333 n. 2.

44. J. Jeremias, *Jesus' Promise to the Nations*, SCM Press 1958, p.39, following O. Michel.

45. II Sam. 15.32; Ezek. 11.23.

46. Zech. 14.4; Josephus *Antt.*, XX, 8.6; *War*, II, 13.5; see Goodenough, op. cit., Vol. X, p.180 n. 70.

47. Acts 1.6f.

48. Acts 7.56.

49. See J. A. T. Robinson, *Jesus and his Coming*, SCM Press 1957, pp.43ff.; Sidebottom, op. cit., p.112; Taylor, op. cit., p.569.

50. *Sanhedrin* 98a.

13 *The New Creation*

As the eschatological teaching of the prophetic and apocalyptic writers developed in Judaism, the idea of a transformation of nature came to occupy an increasingly important place. In this scheme of thought Jerusalem was credited with a particularly significant role. With the creation of a new heaven and earth would come a new Jerusalem. Indeed, the founding of the new city, the exaltation of its mountain and the building of its temple virtually constitute the new creation. The transformation of the earth and of Jerusalem are placed in parallel with one another.[1] With the shaking and fall of Zion, the world comes to an end, but only that it may be raised again and become more glorious than ever when God renews his world.[2]

The rabbis developed this earlier thought and read it back into the mythology of the old creation. Because eschatological acts were invariably understood to conform to their cosmogonic archetypes, it was inferred that the old creation had begun in the same way that the new would come. So the rabbis taught that 'Palestine was created first and then the rest of the world'.[3] The creation had begun with Zion its centre.[4] The old creation had spread out from Zion as the new one would do.[5] The preeminence of Jerusalem as the spiritual centre of the new world was now expressed in terms of its temporal priority to all other places on earth in the old creation.

Two models were constantly used in order to set forth this complex of ideas. One of these spoke of the world as a living body, and referred to its centre as the navel. The other likened creation to the construction of a great building and located its foundation rock at the centre of the earth. Both models provided imagery in which to speak of the special role played by the holy city of Judaism.

THE NAVEL

Understanding of the idea of the world-navel has grown steadily during the present century as a result of the work done by a number of scholars. Much of this was already summarized by Wensinck in his important work on the idea among the western Semites. He was able to show that the world-navel was a basic concept around which many others gathered. It was regarded as the centre of the earth, higher than the rest of the world, the place of communication between the upper and nether worlds, the point from which nourishment was distributed over the whole earth and the first part of the earth to be created.[6] This complex of ideas was found to have been widespread. The honour of being the navel of the earth was claimed by Nineveh, Eleusis, Delphi, Paphos, Delos, Epidaurus, Athens and Rome.[7] In consequence, archaeologists have discovered a number of navel stones or *omphaloi* in various places in the Near East. The pervasiveness of the concept directly reflects the virtually universal appeal in ancient times of the animistic outlook.

In Israel the idea appears to have been an ancient one. Judg. 9.37 refers to Gerizim as the navel of the earth,[8] and this was probably a very old tradition. It is also likely that Mount Tabor had been regarded as the navel-mountain at one time. The mountain itself was shaped like the traditional *omphalos* symbol, and its name may derive from a word meaning navel.[9] It is likely, therefore, that the idea was prevalent in the early religious thinking of the Hebrew people long before the honour associated with this title was claimed by Israel for Jerusalem. The exaltation of Jerusalem to spiritual supremacy would inevitably have led to this development in the mythological thinking of the ancient world. So Jub. 8.19 asserts that Jerusalem is 'the centre of the navel of the earth'.[10] The idea was well known to the rabbis. The midrash on the Song of Songs explained that the Sanhedrin had been compared to a navel because 'as the navel is placed in the centre of the body, so Israel's Sanhedrin was placed in the centre of the Temple' in Jerusalem, which was the centre of the world.[11] The altar of incense as the centre of Israel's cultic practice was also identified with the navel.[12] The hill of Zion and all that rested upon it was seen as situated at the *omphalos* of the world, and so understood to have been the navel from which the embryo created and nurtured by God had grown.[13] In closely related imagery, therefore, Mount Moriah could be described as 'the womb of the world'.[14] At Jerusalem the birth of the old creation had taken place.

Judaism also appears to have been familiar with the representation of the navel by a stone.[15] When Israel referred to the world-stone or rock, however, another concept was usually in mind.

THE FOUNDATION OF THE WORLD

The slab of rock which is to be found in the temple area of the Dome of the Rock in Jerusalem is called the *Eben Shetiyah* or foundation stone. According to *Lev. R.* 20.4, 'after the disappearance of the ark there was a foundation stone in its place'. Similarly *Yoma* 5.2 of the Mishnah says that 'after the Ark was taken away a stone remained there from the time of the early Prophets, and it was called "Shetiyah". It was higher than the ground by three fingerbreadths.' In all probability, however, its cultic life began even before the first Hebrew temple was built.

The original significance of the stone is still a matter for dispute. There is a tradition that the stone was the base of the great altar of sacrifice in the Jewish temple. If this was so, then it is likely that it had earlier been a sacrificial rock in Jebusite times.[16] A. C. Bouquet suggested that a Jebusite megalith may once have stood there and that blood libations were poured into a hole in the rock, the whole being enclosed later, just as the Kaaba was built for the black stone of Mecca.[17] On one point, however, there is little room for dispute. The *Eben Shetiyah* came to be regarded as the foundation on which God had built the world. This notion appears in Islamic tradition, which undoubtedly borrowed it from Israel via rabbinic Judaism.

The model of the earth as a great building resting on foundations laid by God was a commonplace of Hebraic usage.[18] These foundations were established in the *tehōm* which Yahweh had overcome by his creative word. There they rested secure, a firm base for the world and its life.[19]

Exaggerated importance would seem to have been attached to the foundations of the temple and their security extolled beyond reason, if it is not recognized that they are one with the rock on which the world was built.[20] The temple and its city are secure above all others because they stand on the very base of the earth. They are supreme over the chaotic waters because they rest on the pillars of rock which penetrate their depths.[21] The foundations of the earth and of Zion are therefore the same.[22] When the builders lay the foundation of the second temple in place, the people rightly shout for joy, as the sons of God had done when God had set down the base of the earth.[23] The building of the world and of the temple are parallel with one another, so explaining the mythological and cultic origin of the rabbinic tradition that the earth was not built until the temple was raised.[24]

This whole complex of ideas may be conveniently illustrated from *Mid. Tel.* Ps. 91.7. 'What did the Holy One, blessed be He, do? Like a man setting in place the central pole of a tent, He raised His right foot and drove the stone down into the very bottom of the deeps and made it the pillar of the earth. Therefore, it is called the spindle stone, for it is the very navel of the earth, from which the whole earth is stretched out. And upon the stone is the house of the Lord.'[25] This is said of the stone set up by Jacob at Bethel, but this is identical for the rabbis with the rock of Jerusalem. So the *Eben Shetiyah* of the holy city was identified as the primeval rock on which the world was originally founded.

The imagery of the two models was therefore easily combined. Both could be used to assert the temporal and spatial priority of Jerusalem in both the old creation and the new. When it became again the navel point of the new birth, Zion would possess 'the cornerstone of the new creation'.[26] This was asserted against all the competing claims of other nations. Babylon might imagine itself destined to become the world empire of the future, but Jeremiah dubs it a 'destroying mountain' which can furnish 'no stone for a foundation' of the world. Indeed it is to become 'a burnt mountain', and its imagined role is to be taken over by Zion.[27] When we turn to the gospels, however, this Hebraic claim is challenged. While the symbolism of the holy city of the Jews as the point of the world's creation is used, this is done in a way which points to its replacement by another rock which, though rejected, would become the foundation of the new world. In the gospels this symbolism is used to proclaim that in Jesus a new creation has taken place, and a new creative spirit spread abroad from the navel of the earth.

THE NEW FOUNDATION

The imagery of the foundation rock lies behind a number of sayings attributed to Jesus. It appears at first merely to heighten the metaphorical power of Jesus' teaching, but further consideration speedily leads to the conclusion that these sayings are no less than revolutionary in character.

In Matt. 7.24–27 and Luke 6.47–49 Jesus makes a simple comparison between the man who builds his house upon a rock and one who is foolish enough to build upon sand. His audience are exhorted to build their houses upon the rock, so that they will withstand the tempests of nature. Now while this would be sound advice to a builder in any country, the words would have an immediate and obvious exemplification in the mind of Jesus' hearers. Of what other house could it be more aptly said that it was built upon a rock than the temple of the Lord at Jerusalem? But further, the saying declares that the man who builds upon a rock is the one who hears and does the word of Jesus. The rock is given an unaccustomed meaning which strikes at the very roots of contemporary Jewish faith. The identification of the rock with the words of the man from Nazareth would have been regarded as totally unacceptable to the scribes. They were accustomed to interpreting the rock as Yahweh.[28] To claim that when a man trusted in the word of Jesus, he could be founded like the temple on the impregnable rock, would appear to be a clear case of blasphemy. Hidden in an apparently harmless analogy lay an idea which was eventually to break the allegiance of the disciples of Christ to their Jewish faith.

The faithful are also likened to a city set on a hill so that it cannot be hid.[29] Here again there is almost certainly an allusion to Jerusalem which towered over the world, at least in its spiritual splendour. The myth of the navel mountain is now recalled, however, in the context of discipleship to Jesus. His followers, rather than Jerusalem, are to be a light to the world of the future.

From these two passages it is already possible to see that the imagery of the mountain is being put to new use. The two sayings were not unnaturally combined and appear as one in the Oxyrhynchus papyri. 'A city which is erected on the top of a high mountain and firmly stablished, can neither fall nor remain hidden.'[30] This version makes the mythological origin of the ideas involved even clearer. It points us back decisively to the concept of the inviolate city built on the summit of the holy mountain. But it is the new community founded on the word of Christ which is to be the holy city of the future.

In Mark 11.23 Jesus is recorded as telling his disciples that faith can enable them to command 'this mountain' to be uprooted and cast into the sea.[31] The mountain clearly represents an obstacle of some kind which has to be removed, but its identification has been disputed. Some scholars have connected the saying with the rabbinic description of one who removed the difficulties of exegesis as a mountain-remover, while others see it as saying that faith can accomplish what appears to be impossible.[32] In the light of the controversies documented so fully in the gospels, it has also seemed reasonable to see in the mountain the legal righteousness of the Pharisees which had to be replaced by simple reliance on God's grace. The particularization of the mountain, however, must surely make it refer to the hill of Jerusalem, and so to the complex of mountain imagery which was connected with it in Jewish thought.[33]

The saying makes use of the familiar contrast between creation and chaos under the imagery of the mountain and the sea. The casting of the mountain into the sea represents the destruction of the world in mythological terms. That this is the intention of the saying also seems to be indicated by its position in the Markan scheme and by the Lukan variation. In Mark, the saying appears immediately after the discovery that the fig tree which Jesus cursed has withered, and is given to further the disciples' understanding of that event. In Luke 17.6 a saying similar in form is given, but the mountain is replaced by the sycamine tree. It would appear, therefore, that the tree and the mountain are used as complementary symbols and were to some extent interchangeable. The relationship of the tree with the mountain is an important pointer to interpretation, for the tree was also used as a centre symbol and to represent the cos-

mos.[34] By means of both symbols, therefore, the assertion
is made that by faith the old order may be brought to an
end.

Further help is given by a comparison with Zech. 4.6–9. In
this passage a 'great mountain' is to become a plain before
Zerubbabel, who then lays the foundation of the new temple.
The 'great mountain' in Zechariah probably stands for the
prince appointed by Persia who must fall before the Jewish
prince, whose glory will be his renewal of the temple.[35] In the
Markan saying, the high mountain is now identified not with
Persia but with Judaism. This is now the obstacle to the new
creation which must be destroyed. The saying, therefore, is an
invitation to act on faith and to reject the old order of creation
as set forth in the cultic centre of Jerusalem, in order that a
new order may come into being founded on a new and different
kind of rock.

In Zech. 4.7 it is said that Zerubbabel would bring forth the
head-stone of the new temple to be greeted by the people with
joy. When the stone comes which was to be 'the head of the
corner' in the new building of which the evangelists speak,
it is not welcomed but rejected. Mark 12.10 makes this point
by a quotation from Ps.118.22f. It is placed at the end of the
parable of the wicked husbandmen, the theme of which is the
rejection of the son of the owner of the vineyard. In this way
Mark ensures that the reader will understand that this rejection
was foretold in Israel, but that the rejected one was destined to
become fundamental to the structure of the new building either
as the coping-stone which completed the building or as a stone
in the foundation which bound it to the walls.[36]

Added to the Lukan version of the parable are statements
which elaborate the concept of Jesus as the stone. He is identified with the stone which breaks men who fall on it and which
scatters as dust those on whom it falls.[37] The background to
these statements is to be found in Dan. 2.28–49.[38] Daniel speaks
of a stone which smites the feet of the great image and breaks
them in pieces. This results in the whole structure crumbling
and being blown away like chaff during the summer threshing.
It then becomes a great mountain or rock which fills the whole
earth. Not only is the towering image destroyed, but it is replaced by the stone which brings about its downfall. The stone

here stands for the kingdom which God is to set up and which will become the world mountain of the future. It is almost certainly an allusion to Israel under imagery similar to that used in Isa. 2.1ff., which speaks of the mountain to be raised above all others.[39] The stone can also be taken as an image of the Messiah, as it was by the rabbis, the king of the new age representing the Israel of the future. Luke has interpreted the stone in a Messianic sense also, but has seen the fulfilment of the prophecy in Jesus. He is the stone destined to destroy what has gone before and become the world mountain of the future. It would seem to follow, moreover, from the place at which Luke has chosen to make use of this imagery, that he identified the structure which the stone must destroy with the old Israel of the wicked husbandmen. The one who brought into being the kingdom of the future would also be one who must destroy all who hinder its coming.

Isa. 8.14 is also probably in the background here, and at Luke 2.34 Jesus is the child grown to be the stone set for the 'falling and rising up of many in Israel'. On him the fate of Israel depends. Rom. 9.33 most significantly draws together Isa. 8.14 with 28.16. The stone of stumbling and the rock of offence are thus connected with the valuable, choice and honourable cornerstone laid for the foundation of Zion which will not disappoint the believer.[40] The stone of offence is therefore for Paul none other than that laid as the foundation of the new temple. Psalm 118.12, Isa. 8.14 and 28.16 are all brought together in I Peter 2.4–8 to form a pattern of testimonies to the new teaching. Men stumble on this rock and are offended by it because it replaces the foundation on which they have built their culture and their faith in the past. The idea of this rock which is to replace the old as the foundation of the new order is given most explicit expression in Matt. 16.18.

This verse has been the centre of denominational debate through a long period of the church's history and this has tended to obscure its fundamental message. The rock mentioned has been identified with Peter, with faith in Christ and with Christ himself. All these interpretations are conceivable. The text is probably done most justice, however, when room is made for all three. The saying is clearly a play upon words. The name Peter was probably derived from the Greek word *petros*, meaning a fragment of *petra* or rock. If this was the case, then the text asserts that Christ himself is the rock on which the church is to be built, but that Peter, by virtue of his faith in Jesus, has become one with that rock, and so shares with Christ a part in being the foundation of the new temple. These considerations, however, must be subordinated to the main burden of the text. A new rock is found to replace the *Eben Shetiyah*. The church built upon it is immediately invested with the inviolability attributed to the temple[41] and opposed like Zion to Hades.

That the rock should have been identified with Jesus, with faith in him or even with Peter, is not altogether a new departure. The demythologization accomplished by the prophets had gone so far that the rock of the myth could be equated not only with Yahweh but also with his people.[42] The Christian gospel here therefore merely continues a usage which is also taken up in rabbinic literature. There the patriarchs could also be called the 'pillars of the earth', and the rock of foundation over the *tehōm*, because they embodied a stability lacking in the wicked.[43] Abraham in particular came to be spoken of as the rock found and chosen by God to become the foundation of the world.[44] Matthew 16.18 has attributed just such a character and role to Peter by virtue of his faith in Christ.[45] Jesus looked among his followers for those who could form the foundation of the new earth over the threats of nihilism, and in Peter discovered one whom he could call upon to walk on the water. Jesus was himself rejected as the stone and was a rock on which many of his people stumbled, but the faith of the first Christians asserted that nevertheless he was chosen by God to be the foundation and the chief corner-stone of the new temple with his disciples sharing in his work as pillars of the new community.[46] And with the building of the new temple, creation was renewed. Christ and his apostles were the base on which a new order was being built.

THE PLACE OF THE NEW CREATION

It was the function of the world navel to denote the place at which creation had begun and where it is renewed. The Jews had identified this place with Jerusalem, and there are some indications that this notion was shared by the evangelists,

especially by Luke and John. If this was the case, then certain
passages in their writings gain in significance and one of the
outstanding problems of contemporary gospel exegesis may be
at least in part explained.

In Mark the death of Christ in Jerusalem already constituted
the end of the world.[47] In Matthew this idea is further suggested
by the shaking of the earth and the resurrection of the dead.[48]
From that moment the world is being made anew and it begins
in Jerusalem. In Luke and John the ascension and the gift of the
Spirit follow necessarily on the resurrection of Christ, and in
both gospels these events which bring the new world into being
are associated most specifically with the holy city of Judaea.

For many years the discrepancy between the gospel accounts
of the resurrection appearances has been the cause of much
scholarly debate. In Mark the resurrection itself takes place in
Jerusalem, but the narrative immediately points away from the
holy city in Galilee. Mark says that the disciples will see the
risen Christ to Galilee, and both Matthew and John describe
an appearance there. This Galilean tradition is completely
rejected in Luke's gospel, while John seems to end with the
record of appearances in Jerusalem at John 20.31, ch. 21 standing as a postscript furnishing the gospel with a second ending.
There were clearly two traditions, a Jerusalem and a Galilean,
and Luke's emendation of Mark's text makes reconciliation
between them virtually impossible.[49] According to Luke, the
disciples are not sent into Galilee to meet the risen Christ but
told to remain in Jerusalem until the Spirit is given. Attempts
have been made to resolve the problem by historical criticism,
but with little success. An approach in theological or mythological terms may at least explain the Jerusalem tradition.

It is possible that an early Christian tradition which associated the appearances of the risen Jesus with the coming of the
eschaton in Galilee[50] was replaced by another which drew its
inspiration from the mythological cosmography of Jerusalem.
By keeping the disciples in Jerusalem, Luke ensures that the
post-resurrection events all take place at the navel of the earth,
where the new creation was expected to begin. Both his gospel
and Acts are dominated by the sacred city.[51] This is most easily
explicable on the assumption that Luke wished to retain the
symbolism attached to the city in presenting Christ as the

creator of a new world. It may well be that he did not record
the saying about throwing the mountain into the sea, because
he wished to retain the value of Zion in his scheme. Jerusalem
is to remain the centre of the new creation as it was of the old.[52]
It is here that the divine nourishment of the Spirit, which vivi-
fies the men of the new creation, is given and distributed
throughout the world.

The identification of Jerusalem as the place at which the
first man of the old creation was made is found in rabbinic
literature. According to *Gen. R.* 14.8 Adam was created 'from
the place of his atonement'. *Mid. Tel.* Ps. 92.6 also explains that
Adam was taken from Mount Moriah at his creation and returned there after being expelled from Eden, to the place where
the temple was subsequently built. If this represents the continuation of a more ancient tradition, the Lukan and Johannine
stories of the gift of the Spirit were aptly located in Jerusalem.

Acts 2.2–4 makes use of symbolism derived from the Hebrew
creation myth of Genesis. As the great wind of God had once
stirred the primeval ocean and brought the old creation into
being, so now it comes from heaven to fill the house where the
apostles are, engendering the new creation. As God had once
breathed into the work of his hands and made Adam a living
spirit, so now the breath of God fills each of the disciples so that
they are able by speaking with tongues to show that they have
been born anew.

The continuity of Johannine symbolism with that used in the
Hebrew and other ancient myths is even more apparent. Early
in his gospel John had introduced the idea of the new birth
and made use of the imagery of the wind of creation.[53] Later,
he tells how Jesus restored the sight of a blind man in a manner
reminiscent of the story of Adam being made from the dust of
the earth.[54] The creation of Adam as given in Gen. 2.7 finds its
closest parallel, however, in John 20.22.[55] Just as Yahweh
breathed life into Adam, so the risen Christ breathes the Spirit
into his disciples. Christ has communicated his selfhood to the
disciples that he might be with them for ever.[56] John suggests
that a new race of men is being created in Jerusalem by the
infusion of breath from the risen Christ. The new creation has
begun where for the Jew it had begun in primordial time, in the
holy city at the very centre of the world.

THE NEW BODY

Finally, we must notice that the concept of the new community as the body of Christ may owe something to the ancient animistic notion of the universe, and in particular to the way this had influenced the portrayal of the first man.

Although the animistic concept of the world as a gigantic human being does not figure in the creation account of Genesis, it does appear to have been known in Old Testament times. It survives in the anthropomorphization of nature such as we find in Hebraic poetry,[57] as well as in the concept of the navel just examined. It is particularly noteworthy in Ps. 90.2, which W. Eichrodt interprets as meaning that 'the earth comes forth from the travail of a mighty primal being, and the mountains are born',[58] thus reflecting the myth of the cosmic or primal Man. The idea may also lie behind the description of Adam in the *Wisdom of Solomon* 10.1 as the 'father of the cosmos'. From the end of the first century onwards it is evident that the myth of the cosmic Man had begun to play a regular role in the depiction of Adam. He is described as having been of gigantic size, so that he stretched from one end of the earth to the other and from earth to heaven.[59] *Gen. R.* 8.1 says that Adam was 'a lifeless mass extending from one end of the world to the other'. This idea appears as part of the general tendency to exalt the person of the first man, but the form which it takes in this instance is hardly explicable except as a renewal of the idea of cosmic Man whose body is co-extensive with the earth and the heavens.[60]

This concept may also lie behind the frequent rabbinic references to Adam having been made from various parts of the cosmos. Adam is said in *Sanhedrin* 38a–b to have been representative of all men, because the dust from which he was made had been taken from places all over the world. Even more suggestive is the description of Adam's creation given in II Enoch 30.8. Here it is said that his flesh was taken from the earth, his blood from the dew, his eyes from the sun, his bones from the stones, his intelligence from the swiftness of angels and from cloud, his veins and hair from the grass and his soul from the breath and wind of God. This account has a remarkable similarity to the concept of the *purusha* in the mythology of ancient

India, which may be regarded as having given classic expression to the cosmic Man idea.[61] In both cases the various parts of the primal Man correspond to elements within the cosmos. It is noteworthy, however, that in the Judaic version the order of events has been reversed. Adam is made from the natural elements, whereas in the Indian myth the body of the primal Man is dismembered and its parts transformed into them. In this way the rabbinic tradition tended to eliminate the pantheism to which the myth in its more original form could give rise when translated into the conceptual language of theology.

Finally, we must note that the concept of Adam as a microcosm remained in the idea that the whole cosmos was involved in his fall and was therefore the object of the Messiah's redemptive activity.[62]

There are one or two pointers to the possibility that this complex of ideas may have played a part in early Christian thought. It certainly seems to have influenced the author of the *Gospel of Peter*, who relates that the stature of the resurrected Christ was such that he reached to the heavens.[63] By the use of this mythological symbolism it appears to be suggested that the risen Christ has regained the height lost by Adam at his fall, and so is the cosmic Adam of the new creation. The canonical literature does not contain such an overtly mythological form of the concept, but it may lie behind certain metaphorical expressions used. Paul clearly thought of the salvation wrought by Christ in cosmic terms. At Rom. 8.22 he is even prepared to speak of the whole creation as though it were capable of passion, awaiting the glory to come. In I Cor. 15.22,45 he speaks of the first Adam as one in whom all die, and of Christ as the second Adam in whom all will be made alive. This language is suggestive of the cosmic Man concept. Adam is a figure in whom all men can be said to exist. Similarly, Christ is to be one in whom all may find life. The gospels never speak of Christ as the second Adam in so direct a manner, but we have seen that the concept is often just beneath the surface. Similarly, they do not indulge in the kind of mythological symbolism favoured by the *Gospel of Peter*. On the other hand, the idea of the cosmic Man is suggested by one of the themes which they share with the Pauline epistles. They tell how the earthly body of Jesus was slain in order that through the resurrection a new body of Christ would come into being. This is a body which is not restricted to time and space. It is at least potentially co-extensive with mankind. This body is the new temple or church made up of those who are nourished on the flesh and blood of the crucified. From him they receive their life and in him they live.[64] In these metaphors it is possible to see an adaptation of the ancient myth of the cosmic Man. It had originally been a cosmological and animistic myth. Now its terminology serves the interests of Christian soteriology. What had once been used to characterize the physical constitution of the cosmos was now used of spiritual renewal

Although imaginative extravagances have been constantly resisted, it is clear that the two fundamental images used in the mythological description of the cosmos have been of significant importance in the New Testament. They provided the basic metaphors in which the new creation wrought by Christ could be given expression. He laid and was the foundation of a new cosmos. He brought into being a new body into which he breathed the Spirit of God at the price of his own life. By his death at the old centre, he brought its claims to an end and himself became the navel through whom the nourishment of the divine life poured into the world born anew.

NOTES

1. Isa. 65.17f.; Jub. 1.29.
2. II Bar. 32.1–6; 44.5,7,12.
3. *Taanith* 10a.
4. *Yoma* 54b.
5. *Mid. Tel.* Ps. 50.1.
6. Wensinck, op. cit., p.xi.
7. Stadelmann, op. cit., p.149.
8. Stadelmann, op. cit., pp.147f.
9. Burrows, op. cit., p.51.
10. Cf. Jub. 8.12.
11. *Num. R.* 1.4.
12. Clem. Alex., *Strom.* V, 6.
13. Wensinck, op. cit., p.19.
14. *Gen. R.* 39.8; see Freedman and Simon, op. cit., Vol. I, p.317, nn. 1 and 2.

15. See Goodenough, op. cit., Vol. II, pp.24f.; Vol. III, illus. no. 781.
16. See Clements, op. cit., p.61; Every, op. cit., p.52.
17. A. C. Bouquet, 'A Note on the Dome of the Rock', *Theology* LIX, 1956, pp.415–8; cf. Butterworth, op. cit., pp.19ff.
18. II Sam. 22.16; Job 38.4–6; Pss. 102.25; 104.5; Isa. 48.13; 51.13, 16; Micah 6.2; Zech. 12.1.
19. *Yoma* 54b; cf. Wensinck, op. cit., p.2; Ginzberg, op. cit., pp.5f.
20. Ps. 87.1; Isa. 28.16; 44.28; Lam. 4.11; *Mid. Tel.* Ps. 11.2; 87.3.
21. Pss. 29.10; 93; Prov. 8.29; *Gen. R.* 33.1; *Ex. R.* 15.7; *Pirke de R. Eliezer*, ch. 10; cf. *Sukkah* 53a.
22. Isa. 51.16.
23. Ezra 3.10–13; Job. 38.4–7.
24. *Gen. R.* 3.9; cf. 2.5.
25. Cf. Wensinck, op. cit., p.41.
26. Childs, op. cit., p.86.
27. Jer. 51.24–26.
28. E.g. II Sam. 22.2f.; Pss. 31.3; 42.9.
29. Matt. 5.14.
30. Pap. Ox. I, lines 37–42.
31. Cf. I Cor. 13.2.
32. A. E. J. Rawlinson, *St Mark*, Methuen 1925, p.158; Taylor, op. cit., p.467.
33. Cf. Manson, *Jesus the Messiah*, pp.29f., who refers it to the Mount of Olives, connecting the saying with Zech. 14.4.
34. See p. 276 below.
35. See Hooke, *Alpha and Omega*, p. 197.
36. J. Jeremias, '*Lithos*', *Theological Dictionary of the New Testament*, ed. Kittel and Friedrich, Vol. IV, pp.274f.
37. Luke 20.18.
38. Jeremias, '*Lithos*' etc., pp.275,281.
39. See N. W. Porteous, *Daniel*, SCM Press 1965, p.50.
40. See LXX of Isa. 28.16; *Acts of Peter* 24.
41. Ps. 46.5; 48.2,8.
42. Isa. 51.16; cf. Gen. 49.24; Deut. 32.3,15,30,31; Qumran, *Community Rule*, V, 8.
43. *Ex. R.* 15.7; cf. *Hagigah* 12b; *Mid. Tel.* Ps. 34.1.
44. *Mid. Tel.* Ps. 53.2. Compare the use of temple foundation symbolism in the Qumran literature, see Gärtner, op. cit., pp.26f.
45. Cf. O. Cullmann, '*Petra*', *Theological Dictionary of the New Testament*, ed. Kittel and Friedrich, Vol. VI, p.96.
46. Acts 4.11; I Cor. 3.11–17; Gal. 2.9; Eph. 2.20f.; I Peter 2.4–8; Rev. 3.12.
47. See pp.60,77 above.
48. See *Gen. R.* 74.1; 96.5; cf. I Thess. 4.16. The rising of men from the ground is r miniscent of some creation myths, see Wales, op. cit., p.13.
49 Mark 16.7; Luke 24.6; cf. 24.49.
50. See Grant, op. cit., pp.125–47.
51. Flender, op. cit., pp.107f.

52. Acts 2.46; 3.1,3,8; 5.20f., 25,42; 9.27f.; 15.2,22ff.

53. John 3.3–8.

54. See further p.290 below.

55. Cf. Wisd. 15.11; II (4) Esd. 3.5.

56. For breath as a means of communicating the self see Gaster, *Myth, Legend and Custom in the Old Testament*, p.19; Philo, *De Specialibus Legibus* IV, 123.

57. Job 38.8.

58. Eichrodt, op. cit., Vol. II, p.115 n. 1. Eichrodt is, however, concerned to argue that such mythology 'is of no consequence for Israel's understanding of the world', p.115; cf. p.114 n. 4.

59. *Hagigah* 12a; *Sanhedrin* 38b; *Gen. R.* 12.6; 14.8; 19.9; 21.3; 24.2; cf. Rappoport, op. cit., Vol. I, pp.8f.

60. See *Gen. R.* 2.3; 14.8.

61. See Mowinckel, *He That Cometh*, p.423; R. C. Zaehner, *The Dawn and Twilight of Zoroastrianism*, Weidenfeld and Nicolson 1961, p.259.

62. Jub. 3.25,28; cf. II (4) Esd. 7.29, 31f.; II Bar. 23.4; *Sanhedrin* 4.5; 38a; *Gen. R.* 23.6; Ginzberg, op. cit., pp.17,26.

63. *Gospel of Peter* 10.40; cf. Hippolytus, *Ref.* IX, 13,1–3; Epiphanius, *Haer.* XXX, 17.7.

64. Matt. 26.61; Mark 14.58; John 2.21; 6.51ff.; Rom. 12.4; I Cor. 3.16; 6.19; 10.16f.; II Cor. 6.16; Eph. 1.22; 4.15f.; 5.23; Col. 1.18.

PART FOUR

Paradise

14 Paradise Lost and Regained

THE INACCESSIBLE EDEN

Inextricably linked in Hebrew mythology with the story of creation was that of the garden of Eden. This is a typical primordial tale, speaking of that which once was in order to express a belief about what should be. In the garden, Adam and Eve live in the state which the creator had intended. The abundance of nature provided for their needs and God was their intimate companion. The story progresses speedily, however, towards disaster. Through disobedience and the loss of innocence Adam and Eve lose their idyllic paradise. This story of apparently irreparable loss thus sets forth man's condition in the world, in which he is alienated from that for which his whole being craves. From the convictions born out of the depths of man's own awareness of the character of his existence comes a story which lays bare the tragedy of the human situation. He is placed under sentence of hard labour, pain and death. He is excluded from the garden and the completion of his being.

In order to represent the idea that what man craves is always just beyond his grasp, two types of symbolic complex were employed. In one, Eden remains on earth and the primordial pair are driven out of it. In the other, paradise itself is taken away from the earth to heaven, leaving man in a world entirely bereft of its treasures.

In the first of these symbolic schemes the inaccessibility of paradise was first of all set forth under the imagery of closed gates. When Adam and Eve are driven out into the wilderness, the gates of Eden are closed shut behind them and cherubim are placed as sentinels armed with swords to prevent man regaining entry.[1] These angelic weapons are compared by Gaster with the revolving, spiked portcullis at the entrance to the

castle of the underworld in Celtic romances.[2] Certainly the
Genesis narrative shares a common motif with other traditions.
It is part of a virtually universal recognition that man in this
life is separated from the realms beyond by a terrible divide.

The inaccessibility of paradise was also ensured by locating
it on the summit of the holy mountain at a fabulous distance
from the habitations of mankind.[3] This idea appears in a number of cultures. In the Muslim tradition, for example, it was
said to be on the top of a jacinth mountain in the east. In the
mythology underlying Mithraism it was probably understood
originally to have been situated at the summit of Mount
Hara.[4] In Hebrew literature, paradise is also located on a mountain. In some cases it appears, moreover, to be in the north.
The book of Genesis is ambiguous, but may be understood as
indicating that Eden lay in a northerly direction.[5] In some
passages of the book of Enoch it is in the east, but in many
others it is to be found among the mountains in the north.[6]
When we remember that the mountain of God was thought of
as being situated in the far north even in prophetic times, it is
fairly clear that these passages reflect a tradition which placed
paradise on the summit of the polar mountain. The inaccessibility of paradise was thus guaranteed by making it one with the
distant mountainous dwelling of the Most High.

The identification of paradise with the summit of the holy
mountain led eventually to a further development which made
its inaccessibility even more sure. The book of Ezekiel seems to
represent a transitionary stage in this process. Eden is described
in terms which derive from the concept of the mountain paradise.[7] On the other hand the idea of a heavenly paradise
appears to intrude on the scene. The primordial man is not
only on the heights of the sacred mountain, but walks among
the stars.[8] This transition was easily made, for the central
mountain was said to reach up into heaven.[9] Eventually the two
ideas were separated, and later apocalyptic literature tended
to make prominent use of the idea of a heavenly paradise.[10]
This development may have been assisted, as A. S. Rappoport
suggested, by Persian, Egyptian and Greek influence,[11] but the
original idea of the paradisal mountain whose tip penetrated
the clouds was more than an adequate basis for it. In mythological terms paradise had been lifted from earth to heaven,[12]

and its inviolability to man's profanation made yet more certain. As the doctrine of divine transcendence came to be increasingly emphasized, paradise was further removed from the world of men. It was located far above the earth in the third heaven.[13]

The old idea of an earthly Eden, however, was not allowed to disappear. The mythological cosmography of late Judaism had to reflect not only the sense of God's absence but also the experience of his presence. The fullness of God's gifts might be denied to man, but in some measure they were to be found on the earth. There grew up, therefore, the notion of two Edens, one above and the other below. The heavenly paradise was clearly a copy of that which had once been thought of as lying on the mountain of earth. In it were the tree, the waters of life and the food of immortality.[14] Even in heaven, Eden was provided with gates.[15] And so the symbolism of Eden was fitted into the developing scheme of heavenly counterparts for earthly things. In this way the old and the new traditions were brought into a rational relationship with one another. Paradise above stood directly over the garden of Eden below.[16] As one was to be found at the navel of heaven, the other would be found at the navel of earth.[17] Both were, however, totally inaccessible to man in this life. There was only one way in which either paradise might be reached. Only through death might man attain to the tree of life.

When a remote, earthly Eden had been pictured, the journey to it was said to involve a passage through various hazards. In II (4) Esdras, for example, the Son of Man comes from a distant land which is only reached by travelling underground for a year and a half.[18] Josephus records that the Essenes thought that Eden lay 'beyond the ocean'.[19] In these passages we can recognize two recurring symbols of death. As the dead were buried beneath the ground, so it was a widespread idea that they had to undertake a netherworld journey. The crossing other midrashic traditions in which Adam is said to have been While it is not impossible that J. Jeremias may be correct in interpreting Josephus to mean that the Essenes thought of paradise as lying in the west beyond the Mediterranean, it is likely that the ocean here reflects the ancient image of death as a passage on or through the waters.[20] The notion is as old as

the Gilgamesh epic and the Greek myth of the Styx. When a
heavenly paradise was envisaged, on the other hand, it was
natural that the death of the faithful should be spoken of as
an ascent. In special cases, the body was held to have ascended,
as in the case of Elijah. In other cases, later Judaism thought
only of their souls coming to rest in the heavenly garden of the
righteous.[21] But while mythological cosmography in one form or
the other had placed paradisal life beyond the reach of mortal
man, there were nevertheless means whereby its delights
might be anticipated.

THE FORETASTE OF PARADISE

The inaccessibility of paradise was in part overcome by the
ability of man to reach a place which could function as the
mountain of God. For the Hebrew, Jerusalem and its temple was
such a place.

The functional identification of Zion with the sacred mountain made it possible for the Hebrew to see in it Eden in their
midst.[22] This may be seen in the regulations which governed
the use of this sacred place, in the symbolism employed in its
architecture and in the traditions which were developed about
it.

Because Jerusalem and its temple were regarded as the place
of life in the midst of a world of decay, all that was connected
with death in the Hebrew mind was excluded. The restrictions
placed on the presence of the leper, the sick and the dead applied with particular force to Jerusalem and the temple
mount.[23] Like Eden, the temple was a holy place in which
nothing defiling was permitted.[24] The garden was indeed 'the
holy of holies'.[25]

Embodied in the decoration of the temple were symbols
which were suggestive of paradise. Here the palm and the
pomegranate represented the gift of life, and upon the doors of
the shrine the worshipper saw cherubim guarding the entrance
to the architectural representation as they were said to have
stood sentry over the entrance to its primordial archetype.[26] It
is likely, moreover, that Jerusalem and its temple were made
to reflect the notion that both Eden and heaven were rectangu-
lar in shape, thus having four sides facing towards the four

quarters of the compass.[27] This symbolism was used to indicate that a holy place lay at the centre of the world, and is
found in some of the holy places excavated at Petra, and in the
Dome of the Rock which had four doors set to the four points.[28]
This basic idea is represented in the temple of Solomon. Twelve
oxen supported the great sea and were divided into groups of
three, each group to face one of the four quarters.[29]

Of the traditions developed about Jerusalem, it may be noted
first that Jerusalem was sometimes invested in Old Testament
times with the impregnability ascribed to paradise.[30] What was
intended in the cultus to represent a spiritual fact was turned
into a political conviction. Although of a somewhat confusing
nature, the developing tradition in late Judaism concerning the
location of Eden in or near Jerusalem is also of some importance. By this time the sacramental symbolism of the Jerusalem
area is obscured by a tendency to identify it geographically
with the region in which Eden was situated. It would seem that
the author of II Bar. 4.3 thought of the temple as having been
located in paradise, for Adam loses the first along with the
second. In rabbinic tradition, however, a distinction between
the temple and Eden is usually maintained, although they are
brought into the closest possible relationship with each other.
Mid. Tel. Ps. 146.9 says that 'He decrees that all, the righteous
and the wicked, should go up to Jerusalem and to the Garden
of Eden, for the same way leads to both places, and both the
righteous and the wicked come to Jerusalem. As soon as they
arrive there, the Holy One, blessed be He, brings the righteous
into the Garden of Eden; but He twists the way of the wicked
and leads them onto the road to Gehenna.' Underlying this
passage is undoubtedly the derivation of the Hebrew Gehenna
from the valley of Gehinnom adjoining Jerusalem. In view of
this, it is likely that Eden is here associated with another site
nearby. This is identified as the Mount of Olives in *Gen. R.* 33.6.
and *Lev. R.* 31.10, which speak of Noah's dove having brought
her olive leaf back from this place. This throws further light on
other midrashic traditions in which Adam is said to have been
made from the ground on which the temple was subsequently
built, to have been moved to the garden of Eden and then back
again to the place of his creation after the fall.[31] In this rabbinic
scheme all the places mentioned in the Eden story are to be

found in or near the mount of the temple. The two journeys of
Adam, therefore, covered very little ground. They took him
from Zion to Olivet and back again.

It would appear, therefore, that the association of Jerusalem
with the primeval paradise was maintained in one form or another over a very long period of Jewish thought. While the
temple stood, the Jew was continuously reminded of the paradise he had lost through his sin, and given in cultic form something of its blessedness. When the temple had been destroyed, he
might look forward to its restoration when what had been
merely represented by it would become a reality.

THE ESCHATOLOGICAL PROMISE

From the time of Isaiah onwards, it became customary to
describe the reign of the coming king in terms derived from the
paradise myth.[32] In the later prophets the idea of an eschatological Eden becomes more explicit, and it plays a prominent
part in the apocalyptic writers.[33] In rabbinic literature, the
mundane Messianic age is usually distinguished from the paradisal world to come, but even the first of these is described in the
symbolism of the Eden myth.[34]

After the idea of Eden's translation into heaven had been
developed, it was inevitable that the eschaton should be pictured as a time when paradise should descend from heaven. The
theory of heavenly counterparts had led to the notion of a
heavenly Jerusalem[35] which is virtually identified with the
heavenly Eden. The descent of paradise, therefore, would come
as the descent of the new and paradisal Jerusalem.[36] The tree of
life will be planted in its temple.[37]

> And the saints shall rest in Eden,
> And in the New Jerusalem shall the righteous rejoice.[38]

This concept was clearly developed by the middle of the second
century BC, and may have emerged even earlier.[39] At all events,
it was a well-established idea by New Testament times.[40] In
Jerusalem, the Jew might confidently wait for the re-opening of
paradise.

OLD AND NEW IDEAS OF PARADISE IN THE GOSPELS

In many respects Jesus and his disciples appear to have shared the basic notions of contemporary Judaic thought concerning paradise. Jesus had no doubt been familiar with the biblical story from childhood and he accepts its authority in his teaching.[41] Allusions to the symbolism of paradise are not, however, restricted to that found in Genesis. From the evidence of the gospels, it is likely that Jesus and the evangelists were also familiar with at least some of the ideas which had grown up around it in later Jewish thought.

Despite a constant concern for life within this world, this is never allowed to obscure the belief that man's present life is set within a larger context than that bounded by birth and death. Jesus confidently looks towards the enjoyment of paradise beyond the grave.[42] The promise made by Jesus to the thief on the cross is most explicit evidence of a belief in the immediate enjoyment of paradise after death, and shows, moreover, that the now common belief in a heavenly paradise had been accepted.[43] The story of Eden was not merely a tale of primordial times, but of vital significance for the hope on which the life of faith was founded. It was a hope which entailed the renunciation of a life founded on the possession of earthly goods, and demanded a righteousness exceeding that of the scribes and Pharisees.[44] The concept of righteousness was enriched and purified of debasing elements, so that many Jews were shocked by the radicalism of Jesus' demand, but this was only an extension of their own ethical outlook. Jesus declared the grace of God to the sinner, but only on condition that his sin came to an end.[45] In the life to come there was no room for the man or woman who persisted in the sin of Adam.

The word paradise rarely occurs, because it is often replaced by the kingdom of God or of heaven. That this is the case is apparent from the fact that the symbols used in speaking of this kingdom are frequently those which are generally associated with the paradise myth. It is not always made clear whether the kingdom so spoken of is gained at death or in the eschaton, but the imagery in either case is frequently derived from the concept of paradise. In Mark 9.43–48 the fate of the wicked is to be thrown into the unquenchable fire of Gehenna, while the righteous enter into the kingdom. In this passage we have exactly the same sort of contrast which rabbinic literature frequently makes between Gehenna and paradise, represented respectively by the valley of Hinnom where the fires of Moloch had once burned, and the Mount of Olives unsubmerged by the flood. The kingdom is clearly understood to be at the centre, as was paradise. To it come the living and the dead from the four winds.[46] Corruption has no place in the kingdom at Luke 12.33. This is an idea which receives constant expression with regard to paradise, and at Luke 20.36 another saying of Jesus is recorded which exactly reflects this paradisal tradition.[47] In the resurrection he declares that men and women will not die any more, but will be like angels. They will gain the life forfeited by Adam and regain their status as sons of God. Two other features of the developed Adamic myth also appear in descriptions of the kingdom to come. Jesus tells his disciples that both he and they will be raised to the royal status once enjoyed by primeval man,[48] and that like Adam, the righteous will shine as the sun in the Father's kingdom.[49] The hope expressed in the literature of Qumran is also found here that 'all the glory of Adam shall be theirs'.[50] While the wicked will be cast into outer darkness, the righteous will enjoy the Adamic exaltation and the primordial light reserved for them.[51]

On the other hand, the paradisal tradition is also used in new ways in the gospels. 'The new thing as compared with the Old Testament and later Judaism, however, is the fact that the message of the Gospels goes much further when it says that the return of Paradise has come already with the coming of Jesus.'[52] In the life and work of Jesus the hoped-for miracle had come. Jesus is shown as one who in himself is the epitome of paradisal blessing and its bountiful bestower. This is shown in a variety of ways, but most prominently in the healing ministry attributed to him.

The prophets had spoken of a Messianic age in which the lame would walk, the deaf would hear, the blind see and the lepers be cleansed, and so it is of course correct to see in Jesus' ministry the fulfilment of these prophetic hopes. But these prophecies were picturing the restoration of paradise. Indeed, the basic concept of the garden of Eden was of a place in which all things were good, and life could be lived without thought of death or disease.[53] When Jesus is presented as one who restores men to health, it is clear, therefore, that he is seen as one who restores the paradisal situation. In doing this he had overcome the gulf which normally separated man from the source of life and healing. He had opened the gates of paradise. In the gospels, this notion of the renewed accessibility of the source of life is given prominent expression by emphasis on the symbolism of physical contact.

The idea that divine power could flow through contact with a sacred thing or person was common in Hebraic thought and widespread among other peoples. The sources of such power were regarded as holy and debarred from profane contact. In the Hebrew tradition, there are many instances of this, but most are associated in some way with the concept of the holy mountain. In the wilderness Mount Sinai is regarded as sacred and may not be trodden upon or touched by the people. Only Moses is allowed to ascend its height to speak with God.[54] The same pattern of thought was also applied to Mount Zion and to the temple which it sanctified. The mount itself was set about with numerous restrictions, so that its sacrality should remain undefiled. Only one person was allowed to ascend the mount and to enter the innermost shrine, the holy of holies. And when he did so, the high priest himself partook of the sanctity of the place and became untouchable.[55] Thus both Mount Sinai and Mount Zion were made inviolate, like their mythological archetype, the garden of Eden.[56] The summit of the first and the holy of holies on the second were the cultic equivalent of the centre of the garden, and denoted the place from which the life and power of God flowed into the world.[57] In the New Testament, however, the alienation of man from God represented by this cultic structure was held to have been destroyed by Christ. What had been untouchable became touchable in the teacher from Galilee. In the Epistle to the Hebrews, particular attention is paid to this. The author contrasts the untouchability of the mountain and of the high priest with the heavenly Zion and its Christ who may be touched with the infirmities of men.[58] It is likely, therefore, that the references in the gospels to the availability of Jesus to physical contact should also be seen against this background.

Time and again the synoptists stress the fact that Jesus allowed himself to come into contact with the leper, the blind and the possessed.[59] This is not the result of a desire to do away with petty ritual restrictions, but is intended to put forward a vital element of the Christian view of Christ's work. These incidents show that Jesus is the source of healing and life from which Adam and Eve had been debarred by their sin. He is the one who has life in himself, life which he freely bestows on others. Men and women seek contact with his person or his clothes because they recognize that this is so.[60] One example of such an act is given in some detail by the synoptists in order that the reader should be fully aware of this. A woman suffering from internal bleeding seeks Jesus out and surreptitiously touches the hem of his garment in order that she might be healed. When this is done, Jesus is said to have felt the life-power flowing out of him and demands to know who has touched him.[61] When she makes herself known, Jesus assures her that her faith has made her whole, but the story also makes it plain that this could only have happened because Jesus is in his person the source of healing power. That source of divine healing which had been cut off from man was now to be found among the people, as Jesus exposed himself to their immediate contact.

The synoptists speak of such healing taking place during Jesus' earthly life, but there are grounds for thinking that John wished to indicate that Jesus only becomes the touchable source of life after his ascension. He avoids the word *haptomai*, constantly used by the synoptists, until the end of his gospel. His only use of the word occurs then in Jesus' command to Mary Magdalene, that she must not touch him because he is ascending to the Father.[62] Later, however, Jesus invites Thomas to feel his wounds, presumably because his ascension is now accomplished.[63] If we take Hebrews as our guide here, this sequence may be read as suggesting that Jesus is like the high priest who ascends the mount to enter the Holy of Holies. But the ascent of Jesus is not to the earthly but to the heavenly temple and to the heavenly paradise. In the course of his ascension, Jesus is untouchable as was the high priest, but once his exaltation is complete, Jesus becomes available to human contact, for he has overcome the barrier between man and the divine source of life. What had been merely a symbolic act becomes in Jesus a veritable fact. He has entered paradise and thrown open its gates to men. John may well have been suggesting that his story was to be understood in the light of the imagery of paradise when he makes the conversation with Mary take place in a garden. Hippolytus saw an intended parallel here between the command of Jesus to Mary and Eve being driven from the tree of life.[64] Whether or not the garden is understood in this way, however, John has clearly made the point that until the ascension of Christ the possession of Eden is not yet fully vouchsafed to men.

The idea that paradise is only restored to man through the death and resurrection of Christ may also be present in the way Luke and John deal with another of the features regularly associated with it. As Jesus is presented as offering the gift of life in his ministry in anticipation of the resurrection, so also these evangelists show him as one who would give the world the peace which it had lacked since man had first disrupted nature and community by his disobedience. The notion of a return to that peace which had once existed between men and nations in primordial times was a familiar feature of the eschatological hope. It is given eloquent expression in Isa. 11.6–9, where the prophet says that then men would be at peace not only with one another on God's holy mountain but with the animal kingdom as well.[65] The author of the *Protevangelium of James* saw in Christ's coming a return to this paradisal situation. At the birth of Christ there is 'complete quietness and rest in nature and mankind'.[66] Luke had already moved towards a partial expression of this idea. Zacharias is said to have prophesied that the Baptist would prepare the way of him who will guide men into the way of peace, and angels proclaim the coming of that peace at the birth of Jesus.[67] Luke goes on, however, to show that the peace offered by the Messiah was rejected by his people. Jerusalem does not recognize that which belongs to its peace, so that the intended ministry of peace is replaced by that of the sword.[68] And this sword falls first upon the peace-bringer himself. Only through the triumph over death can the heavenly peace eventually come. Not all our manuscripts include a reference to this gift of peace at Luke 24.36, but without it the theme pursued in the gospel remains incomplete.

In the Gospel of John we are left in no doubt that the gift of peace is made by Christ after his resurrection. In this gospel, the role played by Jerusalem in the Lukan scheme is replaced in part by 'the world'. For Jesus and his disciples the world grants only tribulation, but they can be of good cheer, for Jesus has overcome the world.[69] In consequence, Jesus can unequivocally bestow the blessing of peace in a threefold reiteration of the Hebrew greeting.[70] By his resurrection and ascension, the Christ is enabled to fulfil the hope for that peace which the world cannot attain.[71] It belongs to the paradisal realm in which man is one with God and with his world.

We have now noted two ways in which the gospel writers indicated their belief that in Jesus the paradisal age had arrived. In him the inaccessible had been made accessible. Men had seen and handled the Word who was also the life of men.[72] He had restored their bodies and so brought the healing properties of Eden into the midst of men. Through his death on the cross he had also achieved for them the gift of eternal and divine peace. There were, however, many other aspects of the Hebraic hope which can be most conveniently considered in connection with the major paradisal symbols of the tree, the rivers and the banquet.

NOTES

1. Gen. 3.24.
2. Gaster, *Myth, Legend and Custom in the Old Testament*, pp.48f.
3. See A. Jeremias, op. cit., Vol. I, p.205; Wensinck, op. cit., p.14.
4. See I. Gershevitch, *The Avestan Hymn to Mithra*, Cambridge University Press 1967, pp.99,204.
5. Jacob, op. cit., p.198; G. von Rad, *Genesis*, SCM Press ²1963, pp.77,96.
6. I Enoch 32.1,3; 61.1; 70.3; 77.3; cf. Gaster, *Thespis*, p. 181 note.
7. Ezek. 28.13f.
8. See H. G. May, 'The King in the Garden of Eden', *Israel's Prophetic Heritage*, ed. Anderson and Harrelson, p.170.
9. I Enoch 18.8; cf. 25.3.
10. E.g. II (4) Esd. 4.8; Apoc. Moses 37.5.
11. Rappoport, op. cit., Vol. I, p.110.
12. II Baruch 4.3.
13. II Enoch 8.1ff.
14. Ps. 78.23f.; II Enoch 8.2–5.

15. I Enoch 9.2; II Enoch 13; 14; III Bar. 6.13; cf. II (4) Esd. 8.52; Test. Levi 18.10.

16. II Enoch 8.5f.

17. Cf. Wensinck, op. cit., p.47.

18. II (4) Esd. 13.12,39ff.; see Mowinckel, *He That Cometh*, pp.381f.

19. Josephus, *War* II, 8.11.

20. J. Jeremias, *'Paradeisos'*, *Theological Dictionary of the New Testament*, ed. Kittel and Friedrich, Vol. V, p.768 n. 28.

21. Cf. I Enoch 9.10; 22.3.

22. Childs, op. cit., p.88. Note how this idea appears to be represented in the Qumran literature, see Gärtner, op. cit., pp.28f.

23. *Kelim* 1.6–9.

24. II Chron. 23.19; Isa. 35.8; Ezek. 44.9.

25. Jub. 8.19.

26. I Kings 6.29,32; 7.36,42; cf. Exod. 25.18f., 31–40; 28.33f.; I Sam. 14.2; Clements, op. cit., p.65; J. Gray, op. cit., pp.161f.

27. I Enoch 34–36; 76.

28. Wensinck, op. cit., p.40.

29. I Kings 7.25; cf. S. A. Cook, op. cit., p.54.

30. See II Sam. 5.6; Lam. 4.16; Jacob, op. cit., p.332.

31. *Mid. Tel.* Ps. 92.6; Ps. Jon. on Gen. 2.7.

32. Bentzen, op. cit., pp.40ff.; Manson, *Jesus the Messiah*, p.17.

33. Frost, op. cit., p.21; G. Scholem, *The Messianic Idea in Judaism*, Allen and Unwin 1971, p.8.

34. E.g. *Ruth R.* 5.6; see R. A. Stewart, *Rabbinic Theology*, Oliver and Boyd 1961, p.161.

35. See p.211 above.

36. II (4) Esd. 7.26; 8.52; 13.26; I Enoch 90.28f.

37. I Enoch 25.4f.

38. Test. Dan 5.12.

39. N. W. Porteous, *Living the Mystery*, Blackwell 1967, pp.93–111, esp. p.109.

40. Rev. 21.2,10.

41. Mark 10.6.

42. Mark 14.25.

43. Luke 23.43.

44. Matt. 5.20.

45. Matt. 13.41; John 8.11; cf. II (4) Esd. 7.123f; Rev. 21.8; 22.15.

46. Matt. 8.11; Mark 13.27; Luke 13.28f.

47. Isa. 25.8; 26.19; 35.5f.; Zech. 8.4; *Exod. R.* 30.3; *Ecclus. R.* 1.4.3; cf. Rev. 21.4.

48. Matt. 19.28; cf. 25.31.

49. Matt. 13.43.

50. Qumran, *Community Rule* IV.

51. I. Enoch 65.9A; *Hagigah* 12a; *Gen. R.* 3.6; 42.3; *Mid. Tel.* Ps. 27.1; cf. Rev. 22.5.

52. J. Jeremias, *'Paradeisos'*, *Theological Dictionary of the New Testament*, ed. Kittel and Friedrich, Vol. V, p.772.

53. II (4) Esd. 7.123; II Enoch 65.9f.; but cf. 8.5.

54. Exod. 19.12.

55. Exod. 30.10; Lev. 16.32f.; Heb. 9.7; cf. *Yoma* 7.4.

56. See Josephus, *Antt.* III, 6.4; 7.7; cf. *War* V, 5.4.

57. Gen. 3.3,22; cf. I Enoch 24.4–25.7.

58. Heb. 4.14f.; 12.18–24; cf. Gal. 4.24–26.

59. Matt. 8.3,15; 9.29; 17.7; 20.34; Mark 1.41; 7.33; Luke 5.13; 7.14; 22.51.

60. Matt. 14.36; Mark 3.10; 6.56; 8.22; 10.13; Luke 6.19; 7.39; 18.15.

61. Mark 5.30.

62. John 20.17.

63. John 20.27.

64. Hippolytus, *Comm. Cant.* 15; see Daniélou, *Primitive Christian Symbols*, p.32; Lightfoot, *St John's Gospel*, pp.321f.

65. Cf. Isa. 2.4; 9.6; see Childs, op. cit., pp.65ff.

66. Dibelius, *A Fresh Approach to the New Testament and Early Christian Literature*, p.89.

67. Luke 1.79; 2.14.

68. Luke 12.51; 19.42; cf. Matt. 10.34.

69. John 16.33.

70. John 20.19,21,26.

71. John 14.27.

72. Cf. I John 1.1f.

The stunted, shattered tree which recurs in the paintings of Vincent van Gogh epitomizes much of the artist's loss of meaning in the modern world. Use is made of a symbol which has a history as old as man himself. Stretching right back into prehistoric times, the tree is to be found as a primary symbol among a great many peoples.[1] The strength, height and longevity of a great tree seems to have captured the imagination and to have been capable of expressing for innumerable generations something of man's understanding of his world and of himself. The tree will probably never be again the powerful integrating image it once was, but any attempt to appreciate the faith once known in the world must take it fully into account.

Like the navel and the rock, the tree was a centre symbol. It was pictured standing at the summit of the mountain in the very centre of paradise. It stood in the garden of Siduru Sabitu for Gilgamesh to find when he entered into the depths of the mountains. When the departed Pharaoh arrived in the world beyond, he too found the tree ready to sustain him in the midst of the Field of Offerings. As the paradisal situation was to some extent understood to be recaptured in cultic rites, the sacred plot in which they were carried out was seldom thought to be complete without some representation of the sacred tree at or near its centre. Even when basically anti-cultic movements came into being, the power of the tree image often persisted. So the banyan tree of the Buddha came to be identified with the sacred tree of ancient mythology and was declared to be situated at the centre of the world.[2]

The same sort of thing happened amongst the Hebrews. Although prophetic Judaism resisted much of the symbolism embodied in the tree, it continued to play a vital part in Hebraic thinking even into Christian times. The Old Testament provides ample evidence of the existence of the tree cult in the land of Canaan. It figured prominently in the worship of Baal and was *the* symbol of the high places which the prophets sought to destroy.[3] Yet it is likely that the Hebrews themselves had once venerated the tree in a manner akin to the Canaanites. Indeed, the prophetic task was made all the harder because the people were easily drawn back into a form of worship which had probably existed once amongst themselves.[4] The editing of the old histories following the prophetic movement failed to eradicate all traces of these ancient practices. They show that for a long time, the sites of sacred trees had been places of worship, theophany, judgment and burial.[5] Much of the religious and social life of the Hebrew people was in fact once intimately connected with the cultic tree. In view of this, it is hardly surprising to find that the tree image appeared with some prominence in their myth of the garden of Eden.

The prophetic revolution could not do away with tree symbolism, rooted as it was in the history and consciousness of the people, but radical changes were made in its use. As with many other symbols which had once played a full-bodied mythological role, the tree was reinterpreted in historical terms by prophetic writers. The tree had regularly been regarded as divine in itself, or at least as being the dwelling place of sacred power, but in Israel it came to be de-divinized so completely that it could be identified with Israel herself.[6] It was, in fact, reduced to the level of a simile or metaphor in many passages.

With the development of eschatological and apocalyptic thought, however, there was a revival of tree symbolism. It began to regain much of its ancient meaning. A number of elements connected with the tree begin to be used which had probably never disappeared from the popular lore of the people. It assumes particular importance in the book of Ezekiel. The tree is a prominent symbol in the prophet's scheme of paradise restored.[7] In I Enoch 24.4–25.7 there is a picture which recalls much of the ancient tradition as found in non-Hebraic literature. In the midst of six mountains, a host of fragrant trees encircles a seventh and central mountain. Amongst these trees the seer is shown one which is unique. No mortal is allowed to touch it, and on this tree is found the food of immortality. The tree of life forbidden to the sinning Adam is here found in its mythological home, the sacred mountain at the centre of the world. But its fruit will one day be available. It is reserved for the righteous when they attain to the heavenly paradise.[8] The apocalyptic writers also think of a time when the palm of Solomon's temple or the golden vine on the gateway of Herod's temple[9] would be exchanged for the living reality. The day would come when the tree of life itself will be planted in the temple in Jerusalem and become the site of God's eschatological throne.[10]

In the wisdom literature, another line of thought was followed. The tree of life was here identified with Wisdom, for like its mythological archetype it has the power to bestow length of days and divine peace.[11] The Wisdom which is capable of functioning in this way is, of course, to be found for the author of Proverbs in the commandments of God, and it is this idea which is taken up in rabbinic literature. There the tree of life is regularly understood as a symbol of the Torah. 'R. Yudan taught: Why is Torah likened to the tree of life? To tell you that as the tree of life is spread out above all living creatures in the garden of Eden, so Torah is spread out above all living creatures and can bring them into life in the world-to-come.'[12] This comment clearly reflects two motifs which were very ancient. The tree was of tremendous size and it had the power of everlasting life. These were ideas about which the early rabbis were cautious, however, and speculation on tree symbolism is generally to be found only in late rabbinic writing.[13] The reason for this is probably to be found in the orthodox Jews' disgust at the manner in which the tree cult developed in the Graeco-Roman period, and in their fear that the Jewish community would be led astray by this.

Popular Judaism, however, in the first centuries of our era does not appear to have followed the lead of the rabbis. Some Jews, indeed, seem to have been heirs to those who ran off to the high places with the protests of the prophets ringing in their ears. This is perhaps typified by the fact that, despite rabbinic injunction, use was frequently made of the menorah. The seven-branched candlestick is fairly certainly derived from the form of a tree. Not only does it appear to have been a convenient cultic representation of the sacred tree, but it could also evoke memories of Moses' burning bush and so represent both the life and the light of God among men. Such symbolism appears harmless enough today, but the rabbinic directive against any representation of the tree in this way was probably a valid one at that time. It could easily be used for a species of image-worship. From the popularity of the menorah in the face of rabbinic opposition, we learn, however, that the motif of the tree of life was becoming quite an important one amongst many Jews in the early Christian period.[14]

THE TREE IN THE CHRISTIAN TRADITION

Although parts of the New Testament show an affinity on the part of the early Christian movement with the apocalyptic ideas of late Judaism, it appears to have been one with rabbinic Judaism in its distrust of the tree motif. Very little mention is made of the tree of mythology. And even when this occurs, the symbolism usually appears in the form it had taken in pro-phetic literature. From the second century onwards, however, the tree became an important element in Christian hagio-graphy. Christians were no doubt later led to develop their ideas about the tree through contact with other traditions in which it was an important element. Even in this period, how-ever, the principal impetus came from an internal theological development. It arose largely out of the desire to find typological correspondences between the Old and New Testaments. This is very clearly seen in the connection made between the tree of life and the cross of Jesus.

Celsus declared that everywhere Christians '*speak in their writings of the tree of life and of resurrection of the flesh by the tree – I imagine because their master was nailed to a cross and was a carpenter by trade*'.[15] This was something of an exaggeration, but shows that by the end of the second century the tree of life probably figured with some prominence in both orthodox and unorthodox Christianity. The ancient concept of the tree which was the source of immortal life had found a new vitality in popular Christian thought. Celsus points to a movement, which became widespread especially in the West, in which the life-giving act of Jesus on the cross was more and more frequently contrasted with the death-resulting act of Adam, and the cross itself compared with the tree of life. The development of these ideas is seen in the writings of the early Christian fathers.[16] It was probably inevitable that the work of Christ on the cross should have come to be considered as having fulfilled the function which the tree of life had in mythology, but it is also necessary to take note of the way in which the mythological cosmography of Jerusalem contributed towards this development.

Because the site of the paradisal garden tended to be found in the environs of Jerusalem, it was easy for a connection to be made between the primordial myth of Eden and the story of Jesus' crucifixion. A story was eventually developed which linked these two sets of events. Adam, about to die, was said to have sent Seth to the garden of Eden for the oil of mercy from the tree of life. Seth arrives at the gates of Eden and sees the tree of life but is refused the oil. Instead, he is given three seeds from the tree, which are subsequently buried with Adam's body. From the seeds there grow three trees, a palm, a cypress and a cedar, but eventually they become one. Later, Moses made his miraculous rod from the wood of this tree and so was able to sweeten the waters of Marah and draw forth water out of the rock. All the life-giving and healing agents of the Jewish-Christian tradition came to be related to this tree, but in particular it was said to have furnished the wood from which the cross of Christ was made. In medieval times, therefore, it was believed that splinters from the cross had the power to heal the sick and raise the dead. The mythological significance attributed to the location of the crucifixion made it easy to make such a direct connection. It is possible that the place of Christ's crucifixion was early identified with the place of Adam's burial. In the New Testament it is called *Golgotha*, or 'the place of the skull', and there may already have been a tradition that the hill was believed to be a reliquary containing Adam's remains.[17] On the other hand, the name may originally have denoted no more than the shape of the mount, and there is no evidence that such an identification was made by any of the New Testament writers.

The cross is indeed called a tree in Acts 5.30; 10.39; 13.29; Gal. 3.13 and I Peter 2.24, but in none of these texts is there any indication that the tree of Eden was in mind. The source of the description is in fact given by Paul, when he quotes Deut.

21.22f.: 'Cursed is every one that hangeth on a tree', and I
Peter is clearly dominated by the same passage, although there
may also be an echo here of the LXX of Isa. 53.12. The source
of the description of the cross as a tree, therefore, in the New
Testament is not Genesis, but a law which required that a felon
hung for his crime should be buried on the same day as his
execution. Paul saw a neat parallel between such a person being
described as accursed by God and his lord who suffered such a
fate in order to free men from the curse of the law. No connection of any kind is made with the paradisal tree.

In view of this, it is worth pausing to note that there are no
grounds in the New Testament literature for any kind of contention that the story of the cross grew up out of a contemporary
mythology of the tree, either Jewish or Gentile. Comparisons
with other stories in which a divine or semi-divine person has
been hung on a tree or identified with a tree used in a rite of
death and rebirth have frequently been made. These comparisons may well be illuminating when dealing with some of the
later developments in popular Christian lore, but the total
absence of this kind of thinking from the earliest Christian
literature must mean that any conjecture as to the origins of the
crucifixion story based on them must be dismissed. It is particularly noteworthy that in the gospels the cross is never referred
to as a tree. On the other hand, there are a few uses of the symbolism of the tree derived from the prophetic and apocalyptic
thinking of Judaism.

The early Christians appear to have shared with apocalyptic
Judaism the idea of a paradise reserved for the faithful in which
they would find the tree of life. The author of Revelation promises the fruit of the tree in the paradise of God to the victors of
faith. This is, however, still an eschatological hope, and certainly no clear connection is made with the cross of Jesus.[18]
Jesus himself appears to have shared this hope.[19]

More prominent in the gospels is the use of the tree as a symbol for the nation of Israel. In this the gospels continue a line
of thought which was common in Judaism. In particular, use is
made of the symbolism of the fig tree, which had often stood as
an image for the nation.[20] In view of this, there can be little
doubt that Luke's parable of the fig tree was intended to indicate the failure of Israel to produce those good works which

God had demanded of it.[21] This, however, does not go far enough. Lying behind the use of the fig for Israel must be seen the mythological archetype from which the imagery developed. This is certainly true when dealing with Mark's story of the withering of the fig tree. It is often maintained that Luke's parable about the fig tree has been turned into an incident at Mark 11.12–14, 20–22, and this may well be so. At all events, it would appear that Mark has injected deeper meaning into its symbolism. As an acted parable, the point that Israel has been found wanting appears to be made in an unduly dramatic manner. The story, moreover, has inserted into it another, which tells of the cleansing of the temple. Mark undoubtedly intended that the one should illuminate the meaning of the other.

Mark has placed the cursing of the fig tree most carefully as part of the complex in which he tells of Jesus' arrival at Jerusalem to find the temple 'a den of robbers'. At the same time he finds that the fig tree nearby bears no fruit. Both the temple and the tree, therefore, must represent the nation which is failing to carry out the will of God. But we have to go further than this. The temple was, as we have already seen, a representation of the paradisal garden, but it is now no longer functioning as such. Similarly the tree. The fig was sometimes identified with the tree of life, and this may be in mind here.[22] Myth told of how Mithras had eaten of the fig tree before the creation of the world, and now Jesus comes to the tree that he might eat of it. There is, however, no fruit fit to eat. It represents the nation which had been given the function of the tree of life, to dispense its gifts to men, but which had failed to do so. Although it is outwardly healthy and nourished by the law of God, no fruit is available.[23] The role of the nation of Israel as the tree of life is therefore brought to an end. The tree, like the mountain, must be discarded in an act requiring faith to look beyond the present disappointment to the planting of a new tree of life in the garden of the Lord.[24]

It is likely that for all the gospel writers Jesus had replaced Israel as the tree of life, but this is only indicated indirectly by the synoptists. The Fourth Gospel alone makes explicit use of the tree of life as a symbol for Jesus himself by identifying him with the vine in John 15.1–17. The choice of the vine as the symbol here can hardly have been intended to suggest the joy of marriage wine, for that imagery is absent.[25] Like the fig, the vine could stand for Israel,[26] and so the imagery would suggest to a Jew first of all that a claim was being made that Jesus constituted the new Israel, membership of whose community was essential to salvation. But the symbol is here used in a way which suggests that the vine's character as the tree of life is also in view. The vine was widely used to stand for it, and this is found also in post-biblical Judaism.[27] John makes use of this tradition. Jesus is the tree of life outside whom there is only death. He is not only the dispenser of life, but one who draws men into his own being as the tree. Use is thus made of the old idea of the tree as the unitive centre which brings all men to and into itself. The vine is here, as elsewhere in contemporary thought, a symbol of 'unity and of corporate relationship'.[28] There may even be a claim that Jesus is divine at this point, for John has identified him with the symbol which regularly represented the life which only God could give.[29]

Closely related to the concept of the tree as the unitive centre was the idea that it could stand, like the mountain, for the world or cosmos. The menorah seems to have been thought of at times in this way at the beginning of the Christian era, for its seven lamps were said to represent the seven planets.[30] The tree was not, however, a mere alternative to the mountain. It could suggest that which the mountain could not. It could stand for the vitality of the earth made alive by God,[31] and so be a more adequate symbol to denote the idea that life reached up through the cosmos from hell to heaven and spread itself across the earth

This symbolism of the tree could be aptly used to represent the pretensions of a world empire, one which declared itself universal in scope and authority. It was an especially appropriate image to use of a king who aspired to such an empire. This is how the symbol appears in Ezek. 31.3–14, where it stands for the Pharaoh of Egypt, and in Dan. 4.10–12, where it symbolizes Nebuchadrezzar of Babylon. That it is the world tree which is in mind in these passages is clear from the descriptions given of it. The tree is said to stand at the centre of the earth. Its top reaches to heaven, it gives food to all, shelters beasts under its foliage and gives place for birds to dwell in its branches. The imagery of the world tree is being used to denote a claim to omnipotence and omni-provision. There is a clear link between this and the tree which appears in *Gen. R.* 15.6, which 'spread over all living things' and 'covered a five hundred years' journey'.

In Ecclus. 14.26f. this tree is identified with Wisdom. The world tree was also related to the understanding given by God to men and in which they would find life for their souls. In the gospels the same tree appears as an image for the kingdom of God.

In Mark 4.30–32 Jesus compares the kingdom of God to a mustard seed which grows to become a tree. It puts out great branches so that the birds of heaven can lodge in them. Although brief, this description clearly owes something to that found in Ezekiel and Daniel which in turn derives from the mythological archetype. The use of this simple analogy, therefore, was able to evoke a wealth of association. The kingdom of which Jesus spoke was to be universal in scope, rivalling all the territorial ambitions of ancient empires. In it men from all nations would find their home, for it would constitute a bond between all peoples and God like the primordial tree of creation mythology.

In conclusion, we may note again that tree symbolism finds little place in the gospels, and that when it does so, its mythological content is restricted to that which was acceptable to the cautious spirituality of Judaism.

NOTES

1. Gaster, *Myth, Legend and Custom in the Old Testament*, pp.32ff.
2. D. Seckel, *The Art of Buddhism*, Methuen 1964, p.128.
3. Deut. 12.2; 16.21.
4. II Kings 16.4; 17.10; Isa. 1.29; Hos. 4.13f.
5. Gen. 13.18; 18.1; 35.8; Judg. 4.5; 6.11; I Sam. 31.13; cf. Gen. 14.13; I Sam. 14.2; 22.6.
6. Ps. 80.8–16; Isa. 5.7; cf. Num. 24.6f.; Jer. 24; *Gen. R.* 88.5; 98.9; *Lev. R.* 36.2.
7. Ezek. 47.12.
8. II (4) Esd. 7.123; 8.52; Apoc. Moses 28.2–4.
9. Josephus, *Antt.* XV, 11.3; *War* V, 5.4; Tacitus, *Hist.* 5.5; *Middoth* 3.8.
10. I Enoch 25.5; Apoc. Moses 22.4.

11. Prov. 3.18; Ecclus. 24.17–21; cf. Prov. 11.30; 13.12; 15.4.

12. *Mid. Tel.* Ps. 1.19; cf. *Gen. R.* 15.6.

13. Goodenough, op. cit., Vol. XII, pp. 137f.; cf. Vol. VII, pp.126,128f.

14. Goodenough, op. cit., Vol. IV, pp. 73,75–7,95; Butterworth, op. cit. pp.41f.

15. Origen, *Contra Celsum*, 6.34, trans. Chadwick, op. cit.

16. Ignatius, *Trall.* 11.2; *Smyrn.* 1.2; Justin, *Dial. Tryph.* 86; Clem. Alex., *Strom.* V, 11; Tertullian, *Adv. Jud.* 13; see also Daniélou, *Primitive Christian Symbols*, pp.32f.

17. Cf. Every, op. cit., p.51; M. Murray, *The Genesis of Religion*, Routledge and Kegan Paul 1963, pp.75f.; Wensinck, op. cit., p.22.

18. Rev. 2.7; Test. Levi 18.11; see J. Schneider, '*Xulon*', *Theological Dictionary of the New Testament*, ed. Kittel and Friedrich, Vol. V, p.40.

19. Matt. 26.29 par.

20. Jer. 24.1–8; 29.17; *Cant. R.* 7.5.3.

21. Luke 13.6–9; cf. Apoc. Peter 2.

22. Ginzberg, op. cit., p.40. In the Talmud, the tree of which Adam and Eve ate in the garden is sometimes identified as the fig tree.

23. Cf. Pss. 1.3; 92.12; Prov. 11.30; Isa. 5.1–7; 61.3; Matt. 12.33–35.

24. Rev. 22.2f.; cf. Matt. 7.19. In Rom. 11.16–24 the tree of Judaism is not destroyed but pruned, and the wild branches of the Gentiles grafted in.

25. Corell, op. cit., p.73.

26. Ps. 80.8f.; Jer. 6.9; Ezek. 15.1–6; 17.5–10; 19.10–14; Hos. 10.1; 14.7; II (4) Esd. 5.23; cf. Isa. 27.2–6; Jer. 5.10; 12.10f.; II Bar. 39.7ff.

27. E.g. in ancient Assyria and in the Dionysiac and Mandaean cults. See A. Whittick, *Symbols, Signs and Their Meaning*, Leonard Hill 1960, p.289; cf. *Gen. R.* 15.7; *Lev. R.* 12.1; *Num. R.* 10.2.

28. Borsch, op. cit., p.267.

29. Goodenough, op. cit., Vol. XII, p. 137; cf. Vol. VII, pp.87–134.

30. Butterworth, op. cit., p.42.

31. Cf. Wales, op. cit., p.13.

The Hebrew myth of Eden spoke of a river which watered the garden and then divided into four.[1] The identification of these four rivers with known geographical features is made to show that Eden is the source of all the great rivers of known civilization. The picture is clearly dominated by a certain idea and not by geographical observation. That idea is easy enough to discern. All the waters of the world are held to have their origin at the paradisal centre of the earth, beginning from its summit and spreading out to make the whole world fertile. The Hebrew writer has made use of a fairly common paradisal motif according to which 'the mountains are considered as spreading the nutritive element over the earth, because of their communication either with the clouds or with the nether world'.[2]

That the rivers should be four in number is also not difficult to explain. This is determined by the importance which the four points of the compass had for the ancient world. It is reinforced by the formal presentation of the central mountain as a four-sided pyramid. Down each of its four sides a river flows to water the earth as in the Hindu mythology of Mount Meru.

Because of the multiplicity of symbols associated with the centre, the source of the four rivers is variously identified.

In some cases it is considered sufficient to indicate that the rivers derive from the mountain. In China the four streams come down from the Kwan-Lun hills. This is not clearly made out in the Genesis version of the myth, but, as Oesterley pointed out, the four rivers of Eden must logically have had their source on a mountain,[3] and if the inherent logic of the situation is not enough, we have seen ample evidence of the importance which the central mountain had for the Hebrew tradition.

Either as the mountain in miniature or as a symbol on the top of the mountain, the sacred stone or rock may be the source. This may be illustrated from Slav mythology in which the four streams issue from the stone, Alatuir, in the island of Bonyan. From this basic motif there is an important derivative type of story. The life-giver is presented as one who draws forth water from the rock. This is done by Mithras when he aims an arrow at a rock face,[4] and by Moses when he strikes a rock in the holy mountain of Horeb with his rod.[5]

Not unnaturally the source is frequently a fountain, spring or well. In Iran the four streams were said to descend from the fountain of Arduisir in the realm of the blest. In the Scandinavian Edda they come from the spring Hvergelmir in Aṣaheim, the home of the gods. In Homer there are four springs which are located outside the cave of Circe.[6] The tradition also appears, as we shall see, among the Hebrews.

As a particularly important centre symbol the tree is frequently the source of the waters. Their function as life-giving agencies is then made very clear. The Hindu-Buddhist tradition derived the streams from the roots of the four-limbed damba-tree on Sineru, and the same idea is found in Jewish and Christian literature. *Gen. R.* 15.6 says that the primeval waters come from under the tree to fertilize the earth. The seer of the *Apocalypse of Paul* says, 'I saw a tree planted out of whose roots waters flowed, and the source of the four rivers was in it'.[7]

When Israel was identified with paradise eschatologically, it followed that its holy city and its temple would become for the Jew the place from which the world's physical and spiritual nourishment flowed.[8] According to Joel 3.18 a day was coming when the mountains would fill the stream beds of Judah. Ezek. 47.1–12 spoke of healing trees growing on the banks of a river which would flow down from Zion. Zech. 14.8 declared that the day would come when living water would go out from Jerusalem in summer and in winter.

This eschatological hope seems to have derived from the identification of Jerusalem with the navel centre. Zion could already, therefore, be credited with being at the very source of the waters. God's fountains were there and the Gihon could be seen as symbolic of the overflowing river of paradise.[9] So the rabbis identified the source of all fresh water on earth with the

rock of Jerusalem. Jerusalem is favoured above all places, for it
is in the garden of Eden, and the rest of the world receives only
the residue of that water which first spreads through Palestine.[10]
While this was not a physical fact, the symbolism of Eden could
still be used to represent the spiritual fact. In Zion, Jacob's well
gushed forth the divine gift of the law.[11]

In the city raised to such pre-eminence, however, it is the
temple which takes pride of place. The house of God tends,
therefore, to replace all the symbols designating the source of
the rivers. In Ps. 36.8f. the life-giving water which flows from
the mountains of paradise is identified with 'the river of thy
delights', which is part of the abundance furnished by the house
of God.[12] Joel's fountain comes forth from the temple.[13] Ezekiel
is even more specific, and leaves us in no doubt that he thinks of
the temple becoming the new Eden when he says that the
healing river comes from below its threshold.

The Hebrew of Ezek. 47 speaks of two rivers which appear at
first to be in conflict with the usual motif of four rivers. This is
a reference, however, to a related concept. The two rivers are
the sources of the two deeps in Canaanite myth, and come
from the abode of El who lives at their originative junction.[14]
Similarly Utnapishtim lived at 'the mouth of the rivers',[15] and
in the Koran Moses says that he will discover 'the junction of
the two oceans'.[16] One refers to the celestial and the other to the
subterranean waters. Both rivers may become four, those of
paradise then being a counterpart to those of Hades, as in
Greek classical literature. There is no doubt that we are again
faced with the idea of the paradisal source of all waters, and that
Ezekiel has claimed this role for the temple in Jerusalem.

THE CONTENTS OF THE RIVERS

The paradisal rivers were primarily distributors of the rain
given by the heavenly waters.[17] As such they represented the
divine gift of life which was spread over the earth, causing the
land to give of its fruits. The 'river of God' was therefore the
river of grain.[18] Upon this basic idea others grew up which made
use of the richness of meaning potential in the symbol of water.
Water meant prosperity, and so the figure of God's stream
could be used to suggest his gift of an 'untroubled, full, and

prosperous life'.[19] The cleansing power of water led to the river
being thought of as one which washed away sin and impurity.[20]
The fertilizing power of water also suggested the idea of the
river as a stream of immortality. The mythical river flowed
from its divine source with the water which Osiris gave to the
blessed dead, and which was received by the devotee of Mithras.[21] The water of the river was for healing. Both physically and
spiritually the water provided by the Lord was full of saving
power.

The four rivers were not always simply running with water.
Use was often made of other symbols in order to endow the
rivers with greater richness of symbolic meaning. *Deut. R.* 7. 3
compares the Torah not only to water, but also to wine, honey,
milk and oil. As so often, such a rabbinic comparison reflects an
old mythological tradition.[22] It appears also in II Enoch 8.2–5,
where the four rivers which come from the tree to the earthly
Eden are said to run with honey, milk, oil and wine. These are
probably late formalizations of a process which had been going
on for some time. They bring together symbols which had been
associated with the tree of paradise and its blessings.

Honey was a very ancient mythological symbol. 'The idea
that rivers and wadis will flow with honey features prominently
in ancient conceptions of the Golden Age; and it is, in effect,
such a golden age that is inaugurated year by year when Baal
returns to the earth.'[23] Dionysos was said to have discovered
honey, and the rivers to have run with it when the god first
revealed himself.[24] Honey also appears in the regeneration
ritual of Mithraism. The Hebrews appear to have been familiar
with this usage. In Exod. 16.31 the manna provided by God
in the wilderness is said to have tasted like honey. Milk not
unnaturally appeared in the same context of ideas as a symbol
of the nourishment provided by the earth-mother. Throughout
the ancient world, the breasts of the divine mother image were
emphasized for just this reason,[25] and a cup of milk was given
to initiates in some of the mysteries. In addition to discovering
honey, Dionysos was said to have produced milk from wood.[26]
Milk and honey were thus common symbols of divinely provided nourishment. In view of this it is clear that the land promised to the wandering Israelites was given a paradisal character
when described as one flowing with milk and honey.[27] They

would live in the very place where the divine sustenance flowed in abundance. The Christian author of V Ezra was certainly in no doubt about the significance of this description of the promised land, for he said that the milk and the honey came from the very fountains of paradise.[28]

In Isaiah and Joel, wine is brought into association with milk and both are connected with the rivers of the Lord. He who comes to the waters can buy wine and milk without money, says the prophet Isaiah, while Joel declared that when the fountain comes forth from the house of the Lord, the mountains will drip with sweet wine and the hills flow with milk.[29]

Oil is also constantly mentioned as one of the blessings of the land given by Yahweh.[30] Other examples of blessings also appear, but it is clear that milk, honey, wine and oil could be thought of as typifying the paradisal prosperity of the land provided by the Lord.

Of these five blessings, however, only three are relevant to the study of the gospels. Paradisal milk seems to appear briefly in I Peter 2.1–10. There Christians are said to have tasted of the Lord and are now urged to long for the spiritual milk that they may be nourished towards salvation. The writer immediately passes on to talk of Christ as the living stone and the rock. This appears to be abrupt unless allowance is made for the fact that milk, like water, could be thought of as issuing from the rock of paradise.[31] There is not even a passing allusion to the honey of paradise in the New Testament, and so we may confine ourselves to the use made of the symbolism of the oil, the water and the wine.

THE OIL OF IMMORTALITY

Oil figures with some prominence in the post-canonical tradition of Christianity. Moreover, it is explicitly connected with the paradisal tree and with healing and immortality. In the developed myth of Adam, Seth is sent to the garden of Eden for 'the oil of life' from 'the tree of his mercy' which is to save Adam from death.[32] In the *Gospel of Bartholomew* it is Jesus who anoints men with the oil of life.[33] In the *Acts of Thomas* it is called the 'power of the tree', and in the initiation ritual described, oil is poured on the head and used to anoint the body.[34] The *Clementine Recognitions* explain that the Son of God is called Christ because 'Him first God anointed with oil which was taken from the wood of the tree of life'.[35]

These Christian and semi-Christian usages appear to have been a development out of Jewish thought and practice. The idea of oil from the tree of life is found in the apocalyptic writers, and continued in rabbinic Judaism, where it was used in speaking of the Torah. 'Just as oil [gives] life to the world, so too do the words of the Torah.'[36]

In the Old Testament, oil appears in two contexts. It is a common symbol of fertile abundance, and it is used in various rituals. These two types of reference to oil are probably to be connected. As representative of fertility, oil seems to be a life symbol. When objects and people are anointed with oil, it is likely that in early times this was understood 'as the supplying of new life-power mediated through the oil'.[37] That this idea persisted in Israel is indicated by the fact that anointing was connected with the gift of the spirit and that a leper was anointed as part of his purification.[38] It is also significant that in Num. 11.8 the cakes of manna are said to have tasted of oil. If oil was an accepted symbol of life, then we can assume that special importance would be attached to the use of oil in burial rites. Evidence concerning the treatment of the corpse in pre-Christian Jewish practice is almost non-existent. It is significant, however, that the Egyptian practice of embalming was used at the deaths of Jacob and Joseph.[39] At some point in the history of Israel, embalming with its anticipation of future life did find a place. Later Jewish practice appears to have consisted simply of washing and anointing.[40] A purely sacramental act had clearly come to be regarded as all that was necessary. No attempt was made to preserve the body as such, but the treatment of the cadaver with oil must surely have been intended to represent a hope for its life in the future.

Of some importance, as we shall see, is the fact that the oil of anointment was generally reckoned to be extremely fragrant. Its perfume appears to be derived from that of paradise, and especially of its trees.[41] In II Bar. it is said that the 'winds shall go forth from before Me to bring every morning the fragrance of aromatic fruits, and at the close of the day clouds distilling the dew of health'.[42] That this fragrance is not merely an aesthetic pleasure is made clear in I Enoch 25.6, which says that

> . . . its fragrance shall be in their bones,
> And they shall live a long life on earth.

The fragrance of paradise by itself is credited with life-giving properties. In the light of this Jewish tradition, we can readily see the full significance of the statement by V Ezra that '*the tree of life* will be to them for an ointment of sweet fragrance'.[43]

The symbolism of the oil of life appears very little in the New Testament, but the few references made are of some importance. The letter of James informs us that it was the practice of the early Christians to anoint the sick with oil in the name of the Lord, so that the prayer of faith might bring healing.[44] It may be accepted, therefore, that the first Christians continued to understand oil as a sacramental symbol of life and healing as the Jews had done. This is of some importance when considering a group of references to oil which appear in the four gospels in connection with the preparation of Jesus' body for burial. The four gospels, however, are not at one here, but seem to reflect at least three different traditions.

In Luke, Jesus is said to have been buried in some haste, so that the anointing with oil which normally accompanied this act was omitted. He is simply wrapped in a linen shroud.[45] In view of this, Luke stresses that the women left the tomb to prepare aromatic oils (*aroma*) and perfumes (*myron*) with which they would anoint the body on the Sunday morning.[46] Luke tells of an anointing earlier in his narrative, but makes no connection between this and preparation for burial.[47] In the Lukan tradition, therefore, Jesus is at no time prepared for burial with the oil of life. On the contrary, he implies that this is wholly unnecessary, for the women who come to do this find that their Lord has already been raised from the dead. Luke's thought may be that the resurrection of Christ is entirely the work of God. Any suggestion of a sacramental endowment with immortality is avoided.

Matthew and Mark also state that Jesus was buried without the customary anointing, but contrary to Luke record an anointing which is an integral part of their passion narrative. The act is specifically said to be a preparation for burial, and

Jesus commands that the woman who does it is not to be rebuked, for the day is coming when no one will be able to carry
out this rite.[48] This prophecy already anticipates the fact that
the customary burial anointing was not carried out later. Mark
goes on to agree with Luke in stating that the women wished to
anoint the body after the sabbath had passed,[49] but failed to do
so because Jesus had already risen. Matthew records the visit
of the women to the tomb, but gives no hint of any intention on
their part to anoint the body. It would seem from this that Matthew makes the women appreciate the fact that the sacramental
anointing with the oil of resurrection had already taken place
at Bethany. It may well be that an anointing which was originally unconnected with burial rites came to be seen as a prophecy
of the passion and an anticipation of the funerary rites. Mark
would then represent a transitional stage in a process which was
completed in Matthew, when the now anomalous reference to
an intention to anoint the corpse was omitted. In this tradition
the normal Jewish custom was carried out, but during life. And
the resurrection to which it pointed comes not in the far-off
future, but on the third day.

John's account of the anointing by Mary is probably based
on the Lukan story rather than on that of Mark.[50] The feet are
anointed and not the head, as in Mark. John also follows Luke
in not regarding this incident as a substitute for anointing at the
time of burial. But contrary to Luke, when that burial takes
place, John records that Nicodemus came with a mixture of
myrrh and aloes and that '*aroma*' was placed between the linen
cloths on the Friday evening.[51] Jesus was therefore prepared for
entombment with the oil of life in the normal Jewish manner
so that, like Matthew, though for a different reason, John omits
all reference to the women wishing to perform this rite on the
Sunday morning. It had been carried out on the Friday evening.
Although the meaning of John's earlier anointing by Mary is
far from clear in the text, it is connected in some way with the
burial to come.[52] The most likely solution is that John wished
to retain the Markan idea that the anointing should point
forward to the crucifixion, but had to relegate it to a mere for-
shadowing or anticipation of the rite which would be carried
out later. Apart from any other considerations he appears to
have attached a common symbolism to both anointings.

In John's account of Mary's anointing at Bethany, the reader's attention is drawn to the fact that the fragrant perfume of the ointment filled the room. This may have been a statement of fact, but John frequently intends a double reference, and it may well be that there is an allusion here to the fragrance associated with the paradisal oil. If that is the case, then the significance of the oil as a symbol of life-giving power has been emphasized.[53] For a moment all those present enjoy the perfume of paradise. In his story of Christ's entombment, John does not specifically mention this feature, but an extraordinarily large amount of spices is said to have been placed within the burial garments. This abundance of fragrant resin and powdered aromatic sandalwood would naturally have suggested that the sweetest fragrance issued from the body of the dead Christ as it did from that of Osiris[54] and from the garden of Eden.

The growing concern to assert that the body of Jesus was given the funerary anointing with oil, which reaches its fulfilment in John, can hardly have been motivated by a mere desire to see the burial carried out according to custom. A deeper motif is clearly present. In view of the equation of the body of Jesus with the new temple, there is some merit in E. C. Selwyn's suggestion on this point. As the tabernacle was sanctified with oil, so was the body of Christ.[55] It is also worth noting that the extravagance of the rite suggests the burial of a king.[56] When it is remembered, however, that it is John above all the evangelists who stresses the bodily resurrection of Jesus, who speaks of his being touched and of his eating by the sea of Galilee, another solution presents itself. There is a hint of the Egyptian mummification ritual in the reference to the spices in John's account of the burial. Has John turned into narrative symbolism the belief of the early church that the body of its Lord did not see corruption, being preserved by the oil of paradise and raised to life by the will of God?

THE WATER OF LIFE

Of the importance which the symbolism of water had for early Christianity little need be said. The rite of baptism ensured not only the centrality of water in its sacramental thinking, but also a good deal of concern with its typological antecedents in the Old Testament. Paul speedily saw a parallel between the baptismal rite and the crossing of the Red Sea.[57] The post-canonical literature was not content to find the archetypal source in Hebraic history. In truly mythological manner, it saw the gift of water in the new dispensation as an enjoyment of the paradisal waters of Eden. The city of Christ to come becomes the new Eden surrounded by the four rivers flowing from the roots of the life-giving tree.[58] Jesus himself is identified with the source of these waters. An early Christian sarcophagus shows Jesus accompanied by a palm tree, standing on a mountain from which flow the rivers of life to the four quarters.[59] In this graphic manner Jesus was seen to have taken over the role of the paradisal tree in the new creation.

This development was not confined to uncanonical literature. It is already present in the Gospel of John. In the synoptic gospels, Jesus is frequently the recipient of God's blessings, and outstandingly the obedient son. In John this aspect of Christ's role remains, but Jesus is also turned into one who by his obedience to the Father has been made to have life in himself. The Christ of John is thus enabled to take over the role previously assigned to God. Jesus becomes, as Yahweh had been, the 'fountain of life' and of 'living waters'.[60]

The active role assigned to Christ may be considered first in connection with the washing of the disciples' feet in John 13.1–11. This apparently simple act has caused commentators great difficulty, but some understanding of it may be gained when it is understood that the story is set by John in deliberate parallelism with that of the anointing by Mary. Both narratives open by pointing out that the Passover is approaching and that a supper is being eaten. In one the feet of Jesus are anointed, while in the other the feet of the disciples are washed by the Lord. The anointing is objected to by Judas, the washing by Peter. Most important of all is the fact that both acts are set in the context of Jesus' knowledge of his coming death. It would seem, therefore, that John intended these stories to illuminate one another. In that case there would be a presumption that what Jesus had received in the one, he gave to the disciples in the other.

The washing is something which will be understood later.

Only in the light of the resurrection will the meaning of the sacramental act become clear. It is therefore something which the resurrection illuminates, which is connected with the gift of eternal life. Without this washing the disciples can have no part in Jesus, and so cannot share in the new life towards which Jesus is looking. Peter is so anxious to be one with Jesus, that he asks to have his hands and head washed also. In reply, Jesus draws the disciples' attention to the fact that a guest bathed before going to a feast; all that remained on arrival was the necessity to wash the feet. This analogy points again to the resurrection, to the Messianic feast which the disciples will attend. It leads on in turn to the use of the figure of water as a symbol of cleansing, but in view of the story as a whole and its relationship with the anointing, it is also seen to be a vehicle of eternal life. Now, not the oil, but water is the agency of life, and Jesus is not the recipient but the distributor of the paradisal power. For this understanding of the use of water at the last supper the reader has been carefully prepared. By the time this story is reached, John has ensured that the reader will know that it is not merely a figure for spiritual cleansing but for the power which comes from God to make alive.

In the story of Christ's meeting with the Samaritan woman in John 4.4–15, he has already been disclosed as 'the root of immortality and the fount of incorruption'.[61] We have already seen that the passage is concerned to show that in Jesus the claims of both Jerusalem and Gerizim to be the sacred mountain are made obsolete. Now we can take note of the fact that the work of the patriarch of both peoples, Jacob, as the provider of water, is seen to be inadequate and is replaced by the provision which Jesus offers. Jacob had given the people physical sustenance by digging the well, but Jesus offers the water of life drawn from 'the wells of salvation'.[62] The woman is being asked to understand that Jesus offers her eternal life and that in his person he is the fountain of life. Just as Jesus replaced the cultic mountain, so he also replaced the fountain or well which mythology located upon it. The man who receives water from Jesus is rendered free from the need to go in search of the fountain in the mythological paradise or its cultic representation.

In John 5.2–9, the scene is set beside a pool by the sheep gate of Jerusalem. The water of the pool has the capacity to heal

when it is troubled. In some MSS this is explained as due to the
action of the angel of the Lord. One of the sick was unable to
take advantage of this by reason of his infirmity but is healed
instead by Jesus. Jesus takes '*the place of the angel which troubles the
water*'.[63] Jesus is able to do what the water in its troubled state
was able to accomplish. In coming to a full understanding of
this passage, however, its roots in the Hebraic creation myth
must be noted. The association of healing power with the agita-
tion of the waters recalls the initial movement of God over
the waters in Gen. 1.2. As creation came into being by Yahweh's
stirring of the primeval waters, so now the sick are healed by the
movement caused by his angel. A statement in the *Apocalypse of
Paul* may also be significant in this connection. There it is said
that after the creation, the Spirit of God rested above the tree of
paradise, and that water flowed from it only when the Spirit
breathed.[64] This is a simple extension of the symbolism found
in Genesis, which attributes all life-giving power to the action
of the Spirit of God. Jesus has not merely replaced the angel
here, therefore, but has become the primeval creative power of
God. In this narrative, Jesus has already been credited with
being the source of the creative breath with which he later
endows the disciples in the resurrection.[65]

The healing of the blind man at Siloam in John 9.1–7 has
already been seen to contain allusions to creation mythology.
In most healing miracles, the actions of Jesus are extremely
simple. He heals by a word or by a touch. In this case, however,
Jesus is said to have made clay by mixing his spittle with the
dust of the ground, and to have performed the cure by placing
this clay on the blind man's eyes.[66] Such an unusual concern for
the details of the method employed by Jesus is almost certainly
intended to be instructive. In Genesis, Adam is made from the
dust of the ground, but no mention is made of the use of spittle.
It is possible, however, that John was familiar with other versions of the creation myth in which the spittle of God was
mixed with the dust in order to make the clay into which could
be breathed the breath of life.[67] It was another common
anthropomorphism which could be employed with some appro-
priateness to convey the idea that the creation involved God in
allowing man to partake in part of his own life. Jesus' method of
healing on this occasion seems to reflect a symbolism which

declares that the corruption of the old creation is being removed in the new.

The reference to the use of spittle may have further symbolic
value. On this occasion the use of water as part of the healing
process is not excluded, as it was at Bethsaida. Jesus sends the
blind man to wash in the pool of Siloam. John explains that
Siloam means 'sent', so that the reader should understand that
'the pool represents Him who has been sent'.[68] A connection
may therefore be made between the healing spittle and the
water, which also appears in the text of a charm given by
Goodenough. It reads,

> I summon thee, Gabriel, by the spittle
> Which came forth from the mouth of the Father,
> And became a spring of the water of life.[69]

The same combination of motifs is found in the *Odes of Solomon*:

> 1. Fill ye waters for yourselves from the
>   living fountain of the Lord,
> 2. For it has been opened to you;
>   And come all ye thirsty and take a draught,
>   And rest by the fountain of the Lord . . .
> 5. For it flows from the lips of the Lord,
>   And from the heart of the Lord is its name.

Borsch is probably correct in thinking that the Odes and John
have derived this symbolism from a common background of
ideas[70] to complement one another. For John, Jesus was the
one sent by God to endow his people with the spittle of the new
creation which becomes a stream of eternal life.

The most explicit reference to this 'river of living water' is to
be found at John 7.38. This text has given much trouble to
exegetes, but a consideration of it against the background of
Hebraic mythology would seem to offer the most rewarding
approach. It will then be seen that Jesus here refers to a familiar
complex of ideas.

On the last day of the feast of Tabernacles, Jesus offers drink
to the thirsty, saying, 'He who believes in me, as the scripture
said, "out of his *koilia* shall flow rivers of living water"'. The
following verse then explains that this refers to the Spirit which
believers are to receive when Christ is glorified.

It is possible first of all to be fairly certain that it is Christ himself, rather than the believer, who is here the source of these rivers. Both the immediate context and the theology of John's gospel as a whole suggest this interpretation.[71] This is something which John has asserted on several other occasions, as we have seen. In this instance, however, he is said not to replace the well of Jacob, the angel or the spirit of the pool but to become the *koilia*. This word may be rendered in a variety of ways, but most of the meanings attributed to it are related to one another. As used with reference to a human being it refers to the interior of the body and especially to the belly or womb. Unvocalized it may mean fountain. The ambiguity of meaning here seems to reflect the complementary character of a group of symbols all of which were appropriately used in the mythological description of the centre.[72] It denotes, in one way or another, the source of life. This approach to John's meaning is further supported when consideration is paid to the ritual of the feast of Tabernacles and to the probable source of the quotation.

On the last day of the feast, water was drawn from the pool of Siloam, which John is shortly to identify with Christ,[73] and poured into a silver bowl on the altar of burnt offering. This rite is frequently said to have been a rain-making ceremony, but it is likely that even seen as such, it derives from the notion of the fertilizing water which descends on the mountains of God. In the Hebrew tradition, the water-bearing mountain was exemplified by the rock of the wilderness, and there is some support for the view that a connection was made between this rock and the feast of Tabernacles. The Priestly code associated the feast with Israel's time in the wilderness,[74] the water-pouring was accompanied by the lighting of the candelabra which may well have symbolized the accompanying pillar of fire, and one rabbinic source connected the flask used at the feast with the wilderness rock.[75] Also of some importance is the fact that the feast of Tabernacles came to have an eschatological character. It was the feast of paradise regained in the fathers, and Luke 16.9 which speaks of the righteous living in tabernacles in paradise, may indicate that such a view was not unknown in the first century.[76] Bultmann was therefore able to conclude that 'the libation of the water, typical of the feast of Tabernacles, was seen as a symbolic representation of the blessing of water in the final age, and as an anticipation of the reception of the Spirit in the end time'.[77] It would seem, therefore, that for John, Jesus has become the navel from whom the paradisal waters come, and has fulfilled the symbolism of the feast of Tabernacles.[78]

In assigning this role to Jesus, however, John has again denied the function to Jerusalem. Various Old Testament texts have been suggested as possible sources for the quotation made here,[79] but it is clear that John 7.38 is not dependent on any one of them exclusively. The rabbinic source cited by T. F. Glasson connects the wilderness rock and the feast of Tabernacles with Ezek. 47, where the waters come from the temple on Mount Zion. The closest parallel to the text quoted is probably to be found in Zech. 14.8, which speaks of the time to come when living waters would flow out from Jerusalem. Jerusalem had been identified with the navel source of the waters and so might appropriately be referred to as the *koilia*. From the rock of Jerusalem all the world drank, located as it was at the junction with the abyss.[80] What is given as a quotation here, therefore, is a statement of a mythological kind containing the commonly accepted symbolism of Zion as the navel, but with the explicit mention of Jerusalem omitted so that it could be made to refer to Jesus. Jesus is now the rock from which the waters flow. The Christ of John has become in place of Jerusalem the fount of the Spirit of life.

THE FRUIT OF THE VINE

The most outstanding example of the use of wine as a symbol appears in John's story of the wedding at Cana. Because this is without parallel in the synoptic gospels and seems to introduce something of a new element into the story of Christ, scholars have frequently been tempted to find its origin in pagan myth and ritual. The temptation to do this is great in view of the fact that wine appears with such prominence in the Dionysiac cult of Roman times. Dionysos was said to produce wine in a miraculous manner.[81] As early as 1794, Dupuis called attention to the similarity of this to the story of the wedding at Cana. The idea was subsequently taken up by a succession of scholars. Estlin Carpenter spoke of the fourth evangelist transforming 'the miracles of Dionysos into an imaginative symbol of the glory of Christ'.[82] Similarly, the Dionysiac origin of the story seemed likely to Bultmann.[83] These conclusions should not, however, go unchallenged, and may well need to be modified.

Dionysiac elements were undoubtedly Christianized along with many other pagan rites, festivals and stories. As Goodenough points out, Dionysus Dendrites had 'been taken over' and Christianized by the middle of the second century.[84] Moreover, the church connected the Cana story with the Epiphany festival of 6 January, which may have replaced a Dionysiac one.[85] While having considerable importance, these facts do not establish the originative source for the wine symbolism of the Johannine gospel. All that they would suggest is that John may have seen some advantage in setting it forth in a manner recognizable to those familiar with Dionysiac symbolism. All that the two traditions have in common is the use of wine as a symbol and the idea that water may be turned into wine by divine action. But these common elements are surely explicable from the Jewish background out of which the gospel grew, making resort to the religion of Dusares unnecessary by way of explanation. Goodenough says that the four constituents of the paradisal rivers all recall Dionysian symbolism,[86] but as we have seen, they were probably common enough elements of myth, and derive naturally from the Hebraic tradition. This must certainly be held true of the wine.

The provision of abundant wine in the eschaton was a long-established element in the Hebraic tradition. The promise is already made in Isa. 55.1 and Joel 3.18.[87] The symbol continued to be used by Philo and the rabbis. Although E. R. Dodds rightly points out that the *orgia* of Dionysianism were religious experiences rather than drunken revels,[88] it is perhaps significant that Jewish sources wish to avoid any suggestion of insobriety in connection with the wine of God. Philo speaks of a 'divine intoxication' which is 'more sober than sobriety itself',[89] and makes the wine of the Priest-*logos* stand for 'God's gifts of grace, joy, virtue, wisdom, and the like'.[90] The rabbis were very conscious of the evils of intoxication, and looked forward to a paradise in which wine might be enjoyed without this accompanying menace. If Dionysian symbolism found a place in Judaism,[91] the connection between the use of wine and religious ecstasy was carefully safeguarded.

In the synoptic gospels there is little use of wine as a symbol. But Jesus is presented as one who shares the common Jewish hope that the faithful will drink of the fruit of the vine in the kingdom of God. To this he confidently looks forward as his death approaches. On the other hand, the new wine is in a sense already present with the coming of Jesus. This wine is so full of life that it would burst the old bottles of Judaism should any attempt be made to contain it within the old structures of life and thought.[92] At the last supper, Jesus identifies the blood of his own body with the wine. In one of the most striking christological claims made in the synoptic gospels, Jesus is declared to be both the source and the content of the wine of God.[93] This claim is made in anticipation of the sacrifice which he is about to make.

John appears to have shared the synoptic outlook, although he presents it in a manner peculiar to himself. Jesus is set forth as the wine-giver at the very outset of his ministry. Here, too, it is wine which replaces the water of Judaism, but already in this story John hints at the deeper meaning which the gift of wine has in early Christian thought. The miracle at Cana is said to be the first of the signs.[94] But as we know from the passage which immediately follows, there was for John only one sign vouchsafed by Jesus to questioning followers. That one sign was, as in the synoptic gospels, his own death and resurrection, and all others are merely symbolic representations of it.[95] The miracle takes place, therefore, on the third day, symbolizing the resurrection to come.[96] The new life which Jesus would give to his disciples is to be bought at the cost of his own life.

Finally, therefore, note must be taken of the references to the blood in the gospels, especially as it occurs in connection both with the water and the wine. The meaning of one symbol is frequently illuminated by placing it in parallel with others. All the fluids we have considered were to some extent complementary, the milk, honey, oil, wine and water. They were all in particular expressive of life-giving power.[97] To these must be added the symbol of blood, which is so clearly a life-symbol having its roots in Christ as the lamb in Revelation.[98]

Blood was a common life symbol, and is often paralleled by breath. So in creation myths the clay is sometimes made with blood as in the Assyrian myth, the *Enuma Elish*, in the Greek

myth of the Titans and elsewhere.[99] The offering of blood was
the offering of life as in the Osiris myth. Sometimes the river of
life is said to derive its properties from the blood of the god.[100]
So the grave of Adonis was said to lie at the source of the river,
while in the fifth century it seemed entirely appropriate to
show the tomb of Christ giving forth living water.[101] The symbolism of the blood as the gift of life was so potent that it appears
in the gospel story of the last supper, despite the Jew's abhor-
rence for the drinking of blood. The very starkness of Jesus'
words made the point to a Jew with all the greater force. In
John the idea seems to have been conveyed with greater subtlety.

At the crucifixion John says that there came from the side of
Jesus both blood and water. The issue of blood is explained
quite naturally by the piercing of his side by one of the soldiers,
but by adding that water also came forth, John seems to be
pointing to greater significance. Attempts have been made to
explain the circumstances in physical terms, but the physical or
literal meaning is usually accompanied in John by a spiritual
one. In this case the fact that both blood and water were life-
symbols seems to provide the clue.[102] From the death of Christ
there issue the life-giving streams. Further support for this interpretation, moreover, is to be found in Paul's identification
of Christ with the rock in the wilderness.[103] In the Old Testament, the rock gave forth water when struck by Moses, which
sufficiently indicates that John is here thinking of Jesus in his
death as having become the navel stone from which the life-
streams proceed. This is all the more likely when note is taken
of the rabbinic treatment of the Old Testament incident.
According to this Moses smote the rock twice. First it gushed
blood and then water.[104] Selwyn concluded, therefore, that
'the issue of blood and water from the pierced side was proof
that Jesus was the Rock who was the Lord Christ'.[105] It
designated him as the giver of life through his own death. The
lance thrust was intended to prove the death of Christ, but the
blood and water which come forth constitute another testimony to him as the source of life.

NOTES

1. Gen. 2.10.
2. Wensinck, op. cit., p.10.
3. Oesterley, *The Evolution of the Messianic Idea*, p.129.
4. See Vermaseren, op. cit., pp.85–8.
5. Exod. 17.5–6.
6. Cf. Butterworth, op. cit., pp.8,53,116,118.
7. Apoc. Paul 45; cf. *Cant. R.* 6.9.2.
8. Isa. 33.21.
9. Ps. 46.4; 87.7; see Clements, op. cit., pp.71f.
10. *Taanith* 10a.
11. *Gen. R.* 70.8.
12. Cf. Jacob, op. cit., p.325.
13. Joel 3.18; cf. Zech. 13.1.
14. Clements, op. cit., p.107 n 2.
15. Gaster, *Thespis*, p.183 note.
16. Koran, Sura 18.59ff.
17. Ps. 104.13; *Gen. R.* 4.4; *Eccles. R.* 7.1; cf. *Mid. Tel.* Ps. 24.6; Wensinck, op. cit., pp.7f.
18. Ps. 65.9ff.
19. Johnson, op. cit., p.104; cf. Ps. 36.8f.
20. Zech. 13.1.
21. See Borsch, op. cit., p.82; Vermaseren, op. cit., p.88; cf. Luke 16.19–31.
22. Cf. Apoc. Paul 23; Koran, Sura 47.16f.
23. Gaster, *Thespis*, p.222 note.
24. Ovid, *Fasti* 3.736ff.; Euripides, *Bacchae* 143.
25. G. R. Levy, *The Gate of Horn*, Faber 1948, pp.97f.
26. Dodds, op. cit., p.164.
27. E.g. Deut. 31.20 etc.; cf. Sib. Or. III, 746–9; II Enoch 8.5.
28. V Ezra 2.19; Apoc. Paul 22.
29. Isa. 55.1; Joel 3.18; cf. Rev. 21.6.
30. E.g. II Kings 18.32; cf. Job 29.6.
31. Cf. F. W. Beare, *The First Epistle of Peter*, Blackwell 1961, p.95. See the symbolic use of milk in Odes of Solomon 19.1–7.
32. Life of Adam and Eve 36.1f; 40.1f.
33. Gospel of Bartholomew IV, 65; cf. Life of Adam and Eve 42.3f.
34. Acts of Thomas 157.
35. *Clem. Recog.* 1.45, trans. T. Smith, T. and T. Clark, 1868.
36. *Deut. R.* 7.3; cf. II Enoch 8.2–5; 22.8; Chadwick, op. cit., p.342.
37. Noth, op. cit., p.238.
38. Lev. 14.10–32; I Sam. 10.1,6,10; 16.13.
39. Gen. 50.2f.
40. *Shabbath* 23.5.
41. I Enoch 29.2; cf. 24.3; 25.1,4; 32.3–5; Odes of Solomon 11.
42. II Bar. 29.7; cf. *Shabbath* 88b; *Num. R.* 13.2.
43. V Ezra 2.12.

44. James 5.14; cf. Acts of Thomas 119.
45. Luke 23.53.
46. Luke 23.56; 24.1.
47. Luke 7.36–50.
48. Matt. 26.6–13; Mark 14.3–9.
49. Mark 16.1.
50. Bernard, op. cit., Vol. II, pp.409ff.
51. John 19.39f.
52. John 12.7.
53. Cf. Ignatius, *Eph.* 17: 'It was for this reason that the Lord let the ointment be put upon his head – that he might breathe incorruptibility upon the church. Do not be anointed with the foul smell of the teacher of the ruler of this world, so that he may capture us from the life that lies before us', trans. E. J. Goodspeed, *The Apostolic Fathers*, Independent Press 1950, p.212. Clem. Alex., *Paed.* 2.8.
54. Gaster, *Thespis*, pp.384ff.; cf. p.236.
55. Exod. 30.23ff.; Selwyn, *The Oracles of the New Testament*, p.281 note.
56. II Chron 16.14; cf. Jer. 34.5; Brown, op. cit., p.960.
57. I Cor. 10.2.
58. Apoc. Paul 45.
59. See Goodenough, op. cit., Vol. VII, p.116 and fig. 128.
60. Ps. 36.8f.; Jer. 2.13; 17.13.
61. Acts of John 109; cf. Rev. 7.17; 21.6.
62. Isa. 12.3.
63. O. Cullmann, *Early Christian Worship*, SCM Press 1953, p.86.
64. Apoc. Paul 45.
65. John 20.22.
66. Cf. Mark 7.33; 8.23.
67. See W. Crooke, 'Saliva', *Encyclopaedia of Religion and Ethics*, ed. James Hastings, Vol. XI, p.100; Irenaeus, *Adv. Haer.* V, 15.2; Lightfoot, *St John's Gospel*, p.202.
68. Lightfoot, *St John's Gospel*, p.203.
69. Goodenough, op. cit., Vol. II, pp.185f.
70. Odes of Solomon 30, quoted Borsch, op. cit., p.277.
71. See F. J. Badcock, 'The Feast of Tabernacles', *Journal of Theological Studies* XXIV, 1923, pp.169–74; J. A. T. Robinson, *Twelve New Testament Studies*, p.164 n. 9.
72. Cf. Jonah 2.1; Matt. 12.40. Borsch, op. cit., p.277 n. 9 writes that this word does not usually 'refer to the centre of an inanimate object', but its use would be entirely appropriate when the mountain was treated anthropomorphically.
73. See Badcock, op. cit., p.171.
74. Lev. 23.43.
75. See T. F. Glasson, *Moses in the Fourth Gospel*, SCM Press 1963, pp.58f., who cites *Tos. Sukkah* 3.3–13.
76. See Daniélou, *Primitive Christian Symbols*, pp.1–24.
77. Bultmann, *The Gospel of John*, p.305.
78. Goodenough, op. cit., Vol. XII, p.87; cf. Hippolytus, *Ref.* V, 8.20

quoted Borsch, op. cit., p.277, which refers to 'the current of the great ocean flowing from the midst of the Perfect Man' in Naassene teaching.

79. See Num. 20.11; Ps. 105.41; Isa. 43.20; 55.1; Ezek. 47.1; Zech 14.18.
80. See J. Jeremias, '*Lithos*', *Theological Dictionary of the New Testament*, ed. Kittel and Friedrich, Vol. IV, p.278; cf. Bultmann, *The Gospel of John*, p.305 n. 1.
81. Pausanius, *Elis* II, 26.1f.; Hesiod, *Homeric Hymns* 7.35ff.; see further Barrett, *The Gospel according to St John*, p.157.
82. Carpenter, op. cit., p.380.
83. Bultmann, *The Gospel of John*, pp.118f.; cf. Dibelius, *From Tradition to Gospel*, pp.276f.
84. Goodenough, op. cit., Vol. XII, p.137.
85. See Guilding, op. cit., p.185; Bultmann, *The History of the Synoptic Tradition*, p.238.
86. Goodenough, op. cit., Vol. VII, p.126.
87. Cf. Gen. 49.11f.
88. Dodds, op. cit., pp.xiif.
89. Philo, *Legum Allegoria* III, 82; cf. Acts 2.13ff.
90. Dodd, *The Interpretation of the Fourth Gospel*, p.299.
91. Cf. Goodenough, op. cit., Vol. IX, pp.57,80.
92. Mark 2.22.
93. Mark 14.24.
94. John 2.11.
95. John 2.18ff.
96. Cf. Dodd, *The Interpretation of the Fourth Gospel*, pp.299f.
97. Note that wine and oil is a healing mixture at Luke 10.34.
98. Rev. 7.14; 12.11.
99. Gaster, *Myth, Legend and Custom in the Old Testament*, p.20.
100. See Robertson Smith, op. cit., pp.173f.
101. Daniélou, *Primitive Christian Symbols*, pp.49f.
102. Because of this passage Celsus asked if Christ's blood was *ichor* like that of the gods, see Origen, *Contra Celsum* II, 36; but cf. *Lev. R.* 15.2.
103. I Cor. 10.4; cf. Exod. 17.5f.; Num. 20.11.
104. See *Mid. Tel.* Ps. 105.12; cf. *Ex. R.* 3.13.
105. Selwyn, *The Oracles of the New Testament*, p.233.

17   The Eschatological Feast

A recurring feature of Jewish expectations concerning the end-time was the idea of the Messianic feast which God would prepare for his people. It became one of the Jew's favourite images of eschatological bliss, and finds a place in the Old Testament, in apocalyptic and in rabbinic literature. The basic features of the picture are already laid down in Isa. 25.6–8, and are subsequently subjected to continual revision and elaboration. Throughout this development we can see how the eschatological hope is being conformed to the primordial archetype of the garden of Eden. In it, all the fundamental concepts embodied in the ancient myth take on appropriate new forms.

As Adam had been expelled from the garden of Eden because of his sin, it became axiomatic that the righteous alone would enjoy the paradise of the future. Only those 'who honour the true and everlasting God' may come to his table of delights.[1] In it there would be no place for the wicked. The conditions of entry for the future were not to be in any way different from those which were demanded of the inhabitants of the primordial Eden.

In Isa. 25.6 the feast prepared by God is laid on the mountain of Jerusalem. The prophet sees Zion ceasing to be merely a symbol and becoming in fact the Eden of the eschatological age. Throughout the ensuing development there was this inevitable association of the paradisal eschaton with the glory of God's mountain.[2]

The fertility attributed to the garden of Eden also reappears in descriptions of the Messianic age. The mountains of Judah's Messiah will be '*red with* vineyards and his presses will flow with *wine*'. His valleys will be '*white with* corn and with the flocks of sheep' says the *Targum Onkelos* on Gen. 49.12,[3] following an imagery which already has eloquent expression in Isa. 25.6. Men will once again feast on the bounty of God and have no need of the labours to which Adam was condemned.[4]

But this hope of a return to paradisal fertility is not a materialistic one. It is expressive of the Hebrew faith that man would one day be blessed with the heavenly food of Eden which was the sustenance of eternal life. It was natural, therefore, for Isa. 25.8 to associate the future fertility of Zion with the destruction of death and sorrow. Those who ate of the Messianic banquet would have feasted on the tree of life.[5]

The eschatological meal therefore constituted a final victory over the forces of death, chaos and evil. In order to give dramatic expression to this notion, use was made of the ancient symbols which stood for these things. The righteous were pictured as enjoying the abolition of all that opposed the creation of God under the imagery of feasting upon the flesh of Behemoth and Leviathan. The old enemies of mankind would be served as delicacies for the faithful. 'Behemoth shall be revealed from his place and Leviathan shall ascend from the sea' and 'shall be for food for all that are left'.[6] The rabbis saw the eating of 'Behemoth on a thousand mountains' as recompense to the Jew for having been prohibited from eating certain cattle, '*behemoth*',[7] but the basic notion was less particularized than this. The eating of Leviathan and Behemoth represented feasting on the total riches of land and sea. It also symbolized man's enjoyment of God's final victory over the negative forces for which they had stood in the ancient myth.

THE MESSIANIC FEAST IN THE GOSPELS

The popular Jewish expectation of a feast to be enjoyed in the kingdom of God is expressed in Luke 14.15. Someone in the crowd listening to Jesus speaking of earthly meals was immediately reminded of the heavenly feast to come. It was a hope which Jesus himself probably shared and which is certainly taken for granted by the evangelists. Both Matthew and Luke speak of entry into the kingdom under the imagery of taking up a place at table,[8] and the words of Jesus at the last supper look forward to a better feast to come.[9]

There appears to have been such a well-rooted connection made between the respective ideas of the kingdom and of a feast, that the two images tended to suggest one another. This is probably the case in Matt. 6.25–33 and Luke 12.22–34. The words of Jesus are directed to the anxiety of men about the things of this world. They are told to put their fears to one side and consider the bounty of God in the realm of nature. They are not to worry about what they shall wear or what they shall eat. They are to seek first the kingdom and these things will be provided for. Underlying the apparent simplicity of this text is almost certainly an allusion to the notion that in the kingdom God will provide glorious raiment for his faithful and heavenly food for their table. Another allusion is probably to be found in Luke 15.11–32. When the prodigal returns to his father's house, it is to take part in a banquet held in his honour. The most direct use of the imagery is made, however, in Matt. 22.1–10 and Luke 14.16–24. The common element in the parables which these passages contain is the idea of the Messianic feast. The teaching is here reinforced by the additional use made of the symbolism of the wedding. Perhaps deriving originally from Isa. 54.5 and Hos. 2.16, marriage had become an accepted Messianic image.

But while the evangelists reflect the popular Jewish hopes for the time to come, they also inject new elements into them. There will be those sitting at table with the patriarchs whom many in Jesus' audience would have hardly expected. In the kingdom they will find those cast out from their society sitting in the places they had thought reserved for themselves. The image of the eschatological feast becomes a vehicle for teaching the new assessment of religious worth. Entry into the kingdom and its table is now held to be dependent upon a man's relationship with Jesus as the Christ. They are already confronted with the Son of Man with whom they hope to eat in the time to come. What their place will be then is made to depend upon their treatment of his brethren now.[10] In the related imagery of the eschatological wedding, Jesus takes the place of God as the bridegroom. This is perhaps already hinted at in Matt. 25.1–13 and Mark 2.20, and becomes explicit in John 3.28–30.[11]

The time of feasting has already arrived. The disciples are already like men attending a wedding and participating in the joy of the bridegroom. Throughout his ministry as portrayed to us by the evangelists, Jesus acts as though the kingdom were already present, and it may be significant in this context that in 'making all meats clean' he anticipates the rabbinic expectation that this will be so in the time to come.[12] Certainly the pious divisions of Judaism are regularly ignored when Jesus eats with tax-collectors and others regarded as spiritually unclean. And in so doing he anticipates his own teaching regarding the admission of such people to the feast when those privileged with the first invitations have refused the honour accorded to them.

It is, however, in the stories of Jesus providing food for the people that he is shown most clearly in this Messianic role. It may well be, as J. Jeremias suggests, that the Syro-Phoenician woman is accepted by Jesus, not because of her wit or her humility, but because she recognizes in him the dispenser of the bread of life.[13] This interpretation is certainly a likely one in view of the fact that the incident is placed between Mark's two accounts of a feeding, both of which assert Jesus to be the Messianic dispenser of the heavenly food. These stories are heavily laden with symbolic value in order to make this clear.

Mark records that both the four and the five thousand were asked to sit, and this feature is emphasized in John's account of the feeding.[14] Now while this was natural enough, it is probably not accidental that it should recall the common idiom of the evangelists when speaking of feasting in the kingdom. The location of the incidents may also be of some importance. In Mark and John the feeding of the five thousand takes place on a carpet of green grass.[15] John also says that they were on a mountain.[16] It may well be that as the tradition of the feedings developed, it was thought apt to suggest the imagery of the fertile paradisal mount as a setting for this anticipation of the Messianic feast.[17] The symbolism towards which the evangelists most clearly direct our attention is that of the gathering up of the food which remained. This is what the disciples are asked to remember in order that they may attain a proper understanding of these events.[18] The gathering in was an important aspect of the Hebrew notion of the Messianic feast.[19] The evangelists, therefore, are clearly intending to set forth Jesus as one who accomplishes this eschatological task.[20] The bread which he provides is sufficient not only for those present but also for the rest of the twelve

tribes. But the story has to be given twice by Matthew and Mark
in order to make the point that Jesus gathers in not only the
Jews but the Gentiles as well. The Jewish and Gentile character
of the two feedings respectively has always been clear enough
to scholars. The twelve baskets of food could hardly have been
intended to refer to anything other than the twelve tribes of
Israel. Almost as obvious is the use of the number seven to suggest the Gentile nations. This symbolism is, however, supported
by further devices. The point is made at Mark 8.3 that some of
the four thousand have come a long way to be with Jesus on
this occasion. No such assertion is made about the five thousand.
While the Jews were mythologically near at hand, the Gentiles
came from afar off. The numbers of those fed also appear to be
significant. The mention of four thousand immediately suggests
the four quarters in which the Gentile nations were held to
dwell. But if it is correct to see a reference to the points of the
compass in the use of the number four, it is more than likely
that five was deliberately used to indicate the Jews. When the
earth is set out in accordance with mythological cosmography,
the people of the centre were appropriately designated by the
number five. Finally, it is to be noted that the four thousand are
fed after they have been with Jesus three days, while it is indicated that the five thousand were fed late on the day of their
arrival. In this it may well be that we should see an intended
reflection of the idea that the Jews enjoy the Messianic banquet
in the course of Jesus' ministry among them, while the Gentile
in-gathering to the feast takes place through his death and resurrection on the third day.[21]

In John's gospel, the symbolism of the feedings is given added
dimension by the introduction of a contrast with the manna
provided by Moses. That the manna of the wilderness would
again descend in the age to come became a commonplace in
late Judaism. II Baruch 29.8 says that 'it shall come to pass at
that self-same time that the treasury of manna shall again descend from on high, and they will eat of it in those years'. Later
it became a recurring feature of rabbinic writing.[22] It was therefore a prevalent notion from the end of the first century onwards and may well have been earlier.[23] In view of this, it may
be that Matthew and John were concerned to counter the
notion with one of their own. In Matthew's version of the

temptation of Jesus, a quotation is made from Deut. 8.3,16 which speaks of the manna which the fathers 'knew not'. There is an interest here not in the return of the manna given by Moses but in another far more precious. In John the message is clear. The manna of Moses gave purely physical nourishment. In contrast, the bread which Jesus gives is that of paradise and of immortality.[24] The food dispensed by Jesus comes from the tree of life and so bestows on its recipients the eternal life forfeited by Adam, for when a man eats of it, he does not die like the people of the wilderness.[25] If this is manna, it is 'the hidden manna, the food of the heavenly paradise'.[26] This is shown by a number of contrasts made by John 6 with Gen. 3. Those who eat of the bread Jesus offers will never die, but live forever, and will not be driven out.[27] It is, moreover, Jesus himself who is the bread descended from heaven, and even for the other evangelists it is the eating of his body and blood which anticipates the eschatological feast on the food of immortality.[28]

The idea of eating the flesh of Christ has frequently been attributed to pagan influence. Attention has been drawn to Dionysiac and Mithraic rites in which the god was held to have been consumed in theriomorphic form.[29] There are, however, considerable doubts as to the existence of such an idea in either of these cults.[30] Consequently C. H. Dodd argues that although 'theophagy belongs to a deep stratum of primitive thought and practice which, lying submerged in our minds, generates a natural and more or less universal symbolism', scholars have probably exaggerated the extent to which the idea was present in the cults of the New Testament period.[31] Moreover, it is extremely difficult to show that the Christian usage was derived from the mysteries. In any case, non-Jewish sources are quite unnecessary to account for the emergence of the idea that the believer feeds on the flesh and blood of Christ. This central notion of the Christian faith does not have its roots in paganism, but in the Christian transformation of Judaic symbolism. Throughout our study we have had occasion to note how numerous symbols taken over from Hebrew mythology were progressively made to refer to Christ. In the earlier stages of the Christian tradition, Jesus is one with the people and looks with them to share in the glorious blessings of the new creation. As christology develops, however, Jesus as the Christ is seen as the bestower of these gifts. He brings about the new creation and imparts its benefits to his disciples. Finally, Jesus is himself identified with the paradisal gift of life. The mythological symbolism of the evangelists, especially John, centres this upon the very flesh of Jesus. In his person he is the food of immortality, and from his body flows the life-giving streams. All the life-symbols are identified with him. He is the tree and its fruit. He is the bread and the fish[32] which he distributes to the hungry. It is hardly surprising, therefore, that Christians should have rejoiced in the idea that the Judaic hope of the Messianic banquet should be seen as fulfilled in Christ, and have expressed this most starkly by speaking of eating his flesh and drinking his blood.

NOTES

1. Sib. Or. iii, 46–9; cf. *Num R.* 13.2; *Esther R.* 2.4.5.
2. E.g. V Ezra 2.19.
3. Trans. Bowker, *The Targums and Rabbinic Literature*, p.284.
4. Deut. 33.15; Isa. 51.3; Sib. Or. iii, 48; *Shabbath* 30b; *Lev. R.* 27.1.
5. *Ex. R.* 25.8.
6. II Bar. 29.4f.; cf. II (4) Esd. 6.51f.; *Baba Bathra* 74b, 75a.
7. *Lev. R.* 22.10.
8. Matt. 8.11; Luke 13.29.
9. Mark 14.25.
10. Matt. 25.31–46.
11. Cf. Rev. 19.7ff.
12. Mark 7.19; *Mid Tel.* Ps. 146.7.
13. Mark 7.27–29; J. Jeremias, '*Paradeisos*', *Theological Dictionary of the New Testament*, ed. Kittel and Friedrich, Vol. V, p.772 n. 63.
14. Mark 6.40; 8.6; John 6.10f.
15. Mark 6.39; John 6.10.
16. John 6.3,10.
17. Cf. Barrett, *The Gospel according to St John*, p.228, who takes the contrary view.
18. Mark 8.14–21.
19. Isa. 11.12; 27.12; 56.6f.; Jer. 23.1–3; Ezek. 11.17; 20.33ff.; Hos. 1.11.
20. Meeks, op. cit., pp.96ff.
21. Cf. Meeks, op. cit., p.291.
22. E.g. *Ruth. R.* 5.6.
23. See Brown, op. cit., pp.265f.
24. See Dodd, *The Interpretation of the Fourth Gospel*, p.336; Glasson, op. cit., pp.45–7; Meeks, op. cit., pp.91–8.

25. John 6.27–49; see Borsch, op. cit., pp.295f.

26. Ps.-Titus, Hennecke, op. cit., Vol. II, p.166.

27. Cf. John 6.50 and Gen. 3.3; John 6.51 and Gen. 3.22; John 6.37 and Gen. 3.24; see Guilding, op. cit., p.62; Brown, op. cit., p.279.

28. Matt. 26.26; Mark 14.22; Luke 22.19.

29. Frazer, op. cit., Vol. VIII, p.16; cf. p.10; Dodds, op. cit., p.xviii; Goodenough, op. cit., Vol. XII, p.133.

30. See Gore, op. cit., pp.725ff.; Vermaseren, op. cit., p.103.

31. Dodd, *The Interpretation of the Fourth Gospel*, p.339 n. 1.

32. See D. J. Wieand, 'John 5.2 and the Pool of Bethsaida', *New Testament Studies* XII, 1965/6, pp.392–404; Goodenough, op. cit., Vol. XII, pp.99, 101.

Conclusion

GOSPEL MYTHOLOGY AND FAITH TODAY

The history of the debate concerning the relationship of the gospel story to myth is heavy with conclusions rashly drawn on the basis of selected evidence. A degree of caution is therefore called for at the end of our study. From the review of the gospel material now completed, however, it is possible to throw some light on the problems with which we began.

Although each evangelist made use of those elements in current mythological symbolism most appropriate to the expression of his own particular insights into the significance of the man from Nazareth, there is nevertheless a homogeneity of treatment. The evangelists all saw in Jesus one who had a special relationship with God such that it could not be adequately expressed in purely human terms. Inevitably they resorted to the language of myth, and set forth his divine origin in a variety of narrative forms. In their portrayal of the clash which developed between Jesus and the religious establishment of his day, each evangelist attached particular importance to Jesus' relationship with the temple, its hill and its city. The result of that confrontation was for them a dramatic change in their understanding of the ways in which a man might come to God. The mediation of the holy city was replaced by the person of Jesus Christ. Most important of all, they saw in the coming of Jesus the birth of a new creation, and it was this more than anything else which led them into the use of mythological forms.

As the evangelists were constantly able to point up their message with nothing more than allusions to mythological motifs, it is reasonable for us to assume that they were able to draw upon a fairly well-articulated framework of mythological thought current in contemporary Judaism. This was largely

Conclusion 309

centred upon the idea of the eschaton, which in turn was dependent for much of its imagery on the Hebraic mythology of creation. The burden of their developing christology is the repeated assertion that the new creation had begun with Jesus. In him the world was being made anew and a second humanity coming into being.

We have also discovered that this corpus of Judaic mythological thought was not simply something that belonged to the past. On the contrary, it was living myth, and the rabbinic literature is eloquent testimony to its vitality in the period during which the early Christian church was formulating its basic concepts. The importance of the Christian adaptation of Greek philosophical ideas in the development of Christian doctrines had been rightly stressed. But our study does raise the question as to whether adequate consideration has been given to the influence of Judaic mythology on the common faith and practice of the emergent community. Much light may be thrown, for example, on the recurrent attempts at spatial centralization by the church. Within the New Testament period Jerusalem retains much of the charismatic quality for the Christian church which it had earlier possessed for the Jewish community. The story of the Acts of the Apostles and Paul's letter to the Galatians are only fully explicable when due weight is given to the early Christians' retention of the concept of Jerusalem as the divinely designated centre of mankind. Only the pressure of violent historical events force the Christian community to relinquish Jerusalem. Later church history records how other places bid to become the spiritual successor of Jerusalem, until Rome eventually emerged to take over the function of the bond on earth between man and God. The story might be taken much further and consideration paid to the role subsequently claimed for Byzantium and Moscow. The importance of mythological forms must also be acknowledged in the development of the church's piety. While the struggle of Alexandria and Antioch may be of paramount importance when considering the tortuous developments of philosophical Christology, it was the story of Christ's birth, death, descent and resurrection which remained at the centre of Christian faith. There is a continuity of mythological formulation stretching from the gospel story through the exultation of Paul's christological hymns into the living piety of the

Christian centuries. In tracing out the history of this mythological Christology, the works of Christian iconographers and
architects are probably of more value than the records of
church councils.

Other conclusions to which our study points us may perhaps
best be considered in connection with the contemporary situation rather than with past history. Research into the origins and
early development of Christianity can have little to commend
it to the modern reader unless it has something to say to his own
situation. Indeed, the debate about Christian myth has never
been carried on in isolation from contemporary issues of faith.
Whether a mythological presence in the gospels has been asserted or denied, the decision has always been made for or against
faith in Jesus as the supreme revelation of God to man. It is
most appropriate, therefore, that we should end with a consideration, however brief, as to whether the knowledge we
have gained about the evangelists' use of mythology throws any
light upon the contemporary religious dilemma.

We have seen that mythological elements are undoubtedly
present in the gospel story. The history of the debate shows that
this fact has been a constant source of embarrassment in the
modern period. An assessment of the value attaching to the
former may well be illuminated by a consideration of the causes
of embarrassment in the latter.

Many scholars who have accepted the presence of mythology
within the gospel story have been at pains to eliminate it. They
have claimed that the evangelistic presentation of the gospel
is, in consequence of its use of myth, strange and often unintelli-
gible to the twentieth-century mind. For this reason, it is asserted that the Christian theologian must restate the faith of the
evangelists in a non-mythological way. Bultmann has been the
most explicit exponent of this view, but it is one which is shared
by many who reject his terminology. As the Western world has
steadily lost its ability to comprehend the nature of ancient
Near-Eastern mythology, theological exponents and popular
preachers have felt justified in attempting to tell the story of
Christ in other ways. It has been seen as a dramatic portrayal
of philosophical ideas for the benefit of the masses. In an age
dominated by the concept of evolution, the Christ-event has
been seen as a particularly significant moment in human

development. On a more popular level Jesus has been presented as a socialist reformer, a revolutionary agitator and even as a lovable drop-out from a corrupt society. In each case, however, such restatements have lacked anything more than a passing appeal, and it has quickly become apparent that they have been unable to retain the most basic affirmation of evangelistic faith. The liberalization of Christ has always entailed a diminution of his stature and a distortion of the gospel. These views have only made of Christ an outstanding example of whatever value was most currently acceptable. Rather than being a response to what the evangelists have to say, they have been used as pawns in an ideological battle.

If restatement constantly involves the loss of the evangelistic Christ, there would appear to be no substitute for a reiteration of their story. The claim that this leaves the gospel message beyond the capacity of modern man to grasp cannot be sustained. The alienation of the present from the thought-patterns of the past can be easily overstated, for it is erroneous to think of our modern age as post-mythological. While there is always a transient element in the imagery of any particular period, it is precisely the universal and timeless quality of central mythological motifs which has made them a constantly vital element in human culture and enabled them to survive to the present time. The power of mythology to penetrate the technological age is evident in a number of areas of human activity. At the popular religious level, the fascination of various mythologically-based sects is amply testified to in the midst of the impersonalized concrete cities of the Western world. While the use of mythology for the purposes of political ideology and propaganda has been most obvious during the twentieth century in the Germany of the Nazi régime, very little reflection is required to discern that this is also true in many other instances. Perhaps the most important witness of all is furnished by the realm of artistic endeavour and appreciation. The mythological narratives of the past retain their power to move and illuminate the modern audience, whether they are conveyed through the medium of painting, music or drama. This is of particular importance precisely because many of those whose spirit is raised to new heights of inner understanding by such means would often be hard pressed if required to give a verbal account of their discovery.

It is hardly surprising, therefore, that the evangelists were able by the use of mythological forms to break through the barrier of intellectual poverty and speak to all men, or that the story they told should retain its power in the twentieth century. Perhaps the justification of their method even in the modern age is to be seen in the continued ability of their narratives to evoke deeper responses in men and women than the laboured formulations of those who would replace them. In some cases, Christian communities have been bereft of the discursive explanations of theological leadership but have been enabled to survive by the picture of Jesus and his story passed down from the evangelists.

It would appear, therefore, that the choice is not whether modern man shall have a myth but rather which one he shall have. The Christian church possesses a mythology of which it has never been ashamed in the past, and there is no new factor in the present situation to cause it to be so now.

Contrary to the point of view just examined is that which asserts that myth has no place in the biblical tradition. Scholars from both ends of the theological spectrum have united on this platform, although for quite different reasons. Conservative theologians have rejected the idea that mythological elements are to be found in the gospel because they have seen it as an attack in whole or in part upon the historicity of the narrative. There is much excuse for this attitude in view of the anti-historical excesses into which the acknowledgment of a mythological presence has led a number of its exponents. Such scholars have also been led to a negative point of view by the almost invariable comparison of Jesus with the saviours of other mythologies, frequently leading to a denial of his uniqueness and worth. Conservatism has been rightly concerned to safeguard fundamental truths concerning the origins of Christianity. But our study has shown us that the acceptance of mythological usage in the gospel narratives does not entail a denial of Christ's existence or even of the fundamental historicity of his story. We have also seen that comparisons with pagan mythologies have often been misleading and that the forms used by the evangelists are immediately derived from Judaism. Moreover, it is clear that the gospel story is no mere construction even out of Hebraic elements. It has a unique character of its own which is only explicable on the assumption that it was precipitated by the character of that historical phenomenon which was constituted by the life and death of Jesus.

Allied to this conservative approach to scripture is a large band of scholarship which has constantly asserted that the very essence of the biblical literature is largely constituted by its anti-mythological thrust. The prophets of Israel in particular are extolled for their triumph over the superstition engendered by the priests of mythological cultus. It is asserted that Israel raised a historical in place of a mythological structure of religious thought and practice. Stress is laid upon the fact that Israel possessed a unique consciousness of history and a distinctive sense of ethical responsibility. It is impossible to quarrel with this point of view as a statement of the positive contribution of Israel's religious leaders, but it has to be noted that the values emphasized are precisely those most readily accepted in the twentieth century. From this one may suspect that the picture created may be somewhat one-sided, and that it may stress the this-worldliness of the Hebrew to a disproportionate degree. The danger in this assessment of what constituted the core of Israel's faith is easily seen when note is taken of the use to which it has been put in the radical theology of recent times. It is claimed that the Hebrew prophets laid the foundation of modern Western secularity. By rejecting the mythological cultus of their day they are said to have paved the way whereby modern man would achieve the desacralization of the world, his society and of his own life. The prophetic protests against idolatry even become in the end precedents for an atheistic affirmation. At this point theological unease must lead to questions being raised as to the validity of the assessment of Hebrew religion which could form a basis for such views.

Recognition of the mythological dimension of Israel's religious consciousness does much to restore a more balanced view. Then we see that the Hebrew looked beyond the time-span of man and set his history within the framework of a divine story, of the act of God in creation and its renewal beyond the limits of man's endeavours at the eschaton. His unique sense of moral responsibility was founded upon his knowledge that he was confronted by a personal God who demanded an account of his actions. The Hebrew believed that both his society and his cultic structure were divinely ordained media whereby life might be sanctified and the spiritual dimension of the cosmos brought to the threshold of human consciousness. Only a blinkered reading of the Old Testament could see in it the birth of modern secularity with its emphasis on individualistic autonomy. On the contrary, the Hebrew remained aware throughout that his historical existence was lived out within a supra-historical dimension, that the world of his senses was set about by another seen only with the spirit's eye. Other-worldliness may be unpopular in some Christian circles today, but it can hardly be rejected with the aid of the Old Testament. Only by arbitrarily casting aside the mythological language in which the Hebrew couched his talk of the spiritual realm, can such a claim be made. This is even more true of the New Testament, although it has been argued that here too we are to find originative factors in the development of modern secularity. A study of the mythological elements present within the central story of the New Testament points to quite a different conclusion.

Throughout the gospel narrative the closed continuum of empirical time and space is declared to have been broken wide open. The world of men is constantly invaded by the emissaries of the spiritual world. Even the most ordinary events are invested with a supra-mundane character. And this is achieved in the work of the evangelists by the use of mythological symbolism. They did not do this simply with the intention of repeating the common faith of Judaism in the eternal significance of particular history. Jesus was not even just a remarkable instance of the infiltration of the world of man by the divine. The only act of God which they thought comparable to that which had taken place in him was the creation. No other presentation could do justice to the facts as they saw them than one which saw in his life the re-enactment of the central event in Hebrew myth. Only in this way could the finality and absoluteness of the Christ-event be portrayed.

As a result of this assessment of the character of the role of Jesus, the Christian church was able to come into being. The life of Jesus provided the archetypal basis for a new community of humanity with behaviour patterns determined by the example of its Christ. The mythological symbolism of the gospels was first concerned to portray the more-than-history in the life

Conclusion
315

of Jesus, but it also proclaimed that there was a divinely
ordered foundation upon which human behaviour was to be
built. As the life of Jesus was shown by the aid of myth to have
been lived out within a God-determined framework, so too it
was declared that this was true for every man and woman. As
a result, the Christian took his bride in the knowledge that
marriages were made in heaven, that a child was a gift from
God, and that death was a journey into the freedom of the
spirit's paradise. Illuminated by the eye of faith, therefore, the
evangelists were able to set forth the transcendent dimension
of one man's life, so that it could function as the originative
myth of a new humanity. This it continued to do until its transcendent character was increasingly eroded to leave the Christian
trapped in the relativism of an empirical prison.

It is clear, therefore, that denial or rejection of biblical
mythology is attended by dangers to the fullness of Christian
faith. On the other hand, it must be remembered that the
gospels do not invite their readers to re enter the sacral society
and cultus previously supported by myth. On the contrary,
they proclaim man's freedom in Christ from the particularist
bondages imposed on many by mythological cosmography. At
several points in our study it was necessary to note that myth
was both used and transcended in the gospels. The use of myth
therefore appeared to be paradoxical in character. In order to
clarify the nature of this paradox, a comparison may be made
with the treatment of Hebrew law in the New Testament. It is
on the one hand that which is said to have been man's tutor
until Christ. It has therefore a perfectly honourable place in the
scheme of things. On the other, it is ruthlessly cast to one side and
its decrees replaced by the one commandment of love. In much
the same way, it may be seen that Hebrew mythology and its
accompanying cultus served a perfectly valid function until
this, too, was made obsolete for the Christian who saw the full
significance attaching to the role of Jesus as the Christ. Hebraic
mythology, like many others, had established and maintained
the exclusive sacrality of specific places, persons and things.
Painfully at first, but with ever increasing assurance, the Christian
community, imbibing the spiritual freedom of Jesus, disentangled
itself from the mythological cultic system of Judaism. But the
initial momentum was eventually lost, and even the church

sought again the security offered by mythological particularism.

The evangelists proclaimed a new creation in Jesus and the arrival of paradisal beatitude within the world, but the world has not been renewed and paradise has not arrived. The reason for this may well be that men and women still cling to the mythological forms which the evangelistic tradition was ultimately concerned to clear away in the light of the finality which it attached to the Christ-event. Mythology and its cosmography are still used, though often in disguised forms, to maintain the superiority of a particular people, a certain land and local forms of social and ritual behaviour. The concept of entitlement to world leadership on the basis of ancient history and lineage remains a potent force to this day. The peoples of the world have not yet learnt that one piece of ground is no more and no less sacred than any other and that descent does not confer superiority or spiritual authority. And the Christian churches themselves are often quite unaware of the extent to which they ignore the abolition of sacred time and space embodied in their gospels.

Index

The source of bibliographical details is indicated by the use of heavy type